CW00588667

CANINE LIBRARY

THE HERITAGE OF THE DOG

Other titles available or in production

The Kennelgarth Scottish Terrier Book
by Betty Penn-Bull

The Bulldog
A Monograph by Edgar Farman

20th Century Bulldog
by Marjorie Barnard, President, Bulldog Club (limp) (HB)

Keeshond of the World
by Margo Emerson

Staffordshire Bull Terrier in History and Sport
by Mike Homan

The Bullmastiff
by Clifford L B Hubbard

The Butterfly Dog
by Clarice Waud and Pat Chalis (limp)

The German Shepherd Dog
by Joyce Ixer

The Dalmatian
by Clifford L B Hubbard

Toy Dogs — A Comprehensive Guide
by C Waud and Mark Hutchings (HB)

The Versatile Border Collie
by Barbara Beaumont (limp)

Staffordshire Bull Terriers
Editor V C Hollender (limp)

GENERAL DOG BOOKS

Concise Guide to Dog Showing
by Paddy Petch (limp)

Effective Dog Management
by Betty Penn-Bull (limp)

Small Dog Obedience Training
by Mrs R A Foreman (limp)

Pedigree Dogs in Colour
Official Standards and Colour Illustrations by Roy Hodrien
6 volumes limp, plus 6 volumes in one, Hardback

Bird Dogs of the World
by Stanley W C Smith

THE HERITAGE OF THE DOG

by
Colonel David Hancock

NIMROD PRESS LIMITED
15 The Maltings
Turk Street
Alton, Hants GU34 1DL

FIRST PUBLISHED 1990

ISBN 1 85259 228 1

Published by
Nimrod Press Limited
15 The Maltings
Turk Street
Alton, Hants GU34 1DL

Produced by
Jamesway Graphics
18 Hanson Close, Middleton
Manchester M24 2HD

Printed in England

Contents

hounds. The origin of the spotted coach-dog, the dalmatian . . . and the dama-chien or deer-dog of the Middle Ages.

PREFACE

Sources for research

Anyone writing a book on dogs nowadays or indeed even a magazine article seems bound to receive letters from all sorts of dog-devotees ranging from self-appointed dog experts and dog-breed fanatics to quiet country-men with something worth saying and old sportsmen with out-rageous stories to tell. I wonder if Idstone or General Hutchinson had such a response? I say that because it interests me that whilst every modern writer is challenged (and why shouldn't they be), most ancient writers seem revered – sometimes in spite of what they wrote!

Poor old Stonehenge and Dr Caius are usually the first resort of the overnight dog-breed expert and have been over-quoted, mis-quoted and mis-interpreted for most of this century. I value them both but always bear in mind their limitations. Dr Caius was an emi-nent physician with little know-ledge of dogs. Conrad Gessner,

the great naturalist, rejected his first treatise on *English Dogges* as being too inaccurate and in-complete. Neither was Dr Caius a sportsman and I agree with Arthur Croxton-Smith that Dr Caius had his leg pulled by the sportsmen of that day over many matters. But to make matters worse, Dr Caius's Latin treatise was then given a very personal interpretation rather than a translation by Abra-ham Fleming, sometimes making the original even more inaccurate – Fleming himself having no great knowledge of dogs.

The great value to me of Dr Caius's work is the fact that it was the first recorded attempt to list the British dog breeds by their function.

Stonehenge I much enjoy but he is rather weak on foreign breeds, each of his books tends to contradict the last and he him-self produced the odd myth. He initiated the quite unforgivable theory that the mastiff is indigenous to Britain and that the Romans were astonished at seeing such dogs. Edward C. Ash is another source for many writers; his *Dogs: Their History and Development* is a magnificent piece of work but undoubtedly owes a great deal to James Watson and Robert Leighton. I very much admire the scholarship of James Watson's *The Dog Book* published in 1906 and the wide knowledge of Sir Walter Gilbey displayed in his *Hounds in Old Days* of 1913.

In more recent times, Arthur Croxton-Smith and Clifford Hubbard stand out not just for the volume of words they produced but for their individual contribution – Croxton-Smith for covering the first half of this century so painstakingly and Hubbard for making us in the 1940s much better acquainted with the less well-known foreign breeds. I have never quite understood why he classified the Pug in the mastiff group or the Basenji as a terrier, however, I must admit too that I find it hard to forgive Croxton-Smith for his attribution of the origin of the Golden Retriever to a troupe of performing Russian circus-dogs, on sheer hearsay, which he later found himself to be totally without foundation. But people often believe what they want to believe.

Books on sporting dogs and their use I find on the whole not distinguished by their scholarship and those on gundog training add little to General Hutchinson's classic on Dog Breaking. James Wentworth Day is certainly a joy to read; Taplin's *The Sportsman's Cabinet* of 1803–4 is a very good book with really excellent illustrations by such as Reinagle and Bewick. Sydenham Edwards on the other hand had no obvious interest in sport but his *Cynographia Britannica* is extremely important for the coloured plates, all drawn from life by Edwards, of the breeds of his time. Rawdon Lee's *Modern Dogs*, the volume on terriers in particular, is a mine of information, if over-long, but how I wish that the late Dr J. B. Maurice's book on training pointers and setters had contained more words: he made it all sound so simple and his innate modesty led him to underestimate his own achievements.

My favourite post-war writers are Brian Vesey-Fitzgerald and Sonia Lampson – who wrote such beautiful little literary cameos on the various breeds over the years for *Country Life*. But this group in my view compare most unfavourably with their predecessors; where is the painstaking research of Jesse, the illustrative skill of Edwards and Bewick, the descriptive skill of Markham or the quiet authority of Dalziel? I sometimes think too that accuracy counts for less and less despite there being a great more research material available. I read a very expensive book on the Newfoundland recently which claimed that the Newfoundland was a pure American breed developed from indigenous stock! Surely even the presumptuously titled and tendentiously written *The Truth about Sporting Dogs* by

viii

Mrs Bede Maxwell destroyed that theory.

The truth about pedigree dogs is sometimes elusive, especially where origin and ancestry is involved and old beliefs should always be challenged. But knowledge of the development of our modern breeds is so important if we wish to understand them better and appreciate their instinctive behaviour. In this book I have drawn upon my own experiences in over 20 different countries in the past 30 years, my personal researches in many of the museums and art galleries around the world and the researches of others contained in my library of well over 400 books on dogs.

As man's closest animal companion for over twelve millenia it is vital to relate the history of the domestic dog to the social history of man. The astounding adaptability of dog can be witnessed daily; behind that remarkable feature lies a fascinating heritage.

THE ANATOMY OF THE DOG

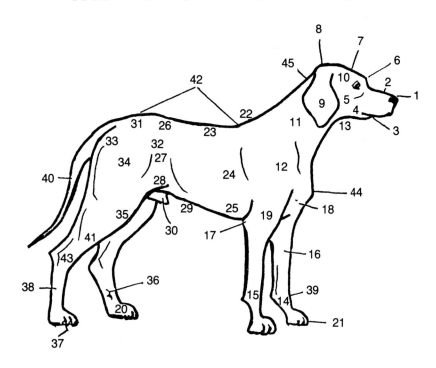

1. Nose	24. Ribs
2. Muzzle	25. Chest
3. Lips	26. Loin
4. Flews	27. Flank
5. Cheek	28. Groin
6. Stop	29. Belly or Abdomen
7. Foreface	30. Sheath
8. Peak or Occiput	31. Croup
9. Ear	32. Hip
10. Brow	33. Rump
11. Neck	34. Thigh (Upper) (First)
12. Shoulder	35. Stifle or Knee
13. Dewlap	36. Dewclaw
14. Pastern or Metacarpus	37. Toenail
15. Wrist or Carpus	38. Metatarsus or Hind Pastern
16. Forearm	39. Knee or Manus
17. Elbow	40. Tail or Stern
18. Brisket	41. Thigh (Lower) (Second)
19. Upper Arm	42. Topline
20. Foot	43. Hock
21. Toes or Digits	44. Sternum or Breast Bone
22. Withers	45. Crest
23. Back	

CHAPTER ONE

The Development of the Breeds

No natural historian has ever conclusively settled the origin of the domestic dog. The wolf, coyote and pariah — origin advocates have always disputed each other's theories. But just as it is incorrect to say that man is descended from monkeys, it is not correct to say that the dog is descended from the wolf, the coyote, the pariah or the wild dog, as we know them today. Man and monkey had common ancestors; dog, wolf, coyote and the fox had common ancestors. It is patently absurd to state that modern wolf is the ancestor of modern dog when each has undergone a separate development over ten millennia. It does admittedly take some degree of imagination to link, in the 20th century, the Chihuahua with the wolf as we see them both today. But man has bred the Chihuahua to suit his design; the wolf is designed solely to survive in the wild, something not all our pedigree breeds would be physically capable of achieving.

If you pick up just about any book on the various breeds of dog, many of the accounts of the contemporary pedigree breeds are likely to be prefaced by flowery descriptions of how that particular breed can be definitively linked with drawings on Egyptian tombs, cave-walls in Scotland, Roman vases and Japanese wall-scrolls. But pedigree breeds have only been recognised for the last 100 years or so, with some of the more ancient breeds sometimes being the last to be recognised. Of course, dogs like Salukis were purpose-bred for many centuries but the variation in type from Algeria to Iran was, predicably, remarkably wide. I have seen them looking like pariah-dogs in Jordan and very similar to our track-greyhounds in Morocco. But man over the centuries bred dogs to suit a function not a stud-book and didn't hesitate to cross a pointer with a foxhound, a greyhound with a bulldog, a setter with a retriever or an otterhound with a terrier when a new breed was identified or working performance required improvement. This was of course how most of our modern pedigree breeds emerged in the first place. Over the centuries, too, breeds like the Talhund, Brabanter, Alpine Spaniel, Drover's Cur, Red Decoy Dog, Black and Tan Rough-coated Terrier and the Tweed Water Spaniel lapsed; more recently the Deerhound, Irish Wolfhound and the Shar-Pei were just saved and the St Bernard, the Cavalier King Charles Spaniel and the Hovawart recreated. Many modern pedigree breeds perpetuate more than one

older breed, the Newfoundland for example having husky, 'water-dogge' and continental sporting dog blood. It is not justifiable therefore to claim too pure a lineage for our modern pedigree breeds.

Inaccurate nomenclature, too, can create myths and misunderstandings. The Great Dane is a German Mastiff, the Dalmatian does not come from Dalmatia nor the Alsatian from Alsace. The Tibetan Terrier is not an earth-dog and the Irish Water Spaniel is a water-retriever not a spaniel. Some breeds too never received the recognition they truly merited, the Welsh Hillman, the Llewellin Setter and the Pyrenean Braque, for example; whilst the sheer whim of man has led to a breed like the Kromfohrlander (a casual creation from a Fox Terrier and a Griffon) being recognised.

Incorrect breed titles as well as mistaken links through physical similarities tend to cloud the issue. The modern Newfoundland is physically very similar to the modern Pyrenean Mountain Dog.

But the originally-imported Newfoundlands were markedly different from the originally-imported Pyreneans.

It is indisputable however that dog has been man's closest animal companion throughout history, man's trade-routes having clear influence on our breeds — the Pug coming to us from

The Tibetan Shepherd dog, mistakenly called a Mastiff

China via Holland and our Spaniels and Pointers from France and Italy (more than Spain, usually claimed as their country of origin). Ascendant empires too led to Chinese, Dutch, Spanish, French and British dogs at different times spreading their influence throughout the civilised world. The Mexican Hairless Dog and the Chihuahua may well be descendants of dwarf dogs, like the Chinese Crested Dog, introduced by Chinese explorers long before Europeans set foot there. The history of the domestic dog is an important part of the history of man.

The encyclopedias tell us that dog has been domesticated for well over 10,000 years and is of the order Carnivora of the family Canidae which also includes wolves, jackals and foxes. The first ancestor of the dog was a forest-dwelling mammal which lived about 40 million years ago – bears and cats also sharing this common ancestor. Dog was the last to become established in its present form – thankfully no one wants to claim that our dogs descend from cats!

Darwin believed the dog to be descended from two species of wolf, Canis Lupus and Canis Latrans, as well as from some European, Indian and African canine species, and from the jackal. The domestic dog, like the wolf, is territorial and the two will interbreed. But the wolf has superb eyesight, the domestic dog rather limited eyesight – with a round pupil to the eye, very different from the oblique pupil of the wolf, and indeed the perpendicular placement in the fox and jackal. Zeuner argued that if dog has a single ancestor it is more likely to belong to the pariah-dingo group. But the oldest remains of domestic dog indicate different varieties and it is likely that simultaneous domestication took place in different parts of the world from different wild species, including the jackal.

The Romans classified the domestic dog into three groups: Canes Venatici or hunting dogs; Canes pastorales or sheepdogs and Canes villatici or watch-dogs. Cuvier in 1800 recognised three main divisions – matins, spaniels and housedogs. Buffon in the late 18th century based his organisation of canine varieties on the various types of ears classified by shape, position and degree of uprightness, (he would have approved the division between Norfolk and Norwich Terriers by the stiffness of their ears!). We owe a much more satisfactory system to Megnin, who in 1897, perfected Cuvier's work by sub-dividing the known breeds into four principal morphological types; lupoids, braccoids, molossoids and graioids. Lupoids, with a head shaped like a pyramid on its side, an elongated narrow nose, straight ears and tight lips, were made up of breeds like the Shepherd and herding dogs, terriers and the spitz group. Braccoids, with the more rounded skull, broader muzzles, well-defined stop, large drop ears and loose lips, consisted of the scent-hounds, setters, spaniels and pointers. Molossoids, with the bulkier almost spherical heads, small drop ears, short muzzle and thick fleshy lips, consisted of the mastiffs and bull-breeds. Graioids, with a head like an elongated cone and a narrow skull with a long fine muzzle and tight lips, were composed of cursorial hounds, the sight-hounds.

An erroneous application of this system of classification has led to breeds like the Pug being incorrectly placed in the mastiff group, perhaps through it once being dubbed even more inaccurately the Dutch Mastiff. All the Oriental short-faced dogs, the Pug, Japanese Chin, Pekingese and Tibetan Spaniel are Braccoids, with a quite different skull conformation from the mastiff group. But even more misleading has been the classification of mountain dogs and big herding breeds into the Molossoid group, with the Tibetan Mastiff quite mistakenly identified as a mastiff. But then so too have the Spanish and Pyrenean Mastiffs; they are neither Molossoid nor mastiff. The four Swiss breeds of mountain dog, with the Hovawart, the Kuvasz, Maremma and Pyrenean Mountain Dog are all Lupoids, like the shepherd dogs and spitz breeds. I suspect however that the English Mastiff played a bigger role when the St Bernard was re-created than is usually acknowledged and that the Pug was used to shorten the face of the 19th century Bulldog more than was ever admitted. Of course as breeds within these four classifications have been intermingled,

sub-divisions have been created, such as molosso-lupoid, lupo-braccoid, molosso-braccoid, and so on. In this way the Newfoundland, created from husky, water-dog and eṕagneul stock, displays the lupo-braccoid characteristics, yet is so often grouped with the Molossoids.

But there is inevitably a degree of conjecture about linking any modern pedigree breed with any ancient breed-type or morphological grouping. There is similar speculation about the stone-age dog Canis familiaris palustris, the so-called peat-dog, first found in Switzerland in the 19th century and more recently in south Sweden. Claims are made that the peat-dog was in fact a peat-spitz and breed enthusiasts straightaway link these preserved remains with present day schnauzer, pinscher and terrier breeds which is, in my view, scarcely justified. Of the four types of stone-age dog Canis familiaris intermedius / leinieri / inostranzewi / palustris, there is further dispute. Canis familiaris intermedius is largely accepted as the principal ancestor of modern scent-hounds and Canis familiaris leinieri that of modern sight-hounds, although, some argue, only the northern ones. Canis familiaris inostranzewi was a larger type of dog, with a powerful head, existing mainly in north and central Europe. Many link it with the big herding breeds and mountain dogs, as well as the Molossian dog, ancestor of the mastiff breeds. My own view however is that the big herding breeds and mountain dogs descend from Canis familiaris palustris of the Stone Age, through Canis familiaris metris optimae, the Bronze Age dog, with Lupoid classification not Molossoid. Undoubtedly many of these big dogs are molosso-lupoid but I consider it is most misleading to claim mastiff-ancestry for a Maremma sheep-dog. But then once the Mongolian Herding Dog became mis-identified as the Tibetan Mastiff, all sorts of claims have been made subsequently giving the Molossian Dog's country of origin as Tibet.

But just as the large herding breeds have a mixed origin, so too do the scent-hound breeds. The Greeks used their 'Hounds of Sparta', Alopecid and Castorian hounds to hunt the hare and Locrian and Cretan hounds to hunt the boar. The Hounds of Sparta and the Cretan hounds were cross-bred to produce the 'Metagon'. Indian hounds, which came from Assyria were used to hunt both the stag and the boar. These 'Indian' hounds, the Assyrian hunting mastiffs, were themselves made up of four different types, Medes, Albanians, Gelonians and Hyreanians. Interbreeding went on between all these types in the pursuit of excellence in the field. It is therefore dangerous to be too defini-

The Podengo Portuĝues has retained its identity

tive in any attribution of pure descent to our modern hounds.

For me, the biggest gap in the study of the genealogy of the dog is however the failure to use genetic evidence to trace ancestry in more recent times of the breeds of dog. The mode of coat-colour inheritance, the way in which hunting instincts are inherited and the herding instinct have considerable relevance when researching modern breeds developed in the last two centuries. We know that the same mode of colour inheritance occurs in toy spaniels, papillons and pekingese as in sporting spaniels. We are aware that breeds like the Airedale, the Collie varieties, the Setter family, the Elkhound and the Cocker Spaniel are mute on the trail but that the Bloodhound, the Foxhound, Beagle, Dachshund and Sussex Spaniel are 'open trailers' i.e. they give tongue on the trail. The 'spotting' of the Dalmatian is related to the 'ticking' found in the hound breeds and the English Setter and remarkably similar to the way in which some English Pointers are marked. Other hunting instincts, the 'treeing' aptitude, the head held high for air-scent or low for ground scent, the tendency to mouth prey rather than kill it quickly and the impulsive 'holding' rather than 'slashing' at a running quarry, are all inherited as distinctly as more visible charac-

The Kooikerhondje of Holland — true to type

teristics. We know that the brindle factor is handed on very similarly in greyhounds, whippets and Great Danes, that Otterhound coat colours are analogous with those of the Bloodhound and that gazehounds are often black or blue but scenthounds rarely are. The inheritance of coat colour in fox terriers and beagles is similar. A geneticist with only a slight knowledge of the history of the breeds of dog could quickly dispel some of the recorded 'facts' on the claimed ancestry of a number of pedigree breeds.

This whole subject presents a fascinating area of research but one confused over the years by

The Dachsbracke — braccoid

perpetuated myths, unproven assertions and sheer wishful thinking. So often the more interesting but less reliable sources such as Stonehenge, Dr Caius and 'Idstone' are quoted again and again to prove a point. Writers like E C Ash, a shameless plagiarist and A Croxton-Smith, who was particularly gullible, are regarded as authorities. The work of Jesse and Watson — so plundered, often inaccurately, by those coming after them is largely unrecognised for its sheer merit. But breed enthusiasts will largely believe what they want to believe and it is unlikely that the Irish Water Spaniel will become known as the Irish Water Retriever, the Tibetan Mastiff As the Tibetan Mountain Dog, the Great Dane as the German Mas-

tiff, the Kerry Blue as the Irish Blue Terrier, the Tibetan Terrier as the Tibetan Sheep Dog or the French Spaniel as the French Setter, as, in my view, they should be. Yet we did manage to replace that quite absurd breed title 'Alsatian Wolf-dog'.

Before the 21st century begins perhaps we could not only sort out the anomalies in our breed-titles but be more conscious of the heritage behind each title and strive hard to breed for correct type. The various breeds emerged because they excelled in their designated role; our ancestors produced pedigree breeds to stabilise the required design. Some of our contemporary breeds have stood the test of time, others sadly have not. Significantly the less intensively developed breeds, mainly foreign ones, have always maintained their old identity, the Stabyhoun and the Kooikerhondje in Holland, the Albanian Wolfhound, the Uruguayan Sheepdog and the Podengo Portugueŝ. But with so many foreign breeds coming into Britain, there would be a great deal to be said for having a 'Year of the British Dog'. Certainly half a dozen of our native breeds could benefit from the interest such a designation would engender. Come on Kennel Club, what about it?

Dogs in Britain

Dog has been man's closest animal companion for some 12,000 years and not surprisingly the history of the dog is inextricably interwoven with that of man. When tribes migrated then their hunting and herding dogs went with them. When primitive communities ceased being nomadic and settled in cities then their dogs adapted to this new life style. As huge wild animals, wild cattle, bison, bear and elk became extinct in Central Europe, then the role of the huge hunting dogs which were used to pursue them, lapsed. Dogs were also used extensively as objects to be traded or presented as prestige gifts. In this way types of dog known to the Phoenicians, the Romans, the Celts, the Chinese, the Ottomans and the Vikings spread far beyond the homelands of those peoples.

From China and India, there comes evidence of hunting dogs in both the Yellow River and the India Valley civilisations of 4,000 years ago. In the Sumerian, Babylonian and Assyrian civilisations of 3,000 years ago, there is testimony to their valuing their dogs. It is worth remembering that the Phoenicians were great travellers, some believing them to be the first navigators to sail out of sight of land. When they travelled their dogs accompanied them and were often used in the barter for goods in the countries they visited. There is an abundance of evidence in the Egyptian, Greek and Roman civilisations of sight and scent hounds, house guards, herding dogs and ornamental dogs, with such dogs accompanying the legions throughout the Roman Empire.

In Central and Northern Europe the endless wandering of the different peoples over many thousands of years has led to the ceaseless introduction of fresh canine blood into the various countries of those areas.

The Megalith builders came from the Eastern Mediterranean by sea to Great Britain and middle Europe around 3,000 B.C. The Windmill Hill culture came overland from North Africa; the Beaker People came from Spain to Great Britain and the Rhineland around 1,500 B.C. The Iron Age Celts came from Central Europe to settle in the British Isles, especially in the north and in Ireland

from the 5th to the 1st century B.C., at a time when there was extensive trading with the Mediterranean people. we had the Romans in Britain from 100 B.C. to the Norman Conquest, we received the Anglo-Saxons, Jutes and Norsemen especially in the east and south of England. This would have brought hunting dogs here from Denmark, Saxony and Normandy. We know that all these people, from the Neolithic hunters in Pembrokeshire 9,000 years ago to the development of firearms in comparatively recent times had a reliance on such hunting dogs which we in modern times have never needed. For primitive hunters voyaging to strange lands their accompanying

Braque Saint-Germain, so like our own pointer

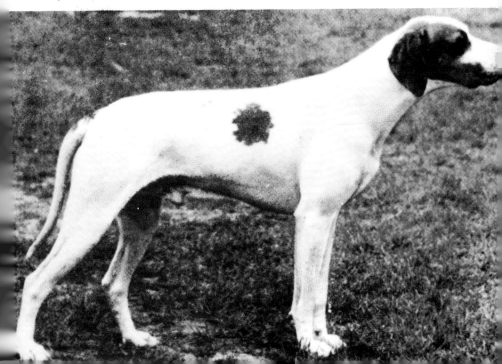

dogs must have had enormous value to them.

From such wanderings, it is possible that smooth-haired sight-hounds, like the modern greyhound, were introduced into Britain by the Phoenicians and that small herding dogs like the modern Swedish Vallhund were introduced into Pembrokeshire by the Vikings to help create the Welsh corgi. The Romans prized small white dogs, like the modern Maltese and took them throughout their empire as companion dogs. These in turn could have come to them from the Far East along the old Silk Route through Parthia. In this way it is possible that small spaniel-like dogs, water-dogs and modern breeds like the Pekingese found their way to Europe. The Iceland Dog could have been the forerunner of our collies and the rough-haired Celtic hunting dogs the ancestors of our Scottish deer-hounds and Irish Wolfhounds.

The Normans were famed for their scent-hounds and introduced big black hounds from which the modern bloodhound may be descended. Many believe that the Brittany hound is the result of Welsh hounds being taken there by Welsh colonists. We know that the Romans imported dogs from Britain which were famous for their size and strength. Officers returning from Service in the Peninsular War brought Spanish pointers back to Britain, just as the German Shepherd Dog was introduced to Britain by soldiers coming back from World Wars 1 and 2. Marlborough's soldiers no

doubt brought continental dogs home with them too.

From all this it is soon apparent that it is always most unwise to talk about British dogs, as though there was a purity of breeding and an isolation which enhanced that purity. The British have long been famed as breeders of livestock, but their skill has been rooted in the judicious blending of good blood not a reverence for British or even pure blood. To someone dependent on his dogs both to protect his flocks and to catch game, the sole criterion was whether the dogs *functioned* and if a stranger had a better dog only a fool would not wish to capitalise on that higher capability.

But if you read the official breed histories for modern pedigree breeds of dog you could be forgiven for thinking that dogs in Britain have been isolated for centuries and pure-breeding revered for several millennia. A neolithic British dog (dating from about 1800 B.C.) was discovered in 1928 during the excavations of the Windmill Hill site near Avebury. Since then I have seen this skeleton claimed in print as a fox terrier, a whippet, a beagle and a Bedlington terrier by breed enthusiasts. But Professor D.M.S. Watson, F.R.S., who made a detailed examination of the skeleton shortly after excavation likened it to the dingo, the hunter-companion of the Australian aborigines.

The fact is that many of our

The Bordeaux Mastiff — often confused with our Bullmastiff

prized 'native' breeds have parallel breeds overseas. Our Old English Sheepdog and Bearded Collies are much like the Owtcharka breeds of Eastern Europe, our Border Terrier is very similar to the little Continental griffon, the Bullmastiff is almost identical with the Dogue de Bordeaux, the English pointer is very much like the Braque Saint-Germain, the Irish Setter could be mistaken for a Langhaar, the Welsh foxhound is very similar to a Griffon Nivernais, an English Springer is easily confused with a Kleine Munsterlander, a Foxhound is much like a Poitevin, a Curly-coated retriever is quickly seen to be related to breeds like the Portugese Water Dog or the Wetterhoun from Holland, a Welsh Springer is similar to a Brittany, a Pembroke corgi is remarkably similar to a Swedish Vallhund and a harrier has distinct resemblances to a German Steinbracke. But none of this should be at all surprising, it would be remarkable indeed for any European country to have native breeds of domestic dog quite unlike those in neighbouring countries. The breeding of modern pedigree dogs has however in the last one hundred years exaggerated many breeds so that they are quite unlike their own immediate ancestors. Dogs from Britain have emerged as world-famous breeds because master-breeders in the last century or so blended the best blood. Respect for pedigrees is very much a modern phenomenon.

Despite the rich and varied heritage of the modern breeds, the absurd claims persist. I read a very expensive book recently on that admirable breed the Newfoundland in which the author claimed it as a native North American breed developed from indigenous stock! This is an area colonised by the British, the French, the Portugese and the Dutch — before the days of anti-mate!

Researching the origin of the Great Dane in Germany some years ago, I came across legitimate local fury about claims from a British authority that this could rightfully be considered a British breed. This British claim was apparently based on the author's inability to trace Great Danes, named as such, in German literature. The Germans call this breed a German Mastiff (Deutsche Dogge). In past centuries the breed has been referred to as Saupacker (member of a pack of boarhounds), Saufanger (boar-catcher), Saurude (boar-hound) and Hetzrude (a pack hound). It may well be that this breed is descended from the Alauntes, referred to by Gaston de Phoebus in the 16th century, with a possibility that the word itself is derived from the Alans, equestrian nomads who came over the Don and the Volga to Gaul between 65 B.C. and 430 A.D. The name Great Dane has never been an accurate breed title. But to claim this as a breed developed in Britain refutes all the available evidence, as does Stonehenge's absurd proposition that the Romans were astounded to see mastiffs in Britain and that they are one of our native breeds.

We have every reason to be proud of our terriers, most British of dogs, our spaniels, our hounds and our sheepdogs. But to claim a wholly British origin for them can never be true. We may well have exported more dogs than any other race, but throughout our own history, foreign dogs have

The Langhaar — often mistaken for an Irish Setter

entered Britain in an endless procession to add to the blood already here. The recent influx of Weimaraners, Rottweilers, Vizslas, Komondorok, German pointers and Belgian shepherd dogs merely perpetuates what has happened throughout our history but with one important difference. With the establishment of pedigrees for dogs, overseas breeds no longer improve the blood of functional dogs already here. For in modern pedigree breeds the gene pool is closed. I wonder how long it will be before sensible sportsmen, eager to obtain prowess in the field, forget about predilections for pedigree dogs and get back to breeding for performance, rather than appearance, once again. I look forward to the day when German pointer blood is being used to improve our British pointers, rather as Continental pointer blood was at the start of the 19th century. For thus, it always was!

The Poitevin — very like a Foxhound

Pure-bred Dogs
The Validity of the Breeds

When I read the official history of quite a number of pedigree breeds of dog, I recall all too easily Henry Ford's famous opinion that 'all history is bunk.' For some of these breed histories were compiled in Victorian days when the knowledge of some still much-quoted dog writers was really quite limited and the inherent chauvinism of those times led to a belief sometimes that anything worthy must have originated in Britain. There was then a quite astonishing lack of awareness of the many varieties of mountain dog, shepherd dog, setter and pointer, mastiff and scent-hound which were really quite well known at that time on the Continent. The red decoy dog, perpetuated to this day in the Nova Scotia Duck Tolling Dog in Canada and the Koikkerhondje in Holland and referred to by some old writers as the tumbler, is still regarded by some as either a lurcher or a terrier. The pointer and the spaniel are still believed to have originated in Spain despite the diligent researches of William Arkwright and the known existence of the old French verb s'espanir, to crouch or sett. The Whiptail is still called the Irish Water *Spaniel* despite the wealth of research available on water-dogs right down the centuries.

I believe it is fair to say that most modern pedigree breeds owe their recognition to the dedicated interest of one strong-minded fancier or a determined group of devotees rather than centuries of pure-breeding producing a distinctive isolated

The Bearded Collie, the type at the turn of the century

breed as such. Men like Dobermann, Korthals, Hamilton, Boulet and King Charles are easily identified, but would we have the Sealyham without Capt. Edwardes, the Irish Wolfhound without Capt. Graham, the Bullterrier without James Hinks, the Leonberger without Heinrich Essing, or the Bullmastiff without S. Moseley?

Men like these produced identifiable breeds rather than any other distinct historically-traceable reason. We could however have just as easily produced Welsh or Devon Cocker Spaniels, Llanidloes setters, Cowley terriers, Land Spaniels, Ossulton setters, St John's retrievers, Bingley terriers, Turnspits and Blue Heelers. We failed to preserve the Norfolk heeler, the Welsh Hillman, the Smithfield sheepdog and the Talbot hound even if we do perpetuate the Norfolk spaniel, the Halifax terrier and the Tweed Water Dog in modern breeds with different names. But it is unwise to claim purity of lineage for any breed and foolish to repeat old falsehoods on origin.

I groan when I read the overnight dog experts and lazy plagarists repeating the old myths, like the Bearded Collie descending from stock swimming ashore

Owczarek Nizinny — Polish Shepherd Dog — very much like our Beardie

from a foreign ship wrecked off Scotland, the Chesapeake Bay Retriever originating from two Newfoundland-like dogs swimming ashore from a comparable ship-wreck or indeed the Newfoundland coming from Pyrenean Mountain dogs taken to Labrador by Breton fishermen. I say this because long-haired sheepdogs have been recorded in Scotland long before this incident is alleged to have occurred; ship's dogs like Chesapeakes travelled aboard countless ships traversing the bay every day in the times

The German long-haired 'pointer' — the Langhaar, at work; easily confused with an English Setter

when this occurrence is said to have happened and why on earth should fishermen in small boats from the coast have taken huge white sheep-guarding breeds from inland areas to the New World with them! I sigh too when I read of the so-called Tibetan Mastiff siring all the mastiff breeds of Western Europe, oh, and the Newfoundland too. The Romans too are alleged to have left breeds like the Rottweiler behind them, yet such dogs preceded them! I have just read a very expensive book on dogs which tells me that the Skye terrier originated from the Maltese, yes, off a Spanish ship wrecked off the coast in 1600! . . . that the Welsh corgi is from the *German*

basset and the Sealyham from the basset of Flanders and the corgi.

I wonder if it is fair to classify the Norfolk and the Norwich terriers as different breeds and to register the Kromfohrlander as a breed at all. The latter came from a misalliance between a wirehaired fox terrier and a griffon fauve de Bretagne on an estate in Germany. Ten years later the lady breeder persuaded the F.C.I., the international kennel club, to recognise the offspring as a new

breed of dog. Based on this sort of precedent, the lurcher breeds of Britain could create a new breed of dog every summer, intentionally. Some breeds too are hard to differentiate, more than one terrier judge having confused a Lakeland with a Welsh terrier. The Bordeaux mastiff is very much like a bullmastiff, the German Langhaar similar to a setter, the Polish Owczarck Nizinny is just like a Beardie and the Cirneco dell'Etna much like a smoothhaired Ibizan hound. I believe it would not be easy to define comprehensively the word 'breed' when used to describe pedigree dogs by recognisable types.

I'm not sure that it is good sense to perpetuate every breed of dog acknowledge as purebred. The gene-pool in such pedigree breeds is now closed and with over 300 inherited defects in dogs, we would be wise to aim for healthy dogs rather than endless in-breeding. The Russians have produced a new guard dog by blending the best blood of the Giant Schnauzer, the Rottweiler and the Airedale in a skilful breeding programme. That is exactly how master breeders the world over developed the superlative breeds we now revere. I am not advocating the developing of new breeds so much as commending the pursuit of excellence, for performance must always rate above pedigree.

The Rottweiler — another breed allegedly left behind by the Romans

Keeping Faith

'For sale, English Springer Spaniel, working type' . . . 'English Setter puppies for sale, from working parents' . . . 'Five Black Lab pups available now, working type'. Advertisements like these in the sporting magazines reveal very clearly and to me all too sadly the emergence since the advent of conformation shows of dogs bred solely for looks. The need for those advertisers to stress the functional ability of their products is illuminating. Man has utilised dogs for perhaps twelve millennia; man has held pedigree dog shows for not much more than a century. The culmination of that century's work is manifesting itself now and in most gundog breeds there is a detectable difference in type between field trial, shooting-field dogs and those being produced on the show circuit.

Over the last few years I have read well-argued articles from well-respected writers in the gundog world about the inevitability even the desirability of such a state of affairs. I remain unconvinced. There can only be one breed in each of the pedigree gundog breeds, or indeed any other group of dogs. Either the dog looks like the breed evolved by the master-breeders of the last century and is *capable* of being, even if not allowed to be, utilised

There is a detectable difference in type between field and show dogs within a breed

in the field. Why should we suddenly be able to discard the well thought-through criteria of those whom we proudly if paradoxically claim as being the founders of the breed? Why surrender the birthright of pedigree stock and ignore the important heritage involved because of what in historic perspective is some purely transient whim?

Conformation shows for pedigree breeds were initiated by the gundog fraternity but have their roots in even earlier hound shows, which in turn developed from the public livestock shows at the end of the eighteenth century. Foxhounds were exhibited for prizes and had their own studbook long before Mr Pape the gunsmith held his '50 bird-dog' show in Newcastle-on-Tyne in 1859. The foxhound today looks and performs very much as its predecessors did in the middle of the last century. Foxhounds do not conform to a standard but are bred to commendable functional excellence and are still extremely handsome canine athletes. The foxhound fraternity have retained control of their hounds, the shooting men seem to have lost control of their dogs. Nowadays a Gordon Setter is expected to be black and tan and would not win in the show ring without being so. That expectation is not historically correct. Bob Truman's superb mainly white Gordon Setter, a quite outstanding field dog, would not be placed at Crufts. The statuesque almost setter-like English Springer Spaniels which do get placed at Crufts are most

unlikely to become field trial champions. But are they really English Springer Spaniels? Slowly but surely, over the last century the shooting men have allowed their breeds to be taken over by the show breeders, not necessarily always because of the strength of the latter, all too often because of the weakness of the shooting men themselves – some of whom surprisingly are breeders of pedigree livestock and know a great deal about breeding in pursuit of function.

It is easy to blame the breed clubs and the show ring circuit for the emergence of say two different types of Labrador, Golden Retriever or Springer. I believe it has been the lack of interest by the shooting men which has allowed the less knowledgeable and less faithful in the show world to take over their breeds. I find plenty of honestly-intentioned breeders of exhibition gundogs who would welcome advice, interest and an involvement from the shooting men. There are very many show gundog fanciers who want to breed a handsome yet still functional animal, just as the master-breeder of English Setters, Edward Laverack strove to do. There are more working tests now as a result of this. But the gap between the field trial world and the conformation dog show need not be so wide. The size of that gap in the end could decide the fate of some of our breeds. The enormous difference between the terriers at a working terrier show and those at a kennel club pedigree dog show illustrates the ultimate effect of such a gap opening up.

The Sealyham terrier has in less than a hundred years gone from being the gamest of terriers, with a weatherproof coconut-matting coat and hound-like marking to a legless, fluffy-coated, hovercraft-like all-white show dog, whose numbers are diminishing alarmingly. But at working terrier shows, you often find real Sealyhams if not in name. It would be so easy to recreate the historically correct breed; the divergence in type may mean the loss of the breed altogether. The breeders of the modern Sealyham have simply not kept faith with Captain Edwardes and his demanding criteria. The breeders of the modern show Labrador are breeding a very different dog from those known to Lorna, Countess Howe. I see Labradors in the show ring which more resemble Rottweilers and Bullmastiffs than the correct type for the breed. In the field I see Labradors which succeed in spite of their anatomy. The wider any divergence in any breed, the worse it is for that breed.

It is sad to see breeds developed by sportsmen like Llewellin, Laverack, Arkwright, Boughey and Cooke subsequently allowed by another generation of sportsmen to degenerate. It is simply not good enough to say 'Let the show people get on with it,' many of those show people would welcome an input from the shooting field. If that input is not forthcoming the penalties are there and many authorities down the years

have made such a point. Dr Konrad Z. Lorenz in his *Man Meets Dog* of 1954 wrote: 'It is a sad but undeniable fact that breeding to a strict standard of points is incompatible with breeding for mental qualities' . . . Dr Michael Fox in his absorbing book *Understanding Your Dog* twenty years later, wrote 'Too many breeders are selecting solely for conformation, for "showy" or "stylish" looks which often become distorted, mimic exaggerations of the original breed stand-

Labradors come in all types — this one has a wavy coat

ards. Insufficient attention is paid to selecting for stable temperament and for trainability' . . . And before him, in his quite admirable book *The Family Dog* (1957), John Holmes, the well-known animal trainer, wrote: 'So popular did this dog game become, that in a short time, a dog that could win in the show ring might be of greater value than a good worker. In other words, for the first time in history, a dog that could do

nothing . . . could be worth more money than one which would work.'

Valuing dogs solely for their looks, ignoring temperament and trainability and breeding to paragraphs rather than the pursuit of function has happened because sportsmen have allowed their sporting breeds to be taken over by non-sportsmen. Just as these breeds were evolved by knowledgeable gundog men, they could so easily be restored by them, it is a matter of whether they wish to.

At a conformation dog show last summer I heard an English Setter breeder proudly stating

Is this the correct mould for the English Springer — or (below) is this smaller, less-feathered, smaller-headed working dog closer to the true type?

that his dog in the ring came from Laverack stock. He had every reason to be proud of its ancestry if not of his dog. It was a terrible specimen with a high lift of the front legs, no drive from the hocks behind, down on its pasterns and out at elbow. I talked to that breeder later and in he had never walked twenty miles over a moor with a pair of dogs. He had no clear idea of what he was breeding for. Edward Laverack did; in his much-valued book *The Setter* of 1872, he wrote: 'The first thing to be attended to in breeding is to consider what object the animal is intended for. My idea is *general utility* for the gun is the great desideratum.'

I believe that the divergence of a breed into a show type and a field type is not inevitable at all, it arises from an abrogation of responsibility by the shooting fraternity. It is thoroughly bad for any breed and already nearly disastrous for one or two. Show breeders are too often maligned, many are well-intentioned but unaware of field requirements in their dogs. It is now for the knowledgeable field-dog breeders and owners to stop standing back and weakly surrendering their breeds to oblivion. Our ancestors developed the best breeds of gundog in the world, some now fast being replaced by more functional Continental breeds. If sportsmen care at all about our native breeds of gundog, they must get thoroughly involved from now on in the perpetuation of these admirable functional animals.

Royal Dogs

Just over fifty years ago, two little girls, daughters of the Duke and Duchess of York, used to go to play with the children of Viscount Weymouth (later the marquess of Bath). The Weymouth children owned a corgi puppy which seemed tireless and quite irrepressible, displaying a remarkably wide repertoire of appealing tricks. The two little sisters, Elizabeth and Margaret, found his boundless energy and lively impishness simply captivating and went home, as all children do, to plead with their parents for a dog like the Weymouth's. An equerry discovered that Viscount Weymouth had bought his corgi pup from Thelma Gray, the famous Surrey corgi breeder, whose Rozavel kennel brought such distinction to the breed. The outcome was that Mrs. Gray took three delightful corgi puppies to 145 Piccadilly for the Duke of York and his daughters to make their selection.

Like most Pembrokeshire Welsh Corgis, two of the puppies were tail-less, and the other sported a tiny stump of a tail. 'We must have the one which has something to wag' ventured the Duchess of York, otherwise how are we going to know whether he is pleased or not?' The chosen pup came from distinguished breeding; his registered name was Rozavel Golden Eagle, son of champion parents, sire Crymmych President and dam Golden Girl. His half-brother became a champion, Rozavel Red Dragon, the most famous show-ring corgi of his day. But the favoured pup himself was not house-trained at this stage and so went back to the Gray Kennels to have his essential education completed.

During this house-training period, Mrs Gray's kennel staff found that the little corgi pup was preparing for his distinguished future by insisting on eating from his own dish and generally acting rather snootily. And so he became dubbed 'The Duke', quickly popularised as 'Dookie', more suitable for a wee pup. But it was with some embarrassment that Mrs Gray, when delivering the pup to his new owners and being asked what name he answered to, had to explain to the Duke of York! Dookie travelled straightaway to Glamis in Scotland with his new owners and at once drew the comment: 'Wha' kind o' doag's that?' from the villagers round the castle. Similar comments echoed round the British Isles as over the coming months Dookie was displayed to public gaze. At this time who could have foretold that Dookie's presence in the Duke of York's family would soon lead to a quite startling rise in popularity for the breed of Pembrokeshire Welsh Corgis and in due course, through his young owner's father succeeding to the Crown, to his being the personal pet of the future Queen of England and the Commonwealth.

Dookie remained the favourite house-pet of the family, from the unexpected move to Buckingham Palace from 145 Piccadilly, to rapturous holidays at Sandringham and Balmoral and joyous weekends at Windsor. The King and Dookie became especially fond of each other's company, 'He really is the greatest personality of a dog that I have ever known,' the King would say, admiringly, 'so intelligent – and so marvellously patient with the children'. Dookie, like all corgis, was an active, energetic, robust and thoroughly entertaining little dog and the young princesses would take him on long rambles in Windsor Great Park, stopping to play his favourite game – leaping to and fro over a kneeling Princess Margaret.

But centuries of working dog ancestry in Wales as a cattle-herder had bequeathed one unacceptable trait on young Dookie, that of nipping the heels of titled guests on formal occasions, and so, on the edict of the King himself, the little red dog was to be shut away on banquet occasions. Despite this he was soon to be joined by a second Rozavel corgi, Lady Jane, as the collection of royal dogs steadily increased. For, quite apart from the shooting dogs at both Sandringham and Windsor, there were now six very special Royal canine pets. Besides the two corgis, there was Mimsey, the King's yellow Labrador, long a favoured breed of the King, her offspring Stiffy and Scrummy, and the 'Tibetan Lion-dog' Choo-Choo, a gift during a Royal Tour before the accession and of a breed well-used to living in royal palaces. Unlike the perky assertive inquisitiveness of the corgis, the aloof Choo-Choo, so named because of his tendency to snore like a train as a puppy, perpetuated the cool detachment of most Far Eastern breeds, the Chow, the Pug and Pekingese in particular.

The King would light-heartedly refer to Choo-Choo as 'that animated dish-cloth' or 'the hairy monster', but held him in great affection. Choo-Choo was permitted one liberty, a nibble at the Queen's nosegay whenever he was held near her lapel.

There is of course nothing new in the Royal Family favouring dogs as pets and having a particular fondness for them. In 1896 when Thomas Fall, the celebrated dog photographer of that time, called on Queen Alexandra to photograph her with one of her Borzois, he recalled more than twenty dogs of various breeds, Borzois, Chows, Japanese Spaniels and Pekes, in the Royal kennels that day. Centuries before that, Henry the Eighth retained a 'Spanyel-keeper', Queen Elizabeth the First had a pack of pocket beagles, which she called her 'glove' or 'singing' beagles, James the First on ascending the English throne very quickly sent to Scotland for his terriers and the unfortunate Charles the First was invariably accompanied by his pack of toy spaniels, a passion shared by his children, Charles the Second, Princess Henrietta of Orleans and James the Second.

Pepys, in the privacy of his famous diary, scolded Charles II for playing with his dogs all the while … 'and not minding the business'. Whilst James II used to infuriate his courtiers by allowing dozens of toy spaniels to over-run the Royal apartments, the Council Chamber and even the Banqueting Halls. William III brought pugs from Holland and George IV, in his Regency days, had a pack of dwarf beagles which he exercised on Brighton Downs. But no monarch before or since has rivalled Queen Victoria's variety of breeds, Skye Terriers and Scotties, Poms and Pekes, Pugs and Maltese, Collies and King Charles Spaniels, Dachshunds, she kept them all, perhaps favouring Skye Terriers. Her husband, Prince Albert, favoured the greyhound in his breeds. In 1891, the man destined to become the dog world's ace showman, Charles Cruft, persuaded Queen Victoria to exhibit her Collie, Darnley, and three of her Pomeranians, whilst the Prince of Wales sent four Bassethounds.

The entries of Queen Victoria, Princess (later Queen) Alexandra (the most active Royal dog-fancier), and King Edward at Crufts were followed in time by those of King George V, the Duke of Windsor as Prince of Wales and the Duke of Gloucester. At the Cruft's Show of 1893 Princess Alexandra entered a St. Bernard and a Basset-hound; this was the show at which the Czar of Russia exhibited a team of 18 Borzois, later presenting a brace to Queen Victoria which became known as Russian fan-tailed greyhounds or Siberian Wolfhounds. In time Basset-hounds became Alexandra's principal breed and by the time her husband became King Edward VII and she was Queen, hers was the most successful Basset-hound kennel in being; when Queen Alexandra was exhibiting, there were often as many as a hundred Bassets, in the entries. King Edward VII was also interested in exotic breeds, once showing a quartet of hairless Rampur Hounds and attempting to introduce the Tibetan Mastiff, although his specimen was rather savage. King Edward was directly responsible for ending the custom of cropping the ears of certain breeds. His last dog, and undoubtedly the one closest to his heart was his wire-haired fox terrier, Caesar, which wore a collar inscribed 'I am Caesar, the King's dog'. At King Edward's funeral in 1910, little Caesar, no doubt puzzled by his much-loved master's disappearance, walked with the King's charger (with empty saddle) in the funeral procession. When King George V died at Sandringham in 1936, among the procession to the nearest railway station at Wolferton was his dog, Jock. 'Wolferton, had become known as the prefix for many of King George's famous Labradors, the breed having been introduced, to complement the Clumbers, in 1911. Wolferton Ben won six Kennel Club challenge certificates whilst at Cruft's in 1934, King George entered a team of Clumbers and won the Championship with Sandringham Spark as well as best brace and team.

King George, when the monarch, was particularly fond of a Cairn Terrier called Bob, but, as the Duke of York, his close friend for eleven years was Heather the Collie. A Fox Terrier called Happy was with him for thirteen years, and Jack a Sealyham for fourteen. Built into the stables' north wall at York Cottages Sandringham, are the gravestones of Heather, Happy and Jack, each stone bearing tribute to 'The constant and faithful companion of His Majesty'.

From this heritage it is scarcely surprising that King George VI was never without a yellow Labrador as a companion dog and that the royal princesses grew up to own and appreciate their dogs. The champion ankle-nipper Dookie was not however to sire his companion Jane's pups to add to the corgi collection of the Royal Household. That honour befell another of Mrs Gray's products, Tafferteffy, a *long tailed* Pembrokeshire Corgi, of all things. Two of this litter became royal pets, Crackers and Carol. Then sadly, in the early days of the Second World War, the celebrated Dookie died, greatly mourned, only to be followed by Carol, after attacks of fits. Crackers, a most handsome dog, in time took Dookie's place and would undoubtedly have won in the show-ring had he been exhibited. Strangely, like Dookie, Crackers would have nothing to do with Jane, who was tragically run over in Windsor Great Park. As a consolation, and as an 18th birthday present, Princess Elizabeth was given, in 1944, a replacement corgi, Susan, whose subsequent offspring Sugar and Honey, went to Prince Charles and the Queen Mother respectively. Their sire was a famous show-winner Champion Rozavel Lucky Strike, the dam being conveyed to him in some style by way of the Royal mail plane.

Meanwhile, Choo-Choo 'the animated dish-cloth', the original Tibetan Lion-dog had been succeeded by his grandson, Ching, whilst another canine character Johnny the Sealyham (Ilmer Johnny Boy, one of Sir Jocelyn Lucas's famous strain) transferred his affection from Princess Margaret, his real owner, to the Queen Mother.

But Susan the corgi initiated a royal corgi dynasty, for the Queen, who takes a keen interest in such breeding now has corgis who are a 9th generation directly descended from Susan, through Honey, Bee, Heather, Foxy, Brush, Geordie to the current dogs Smoky and Sparky. Her Majesty has also produced a new breed, the 'Dorgis' by mating a corgi bitch with Princess Margaret's dachshund Pigskin. There are two Dorgis in the Royal Household, Piper, the bitch and Chipper, the dog. Shadow, Myth, Fable and Diamond are, with Smoky and Sparky, the corgi component.

The Queen looks after her own dogs as much as possible and they move from house to house in the U.K. with Her Majesty and live in her private apartments. When they die, they are buried in the grounds of whichever house the Queen is living in at the time, but three of the longest living corgis — Susan, Sugar and Heather, have grave-stones at Sandringham.

The Queen takes a very great interest in the Sandringham Kennels. Since her accession to the throne in 1952, the breeding programme has gone from strength to strength culminating in the training of four Field Trial Champions, namely, Sandringham Ranger, Sandringham Slipper, Sherry of Biteabout and Sandringham Sydney. The most recent Field Trial Champion, Sandringham Sydney, has become very well known and popular in the field trial world. In 1977 a television film was made called Sandringham Sydney & Co, which showed Sydney at the Field Trials and during training sessions.

Usually the Kennels house approximately 25 fully grown dogs of varying ages from the older and more experienced gundogs, used by members of the Royal Family during the shooting season, to the younger dogs under training as gundogs. In addition to providing dogs for the Royal Family, the Estate Gamekeepers are kept supplied with working Labradors. At certain times of the year, usually in the spring and early summer, there are often as many as forty puppies in the Kennels born to the four or five best bitches which are used for breeding. One or two of the puppies from each litter are kept at the Kennels for training, but the majority are sold at eight weeks old to be trained by other people.

It is the policy of the Sandringham Kennels to attain the highest standard of trained dog possible and to achieve this end a great deal of time is spent training the better dogs up to Field Trial standard. During the summer and autumn, the dog handler attends several working tests and field trials throughout the country in an attempt to create field trial champions and to keep Sandringham dogs at the top of the breed. All the puppies born at Sandringham are given a name by the Queen and are registered at the Kennel Club with the prefix Sandringham. As the Queen is not specifically mentioned in the relevant law, Her majesty has not needed to have dog licences when they have been required by law.

But corgis, dorgis and labradors are not the only 'breeds' in the Royal Family's current collection, greater variety being provided by Her Royal Highness Princess Anne's lurcher Laura, and her Dumfriesshire Fox Hound, Random. Changes of breeds and changes of Monarch however have merely perpetuated the Royal Family's love of dogs.

Just as their Alsatian, Lion, accompanied the late Duke of Kent and Princess Marina on their honeymoon, so too did Susan the corgi go with the Queen and Prince Philip on theirs. The Queen's father, King George VI,

paid two visits to his kennels to check on the health of one of his gundogs who had damaged a paw during the day's shooting, on the very evening of his sad death. Princess Alexandra was brought up with a Chow, Choonam Li Wu T'song — but plain 'Muff' to her. Just before the Second World War, the Duke of Gloucester had a magnificent Bullmastiff Hussar Stingo, who won many prizes for him. And whilst there may appear to be a long gap in time between two young princesses falling for a mischievous corgi in the 20th century and a royal dog-collar in the early 18th century being rather grandly inscribed: 'I am his Highness, dog at Kew; Pray tell me, Sir, whose dog are you?', it merely illustrates an historic trend. From the greyhounds of the Tudors and the toy spaniels of the Stuarts to the corgis of the Windsors; from the Salukis of the Pharoahs to the Borzois of the Czars; from the tiny Papillons of the Louis' of France to the Liondogs of the Dalai Lama and from the huge white Pyrenean Mountain Dogs of the Dauphin's French Court at the end of the 18th century to the fragile Italian greyhounds which were the fondest pets of the Florentine princesses, there is a rich heritage of royal dogs.

Breed Behaviour
'Consider Well His Lineage'

A few years ago I used to sit and write looking out of an upstairs window of the house we lived in then which overlooked the back gardens of some expensive houses on a new estate. In one of these back gardens I could watch the antics of a young Golden Retriever, a handsome energetic dog with an affectionate nature and gleaming good looks. His owners seemed to have two of everything: two children, two cars, two boats, two Siamese cats, perhaps too much. I watched the dog, which was let out into the back garden at 8 in the morning for the rest of the day, with some interest. Once every two hours or so the dog would frantically chase its tail, round and round, round and round, pursuing its own stern with great determination. For some time I wondered what the cause might be: fleas? a tick? worms? blocked anal glands?. Yet there was no persistent irritation, in between bouts of tail-chasing the young dog paid no attention to its rear-end at all. And then one day the answer dawned on me . . . the wretched animal was trying to stop itself going mad. It was young, it had energy to burn up,

The German Shepherd Dog in action — defending the property of its owner

it had affection to give, but no outlet. The young dog just had to do something every so often to release energy, create an interest, occupy itself. Here was a breed specifically developed to possess stamina, endurance, field-prowess and great reserves of energy. Here was a dog of that breed denied any chance of utilising the very qualities which man had spent a century purposely engendering. His owners would have been better off with a stuffed dog on wheels — and so too would their dog. The mind of the dog is a simple one but it depends on stimulation.

The dog is extrovert, exhibitionist and loves knowing things. Not for him man's obsession with himself, dog's interests are external, the sights, sounds and experiences on offer outside himself. This makes dog less selfish, more companionable and often more noble than man. Dogs want to give, to contribute, to serve and be useful. But this usefulness, harnessed by man for the best part of twelve thousand years and developed into specialist skills as sheepdogs, watchdogs and guidedogs exemplify in our daily lives, has given dogs an expectation of being occupied and made more use off, not imprisoned endlessly as pet dogs so often come to be.

I am strongly against the use of dogs in laboratory experiments not just because it is another distressing example of the chilling clinical cruelty which only professional scientists can inflict on living creatures but because I doubt the validity of the empirical evidence obtained from an animal in such a totally alien environment. A beagle running free in a hare field is a different creature from one denied scenthound outlets, deprived of functional usefulness and removed from sensual stimulation. Dogs try so hard to please man that they contrive to produce an appearance of strained well-being for their laboratory keepers which is misconstrued as contentment. The mental suffering must be considerable and therefore the stress. The data produced from such stressful conditions simply must be distorted and therefore be of questionable value.

This canine desire to please their masters illustrates itself both in work and play. Some of the happiest and most vivacious dogs I have ever seen have been those performing in circus acts. I am not entirely in favour of circus acts involving animals but circus dogs genuinely seem to be having the time of their lives. Their performances seem to provide the most stimulating environment attainable for their latent extroversion and innate exhibitionist tendencies. Happy dogs invoke happiness in humans in so many different ways. Our family dogs get enormous pleasure from long walks and I get enormous benefit both from the healthy exercise and their companionship. But there is a huge difference between our two working sheepdogs when taking part in a game. Sam, the dog, regards the game as pure joy, an exercise in exuberant fun. Bess, the bitch, regards the game as a mere substitute for work and takes it desperately seriously. She runs in a curve to cut off the thrown ball, Sam races directly after it and retrieves it without any subtlety. Bess *strong-eyes* the stick in your hand, her concentration never wavering; Sam just wants you to throw the thing, as often as possible. He wants to get rid of his energy, Bess wants to perform, to have a function, to work. It is this instinctive behaviour which has made dog man's closest animal companion.

In all our breeds there are strong predetermined traits of behaviour resulting from specialist breeding with a distinct purpose in mind and this purpose is in the mind of each breed. To keep an Afghan Hound in a London flat is as cruel as keeping a Pekingese in an outhouse. One was bred for a thousand years to run fast over some distance, the other over two thousand as a companion dog. One needs to stretch its legs in order to be alive spiritually, the other needs the stimulation which human company provides. A spaniel needs the smells of a hedgerow, a pointer needs to quarter ground, a terrier ought to ferret around in dense undergrowth occasionally and a bloodhound needs to track. It will never be possible for all of us to use our various breeds in their original role but it is important for the spiritual happiness of the dog for some of its instinctive behaviour to be released. It is one way of saying thank-you to that particular breed for all the service given to man down the ages. Humans follow their aptitude and interests: dogs need to do likewise.

I look askance at some obedience work, for few dogs walk at ease and naturally with their right ear glued to a human knee. With our two sheepdogs I find that one is only happy leading us on a walk, about ten yards ahead, rather as corgis used to lead cattle out to pastures and Old English Sheepdogs did likewise on the droves. The other prefers to 'herd' us from five metres behind, rather as she would work a flock. Both will walk to heel on demand but do so to please me not their instincts. When one is ten yards ahead and the other five yards behind, they are not only under control but relaxed under the control of their instinctive behaviour. Like this they can trot-walk for mile after mile. Why force them to be glued to you towards the end of the twentieth century when in previous centuries their man-made functions decreed that they should walk in a different position? When our dogs are leashed, the bitch *always* takes the outer position and the dog the inner; it's where they feel they should be. We should aim to be considerate towards such instinctive behaviour not crush it and insist on total obedience to our modern whim.

Geneticists might claim that such behavioural habits are passed on in the genes but I have always felt there is more to it than

The Airedale has a strong protective instinct

that. Young dogs learn from old ones as every shepherd and kennel man knows. From each generation of specialist use and by breeding from good functional dogs, our ancestors developed the breeds we now prize and revere. But did the various breeds get better and better in their specialist role solely from their genetic make-up? Dr Rupert Sheldrake has set the scientific world in turmoil by producing his theory of 'formative causation' in which he proposes that living things 'tune in' to the knowledge o their predecessors. In his theory he puts forward the concept of 'morphic resonance' in which across space and time new members of a species can tap an undiscovered force in nature and receive communication from past

members of the same species. In this way, a pointer puppy could receive knowledge of the behaviour expected of a pointer, not from the genetic field but from a morphogenetic field direct into the puppy's mind. Not a theory which endears itself to materialistic scientists and one already attracting all the heated opposition, heaped scorn and arrogant dismissal which all pioneers in any field meet. But it is worthy of some attention by thinking dogmen. The uncanny homing instinct of pigeons and the quite extraordinary feats of some dogs in going back to former homes, sometimes the place where they were born, after an unhappy incident have never been scientifically explained in any convincing way. Could it be morphic resonance – a sixth sensory communication system? Dogs certainly do have powers which humans do not and whilst this may not be entirely relevant to Sheldrake's theory of learning, it is another dimension of the mind of the dog.

How do you explain the behaviour of a dog which goes and sits by the gate half an hour before its master arrives home quite unexpectedly? How do you explain too the behaviour of a dog like R.H. Smythe's (himself a vet) which would greet him on a Monday and Thursday morning with his cartridge bag in its mouth (Smythe's shooting days) and disappear every Tuesday and Satur-

The Weimaraner has an instinct to retrieve

German Shepherd dog on
patrol with the French Army —
a naturally obedient, instinctive
worker

day to go shooting with his former master? Could imprinting, in which say a pup suckled by a ewe, picks up some sheep-like habits – not just by copying – be explained by the as yet undiscovered system of communication proposed by Dr Sheldrake?

Most books on training young dogs treat all breeds the same as though breed-behaviour and specialist-functions inbred and developed over many centuries count for nothing. This is both illogical and unwise. I would no sooner try to train an English Setter in the same way as I would a Bullmastiff, than a Master of Hounds would try to develop a foxhound in the same way as a hunt terrier. We must be more breed-minded when we are training, owning and even showing dogs. The mind of each breed is different and we should have respect for such differences. Why own a Ridgeback or a Lhasa Apso if you are going to ignore its heritage and treat it as a mongrel? Surely you want it to be a Ridgeback or a Lhasa Apso and not merely look like one. The

richness of owning a pedigree dog must come from a deep-rooted respect for the capabilities of the breed. Remember the advice on breeding given to huntsmen by William Somerville in *The Chase* written in 1735: . . . 'Consider well his lineage; what his fathers did of old.' We remember well what our fathers did of old and believe it important that our children are taught the history of nations – the history behind each breed of dog should similarly be important to us, even if only when choosing a dog. But just as the races of human beings differ one from the other, our really basic instincts are similar and not always entirely dissimilar from those of dog. As the gravestones of a dog in the grounds of Berkely Castle records:

'No cold philosophy, no cynic
*   sneer,*
Checks the unhidden and the
*   honest tear,*
What little difference, and how
*   short the span,*
Betwixt thy instinct and the
*   mind of man.'*

CHAPTER TWO

Pastoral Breeds

The Flock Guardians

From Portugal in the west to the Caucasus mountains in the east, from southern Greece to northern Russia there are powerful pastoral dogs to be found, developed over thousands of years to protect man's domesticated animals from the attacks of wild animals. Some are called shepherd dogs, others mountain dogs and a few dubbed 'mastiffs', despite their full length muzzle. Their coat colours vary from pure white to wolf-grey and from a rich red to black and tan. Some are no longer used as herd-protectors and their numbers in north-west Europe dramatically decreased when the use of draught dogs lapsed. A number of common characteristics link these widely-separated breeds: a thick weatherproof coat, a powerful build, an independence of mind, a certain majesty and a strong in-

stinct to protect. As a group, they would be most accurately described as the flock guardians.

In south-west Europe these dogs became known in time as breeds such as the Estrela mountain dog and the Rafeiro do Alentejo of Portugal and the Estremadura mastiff of Spain. To the northeast of the Iberian peninsula, such dogs became known as the Pyrenean mountain dog and, separately, as the Pyrenean mastiff. In the Alps they divided, as different regions favoured different coat colours and textures into the breeds we know today as the Bernese, Appenzell, Entlebuch and Great Swiss mountain dogs and the St Bernard. In Italy, local shepherds favoured the pale colours now found in the Maremma sheepdog and the very heavy coat of the Bergamasco. In the Balkans, similarly differing preferences led to the emergence of the all-white Greek sheepdog and the wolf-grey Sar Tip, Karst and Sar Planina dogs in Yugoslavia.

Further east, other breed-types were stabilised into the Kuvasz and Komondor of Hungary, the Rumanian sheepdog, the Tatra mountain sheepdog of Poland, the Slovakian Kuvasz, the Mendelan of north Russia, the owtcharka of south Russia and the Caucasian sheepdog. In the Himalayan regions appeared the so called Tibetan mastiff, the Bhotia, the Bisben, the Bangara mastiff and the Koochi or Powinder dog of Afghanistan. In central Europe, breeds like the Bouviers des Flandres, Bouviers de Roulers, Giant Schnauzer, Hovawart and, purpose-bred, the Leonberger, emerged. Whilst where Europe and Asia meet, a breed now registered as the Anatolian shepherd dog developed.

The crude way in which the modern breeds of pedigree dog became named has led to all manner of confusion, misunderstanding and false conclusions down the years. Is the Dachshund a hound or a terrier? The German for hound is bracke; hund means dog not hound. Is the Great Dane a Danish dog or a German boarhound? The word Dalmatian may come not from Dalmatia but dama-chien or deer-dog. The Shetland sheepdog is a miniature collie, the Galway sheepdog and the Glenwherry collie work like shepherd dogs, the Old English sheepdog was a drover like the Bouviers and the Entlebuch Sennenhund. Sennenhund does not mean mountain dog but dog of the Alpine high pasture, so the Bernese was originally a drover.

The ancient Dutch hound, the Steenbrak, worked like a scenthound but looked like a sighthound. Sighthounds utilise scent and scenthounds use their eyes; they would be better named speedhounds and staminahounds. Of the Tibetan breeds is the Tibetan terrier an earthdog, the Tibetan spaniel a flushing or game-springing retriever or the Tibetan 'mastiff' a shortfaced, broad-mouthed, smooth-haired holding dog? The Brittany spaniel points game, unlike any other spaniel. The Irish water spaniel is also unlike any other spaniel, actually being a water-dog. What is the difference between a sheepdog and a shepherd dog? If a sheepdog herds sheep, what does a mountain dog do? Sheep and cattle don't graze on mountains but on pastures in valleys, whatever their altitude. Dogs which protect sheep, whatever their modus operandi, are flock guardians.

The breed name Tibetan 'mastiff' has led to a succession of writers to claim this breed as the original mastiff-type, the founder of every mastiff breed. Where is the evidence? Why not claim this distinction for the Bisben or the Bhotia? They both look like a Tibetan mastiff and are just as ancient. Such misnomers can lead fanciers to produce flock guardians looking like modern mastiffs, i.e. loose-lipped, black-masked, short muzzled and ponderous. In the Middle Ages, across Europe, all big powerfully-built dogs were referred to as mastiffs, matins or

Bernese mountain dogs

mastini; the word came to mean big mongrel not a breed. When the word mastiff refers to a short-faced, broad-mouthed, short-coated holding dog it has no connection with the flock guardians which historically had a different purpose and have inherited different instincts. Huge hounds like the hunting mastiffs were owned by the nobility not humble shepherds. Where did the flock guardians therefore come from? Pick up any breed history and its breed record since the first conformation dog show is masterly. But the accounts of its history before this date all too often add up to a mishmash of ill-researched theories, compounded mistakes and blatant plagiarism. But man has used dogs for 12,000 years, what happened before the distinct breeds emerged?

The history of dog is the history of man; when tribes migrated their valuable flock-guarding dogs went with them. The flockguarding breeds have three principal elements in common: their general appearance, their protective instincts and the fact that they are found wherever the Indo-Europeans settled. This latter area stretches from northern India through Iran into NW Asia, E Europe, the northern Mediterranean countries, N and W Europe to the British Isles.

Three thousand or so years ago, the people from the area north of and between the Black and Caspian seas, using their mastery of the horse and their invention of the wheeled chariot migrated to the west, south-west, south-east and due south. These mobile pastoralists, over the next thousand years or so, were to reach the Tibetan plateau and the river Indus in the east, the Taurus mountains in Anatolia and the rivers Tigris and Euphrates in the south and then beyond the rivers Rhine, Danube and Po in the west and south-west to form what eventually became the Celtic, Italic, German, Baltic, Illyrian, Thracian, Slav and Greek settlements.

The earliest known written forms of Indo-European are the second millenium texts from Anatolia, written by such peoples as the Hittites and Luvians. During the first millenium B.C., groups of people known successively as Cimmerians, Scythians and Sarmatians pressed on the eastern frontiers of Europe and again penetrated over the Caucasus and into north-eastern Anatolia, bringing with them huge pastoral dogs and superior kinds of horse-gear. With their spoke-wheeled chariots and hardy little horses from the steppes, the Hittites became powerful warriors. Extensive trade was conducted between western Anatolia and the Mediterranean littoral, from southern Portugal and Spain to southern Italy and Greece. Valuable hunting and flock-guarding dogs would have been coveted and then traded.

Agricultural and social change both affected the way the flock-guarding dogs developed and so too have climate and terrain. What is now the Anatolian shepherd dog was developing in times

*The Karst Shepherd — does the
same job as the Maremma but
is the same colour as a Wolf*

when Roman, Hellenic, Persian and the Turkish empires were successively spreading their influence. But for many breed histories, those of the Rottweiler and the Maremma sheepdog for example, to make so much of the Roman period is quite absurd. A flippant response to such claims would be: 'My Goodness! Is your breed as young as that?' But however sophisticated man became in changing times he still had great need of powerful dogs to guard his sheep. Because such activity is not as dramatic as war and hunting and because shepherds were rarely literate, it does not feature in art or literature.

It was during the eighth and seventh millenia B.C. that man first began to domesticate sheep and goats within the region of western Asia. Man, sheep, goats and dogs have a social system based on a single dominant leader and tend to base themselves on what have become known as home ranges, unlike say gazelles, antelope and bison. They have therefore become inter-dependent. The herdsman becomes the leader and the dog protects man and sheep against the privations of such wild predators as lynx, lion, wolf, tiger, jackal, leopard, cheetah, fox, civets and in some places, huge eagles. Flock-guarding dogs therefore had to be brave, vigilant, determined, alert, resolute and above all protective. Their role, the climate and the terrain demanded excellent feet, tough frames, weatherproof coats, great strength, good hearing and eye-

sight and remarkable robustness. These dogs operated in the hottest, coldest, stoniest, thorniest, windiest, most mountainous and most arid areas of Europe and western Asia. Physical exaggeration does not occur in any of the flock-guarding breeds, shepherds must have entirely functional dogs. Hunting ability is not desired. The size and bravery of these dogs however has led to their being used in bear hunts in Russia and in boar hunts in central Europe where they were used at the kill not as trackers.

Breed historians of the really big breeds make much reference to Molossian dogs in their writings. But the flock guardians and, indeed, the hunting mastiffs predate the dogs of the Molossian people, who probably got their mastiffs from Assyria and merely had their huge flock guarding dogs just as every other sheep-owning community did. Much is made too of the coat colour white, as found in the Maremma, Kuvasz, Greek and Polish breeds, on the grounds that the sheep can quickly distinguish such dogs from wolves. This is a strange theory since most flock guardians are wolf-grey.

We have of course lost most of the flock guarding dogs, including some distinct breed-types, through economic change and the extinction of many wild predators. It is surprising that so many of the breeds have survived, for the dogs of shepherds have been undervalued, underrated and ill-used down the centuries, despite their remarkable service, considerable intelligence and commendable faithfulness.

If you take the Anatolian shepherd dog as an example, this breed has survived the dismissive Turkish attitude towards the domestic dog, the traditional Moslem contempt for all dogs, the harsh terrain and demanding climate of its native land and many millenia of contrasting cultures. The greatest threat to its future, paradoxically, lies in its Kennel Club recognition which, sadly, brings with it deterioration in physique and loss of working use. This breed has survived because of its value to sensible shepherds in remote areas, rather than through the interest of the urban intelligentsia. If it is not to go the way of our own pastoral breeds, it will demand an exceptional breed council or collection of clubs and devotees more interested in sound dogs than a cabinet full of trophies. Dogs from such a distinguished heritage merit honourable custodianship in the future.

There are dangers in the wording of the approved breed standard in such a breed. Phrases like 'heavy head', 'slightly pendulous black lips' and 'rather small eyes' tend to encourage faddists who prefer to pursue such breed points rather than overall sound dogs. In twenty years time you could see Anatolian shepherd dogs as loose-lipped, slobbering, shortmuzzled specimens with tiny piggy eyes, quite unlike their ancestors. Look at the bulldog's

The shepherds of the Caucasus and their big herding dogs

muzzle, the bullterrier's skull, the bloodhound's forehead and the chow's eyes for the evidence of such 'improvement'. Working dogs which wore spiked collars, had their ears cropped, fought wolves, gave birth to their pups in a hole in the ground and slept out of doors in the snow and chill wind deserve a better fate than becoming victim to misguided Western beauty-show breed-point faddists. Arguments about coat colour and mis-marking, shape of ears and carriage of tail are petty relative to the need to breed strapping, soundly-constructed, correctly-moving, congenital disease-free dogs of good temperament. The Anatolian shepherd dog is a truly magnificent breed thoroughly deserving of being perpetuated in its time-honoured mould and not subject to the whim of a dominant breeder or misguided clique. It is depressing therefore to learn of problems in the breed, largely created by fanciers. Would a hard-working Turkish shepherd think colour at all important? Would he want a mastiff, developed to pull down big game by primitive hunters, in charge of his flock? Would he retain sickly pups, unmanageable dogs or 'angstbeissers'?

If we have the privilege of owning a dog from one of these flock guarding breeds, we should respect its origins, revere its lineage and honour its heritage. Humble shepherds from Iberia to the Caucasus have for thousands of years bred these dogs to a high standard and we owe it to them and their splendid dogs to continue this work. We must remember the *essential* criteria which led to these dogs developing as such magnificent examples of the canine race. All breed enthusiasts should keep in their mind the plea on behalf of working dogs made by 'Ikey' Bell the famous foxhound breeder:

> *'Cherish us for our courage*
> *Instead of for our looks:*
> *Look on us more as comrades,*
> *And less as picture books.'*

Entlebucher Sennenhund of Switzerland

Drovers and their Dogs

Do you live near a 'Halfpenny Lane', an inn called 'The Black Ox' or a country track which has a wide grass verge on either side flanked by a hawthorn hedge — which may have a Scots Pine or yew tree planted in it as a landmark? If so then you live near an ancient drovers' way along which as many as 10,000 cattle may have moved at any one time towards the grazing pastures prefacing the great markets or fairs. For centuries the economic survival of Scotland and Wales rested very much on the price the drovers were able to get for their mountain cattle. From the Western Isles to Oban and Glenshira, from Galloway to Dumfries, then on to Carlisle and Newcastle, came the West Highland 'Kyloes'. From Tregaron to Abergwysan (now a metalled road from south of Aberystwyth to west of Builth Wells) and across the Brecon Hills came the Black Welsh cattle. Down The Maiden Way, the Roman road from Hadrian's Wall over Bewcastle Fells, Melmerby Fell and through the Gilderdale Forest; along the Hambledon Drove, the prehistoric route over the Hambledon Hills between Durham and York, and along the Harling Drove, west to east, from Hockwold-cum-Wilton in the Fens through Thetford Forest across Croxton Heath to Roundham Heath came the great herds of black cattle, densely-packed flocks of sheep — even pigs, turkeys and geese, to the 'grazing counties' and then the great fairs and markets of the time: St Faith's Fair at Horsham St Faith near Norwich (sometimes handling 40,000 head at a time), Great Barnet Fair, Smithfield Market, Guildford and Farnham and the Kent sheep markets at Canterbury, Maidstone and Chilham. And as protectors, herders and hunters of game along the way came too the drovers' dogs.

To get the cattle to the main drove-ways, 'heelers' were used, the corgis of today. But most districts in England too had their 'nip'n'duck' dogs, the Ormskirk or Lancashire Heeler can still be found, but there were Yorkshire and Norfolk heelers too. On the main drove-ways the bigger leggier breeds took over, the now - extinct Smithfield sheepdog (very much like a Briard), the old English Bob-tail, the Welsh Hillman, the Black and Tan Sheepdog and the old Welsh Grey, mostly lost to us as distinct breeds. Steadily, at roughly two miles an hour, but for twelve hours a day (except Sundays) over several weeks, the great herds and flocks were driven, guarded and then delivered, usually after a fattening period in good grazing land.

The cattle, sheep and pigs, even turkeys and geese, were given shoes for the journey; many a wise blacksmith siting his forge near a drover's route. The drovers had good stout boots which they could afford for they were well-paid well-respected men, who could be entrusted with large sums of money on the return journey. But the dogs of course had many a sore pad. Not for them either a good night's sleep, for the overnight grazing grounds, usually near an inn, were well known to both sheep-stealers and packs of village-curs. As Edmund Spenser wrote in the sixteenth century:

'Thilk same Shepheard mought
  I well marke;
He had a dogge to byte or to
  barke;
Never had shepheard so kene a
  kurre,
That waketh and if but a leafe
  sturre.'

The drovers' dogs were often very large and very fierce, with those from Sussex and Dorset –

Bouvier des Flandres . . . many resemblances to our Old English Sheepdog

huge bob-tailed sheepdogs – having a fearsome reputation. 'Stonehenge described such dogs in the nineteenth century as:

'. . . a mixed breed ... In the grazing counties he is of great size and strength and some strains are highly valued; but they differ so much as to be incapable of being distinguished from other breeds'.

In 1854, Youatt wrote of the drover's dog and illustrated his writing with what appears to be a much bigger and appreciably less hairy Old English Sheepdog of to-day. But these dogs had need of long legs. Unlike the drovers who often returned home by coach or boat, usually with large sums of money to deliver, the dogs were frequently left to find their way home again – over hundreds and hundreds of miles in the worsen-ing weather of October and November. It is hardly surprising therefore for Stonehenge to de-scribe the old English Sheepdog with the words 'he untiring nature of the dog is very remarkable . . .' Very remarkable indeed!

The Farm Collies

In Britain, we have one surviving breed of working sheepdog, the Border Collie, which appears nowadays to be developing al-most entirely on black and white lines, in the show-ring as well as the shedding ring. And yet there is a rich heritage behind this breed. Wales alone could once

A Smithfield drover and his dog (from W.H. Pyne's The Costumes of Great Britain, *1808)*

sport four sheepdogs, the handsome red and white Welsh Hillman, the Old Welsh Grey, the Black and Tan and the Welsh Collie, mainly black and white: Ireland had the marbled Glenwherry Collie of Antrim in the north and the fine-looking tri-colour dogs of Galway in the south. The Lake District had the leggier shorter-coated sheepdogs, with the shaggier Smithfield sheepdogs featuring more in East Anglia.

The shepherd dog breeds the

world over have themselves been neglected by the authorities in the canine world. In Belgium, for example, their four native varieties of shepherd dog, named after the regions of their development, Tervueren, Groenendael, Malinois and Laekenois, were unrecognised and not bred to type until the invaluable work of Pro-

William Pease (born 1880) with farm collie Fly, West Tilbury

fessor Reul of the Cureghem veterinary school bore fruit at the end of the last century. In Germany, there is but one surviving breed of shepherd dog yet there were other identifiable varieties as well: the white sheepdogs of what was Pomerania, the lighter-coloured cogs of Prussia and the heavier-coated dogs of Bavaria and the south. In the early days of this century wire-coated German Shepherd Dogs existed in the breed, with one well-known bitch of the 1920s, Lori Maier, featuring this coat-texture, now lost to us.

In Holland, we find short-haired, wire-haired and long-haired versions of their shepherd dog, as well as the 'beardie' the Schapendoes; whilst in France, the Beauceron, Briard, Picardy, Pyrenean (not the Mountain Dog) and Languedoc sheepdogs still exist. The quaintly-named Sheep Poodle of Germany, the Catalan, Bergama and Portuguese sheepdogs perpetuate the Bearded variety.

Throughout all these breeds or varieties within a breed there are detectable constants: the dogs respond well to training, they are robust in health yet sensitive in temperament and there is, with the regrettable exception in very recent times of the German Shepherd, no exaggeration of physique. The stamina demanded from

Suffolk Shepherds with their Collies

a sheepdog is considerable, they have to be able to work in any terrain, in any weather, every day. The versatility of such dogs is recognised in their modern use, embracing security work with the police and armed forces; the detection of drugs, arms and explosives for the security agencies and customs service; avalanche rescue, tracking and corpse-locating duties for the police and straightforward guard-dog duties.

Despite fulfilling a wider range of functions for man than any other group of breeds, the sheepherding dogs have had the least written about them, yet day by day they are probably the most valuable. Perhaps because those involved in shooting in the past have been educated people well

able to write and read about their sport, there has never been a shortage of books on gundogs even if at tines they have rather lacked quality. The utility dogs used by artisan sportsmen and farm workers, like lurchers, working terriers and sheepdogs, have however until very recent times been more than neglected. And whilst Phil Drabble in his admirable T.V. series *One Man and his Dog* has redressed this handsomely on film, no one has covered sheepdogs in the way in which, say, Brian Plummer, Ted Walsh and Dan Russell have written about lurchers and terriers. Yet there are more dogs of the

The farm collie preserved in the Natural History Museum

sheep-herding breeds in Britain than any other type, with for example over 19,000 German Shepherd Dogs alone registered in 1986 with the Kennel Club and around 7,000 working sheepdog puppies registered annually with the International Sheepdog Society and twice as many more being unregistered.

Despite an increase from the 54 Alsatians registered with the Kennel Club in 1919 to over 21,000 registered in 1984 however, not one of the breed earns its keep as a sheepdog in the United Kingdom. Despite the introduction of breeds like the Briard, the Tervueren, the Komondor and the

Dutch Shepherd Dog (short-haired)

Maremma since the Second World War and brief flirtations with lesser known sheepdog breeds such as the Pomeranian Sheepdog before that and the New Zealand Huntaway just recently, our renowned Border Collie stands supreme as the working sheepdog here. This contrasts vividly with the growing use of Continental gundogs in Britain in the last 20 years; there might well be well over 1000 being employed in the shooting-field nowadays.

In the United States of America, pedigree breeds like the Cocker Spaniel, the Beagle, the rough-coated Collie, the Boxer, the Boston Terrier and the Dachshund were listed in the 1940s as the most popular. But in his fascinating book *How to Breed Dogs*

of 1947, the veterinary surgeon Leon Whitney described the farm shepherd dog as the most popular breed in America. He wrote of this breed: 'There is a breed which will one day be recognised as a registered breed by the foremost kennel associations, which has no commonly recognised name. It is known variously as the farm shepherd, the barnyard collie, the old-fashioned shepherd, the cow dog, the English shepherd and by other colloquial names. And while I doubt there is a more alert, trustworthy, or American dog, still no breed speciality clubs have. been organised to push it.' I am not exactly sure what Whitney meant by doubting there was a more 'American dog' for he goes on to state: '... and this old fashioned cow-dog have gone hand in hand with the early development of this country. Nowhere have either had greater usefulness, not even in the country of their origin. ' There is no doubt that these mainly black and tan, sable or tricolour sheepdogs came from Britain. In his *The Working Sheep Dog* published in Chicago in 1937, Luke Pasco, the leading New England sheepdog trialler of the 1930s, relates how time and time again he was able to trace outstanding dogs to British stock, usually imported from Scotland with a load of sheep or cattle and often shrewdly included in the deal by American livestock dealers. He referred to them as Border Collies, the name

Nat Seal, a Dorset drover, died 1898

of the contemporary pedigree breed, now favoured as a black and white breed with the distinctive white collar. A more accurate generic term would have been British farm collie.

In *A General History of Quadrupeds* published in 1790 Thomas Bewick illustrated the Shepherd's dog with an engraving which is faithful to the working dog of today. Two hundred, years earlier, Dr Caius listed the shepherd's dog as a distinct breed in his well known treatise on the dogs of England. In his *The Dog* of 1854, Youatt quotes Professor Grognier's description of the shepherd's dog in France: 'In one or other of the varieties it is found in every part of France. Sometimes there is but a single breed, in others there are several varieties... Everywhere it preserves its proper distinguishing type.' These words sum up rather neatly the way in which the terrain, the climate and local preferences produce the differing varieties of shepherd dog in a country. It is interesting to note how the pastoral dog breeds in France match those in Britain, the Briard being comparable with our Old English sheepdog, the Beauceron with our smooth collie, the Pyrenees sheepdog with our bearded collie, the Picardy sheepdog with our rough collie and their little nondescript drovers' dog with the small bob-tailed sheepdogs still found in the Hereford border country. Such dogs were taken by colonists to the overseas territories, so that to this day we have Australian sheepdogs, often featuring the merle colour, and the black and tan farm dogs of the United States.

Wales once featured several distinct breeds of sheepdog, Mr W. Lloyd-Thomas of Llanrhystyd managing to produce very typical examples of the old types just before the Second World War. His Welsh collies were very similar to the Border collie of today and his Old Welsh Grey resembled a less heavily-coated bearded collie. But the Welsh Hillman was a much more imposing breed, bigger than the black and tan sheepdog and in colour a striking golden sable, although some were grey/blue merles. Rawdon Lee considered that these dogs were descended from the Welsh Wolfhounds, employed in the chase by medieval Welsh noblemen. Certainly there is identifiable high breeding a definite 'presence' and an extra pride in dogs of this type which still appear today. Over two feet at the withers and weighing around 50 lbs, these handsome red dogs crop up in litters and would be worth conserving as an ancient native breed. Such atavism indicates to me the surfacing of both the strength and individuality of a distinct breed-type and should be exploited.

David Tolley of Trafford in Cheshire has a fine specimen remarkably similar to the description of the old Welsh Hillman. Anna Pugh has a bitch Jess from Ty Cradoc in the Black Mountains

The farm collie: alert . . .
willing . . . loyal

just off Offa's Dyke which is again very much a re-creation of the old Welsh breed. Wood Cole also of Ty Cradoc has a smooth blue merle bitch which he hopes to mate to David Tolley's dog in an attempt to restore the Hillman type. Wood Cole finds Jess's mother and sister such good workers and the type so firmly imprinted that he is confident of re-establishing a stable line.

But whilst we may have lost the rich variety of regional strains in our herding breeds, the prototypical farm collie has survived the manifold changes in agriculture, the whimsical fancies of showring breeders, the human appetite for new foreign breeds, the hard physical demands made by sheep and cattle driving and sadly all too often down many centuries a distinct lack of care from their owners. As recently as 1953, a survey in Scotland indicated that over 1 in 10 of working sheepdogs there were suffering from a condition known as black tongue resulting from inadequate feeding.

The labrador may be favoured by drivers of range-rovers and Afghan hounds by the fashion-conscious, but no breed can match the record of service to man of the farm collie. My affection for my own two working sheepdogs carries with it my admiration for their character, my appreciation of their labour and my gratitude for the centuries of service given unstintingly by these staunch, undemanding and yet quite irreplaceable farm collies.

Harsh-haired Herding Breeds of Europe

I know of no type of dog which evokes a greater feeling of affection from the public than the long-coated, goat- or harsh-haired sheep-herding dogs found all over Europe. Perhaps this is because they exude an air of sheer lovableness or possibly because they look so mutt-like and lack any look of high breeding or pretension towards aristocratic airs. But whatever the reason it is fair to say, I believe, that everybody loves a 'beardie'.

The group is represented in most areas of Europe: the Cao da Serra de Aires from Portugal, the Briard from France, the Pyrenean sheepdog, the Bergama sheepdog of Italy, the Gos d'Atura of Catalonia, the German Sheep poodle, the lowland sheepdog of Poland, the south Russian Owtcharka, the Schapenpoes of Holland and, from the British Isles, the Bearded Collie, the Old English and Smithfield sheepdogs.

If you compare this distribution with the big flock-guardians of the high pastures like the Maremma, the Estrela mountain dog, the Kuvasz, the Tibetan 'mastiff' and the Anatolian shepherd dog then with the various types of Dutch and Belgian shepherd dogs, the Border collie, the Beauceron, the Algerian sheepdog, Berger de Picardie, the rough and smooth collies and the now extinct Welsh hillman, you can soon see how climate, function and terrain determined type.

It is not unusual for varieties of coat to occur within the same breed-type, as the Portuguese water dog (with its long and curly versions), the Weimaraner (with its long and smooth coated varieties), the German pointer (with its long, wire, smooth and bristle-haired versions), the St Bernard (with its smooth and rough-coated varieties), the Ibizan hound (wire and smooth), the short and rough-haired Italian segugios, the fox terrier and the Vizsla indicate. Throughout Europe, in Holland, Germany, Britain and France for example, there are long-haired, rough-haired and smooth-haired varieties of native herding dogs.

Against that background therefore, I don't believe there is really any need to seek an origin for, say, the bearded collie in dogs off a Polish ship in the 16th century or any other foreign ancestry. If you want a long-haired sheepdog, breed one selectively from the longer-coated specimens of sheepdog stock! The international distribution of dogs that herd sheep, longhaired, rough-coated or smooth, demonstrates that the differing coat-lengths occur naturally and have been perpetuated and enhanced by line-breeding down the centuries to stabilise one particular coat. In time a desired coat length can be fixed and the various breeds, or varieties within a breed, evolved. Not surprisingly, coat lengths can be linked with specific needs in particular areas and developed with other breed characteristics. With pedigree dog-breeding being only just over a century old it is easy to overlook the fact that breed-types evolved in many cases over more than five centuries.

In some areas where prolonged windchill exposure was met, felted coats like those of the Komondor and the Puli were needed. But the coat texture and length produced was originally always in pursuit of a purpose and never appearance. The herding breeds were developed by essentially practical men, in eternal combat against the elements and wild predators, men who quickly discarded weedy or faulty dogs. I know of no old print or early photograph or painting which depicts the longer-haired herding breeds with the excessive length of coat displayed by many of their successor breeds in today's show-rings. Too heavy or too long a coat is a needless handicap to a working breed not traditionally requiring to feature such a characteristic.

Earlier this century Mr H.A. Titley, who contributed so much to the development of the Old English sheepdog, wrote: 'During recent years there has been an increasing tendency to over-development of the coat and especially for show purposes, but it is an adverse handicap for "working" dogs which are exposed to all weathers, mud, and dusty roads.' Forty years or so ago James Garrow wrote to Mrs G.O. Willison, who launched the show career of the bearded collie : 'The Beardie was essentially a worker, famed for fleetness and brains, kept by butchers, farmers, etc ... The coat should not be overlong and of a raw harsh texture ... Have you drawn up the standard for the K.C. yet? You want to emphasise the rule on coat.' Most of the beardies I see in the show ring nowadays display such a length of silky coat as to obscure the natural lines of the dog's body, which is contrary to the breed standard. The standard of the Old English sheepdog places no restriction on the length of coat at all.

I can find no evidence nor any credibility in the stories that the longer-haired herding dogs all originated in one country and spread out from there. I believe it is likely that the herding dogs brought south by the migrating Indo-Europeans two thousand years before Christ had the prototypal dogs and since then they have gradually evolved into the types and with the physical features demanded by location, function and local preferences. In Britain bearded collies have been interbred with the Old English type and the working sheepdogs of the border collie type for centuries. This is not to say of course that in some areas a definite type was not preferred and kept distinct.

The movement of tribes and groups of people over Europe in the last two thousand years, especially in the first millennium A.D., has led to the various modern breeds as we know them today emerging in certain areas. Of course sheep-herding dogs quite often went with flocks of sheep when these changed hands and, sometimes, countries too. It is, in my view, quite absurd to claim that the different herding breeds, especially when they occur in the same country, are completely unrelated. It is entirely fair however to state that line-breeding for distinct type has been practised for several hundred years in a number of areas.

This has led some to claim that Peebleshire is the true home of the beardie, Dorset the real home of the bobtail, The Lake District the original base for the border collie and Snowdonia the home of the old Welsh grey. But beardies have long been favoured in north-west England and, being utilised by drovers, could be found wherever there was a vibrant sheep trade; the Smithfield sheepdog, the bigger beardie, being associated with the sheep market towns and areas of eastern England. There were differences between the longer-haired sheepdogs found in the Highlands and those working in the border regions.

Beardies work in a different style from that of their shorter-haired fellow working sheepdogs; they are not silent or strong-eyed but excel at collecting and then retaining sheep in big groups. This capability made them most useful to drovers and butchers.

I understand that in the early

Shepherd of 1870-80

days of trying to breed pure beardies it was not unusual to find a
couple of pups in a litter looking
more like border collies. The
early registrations of sheepdogs
with the International Sheepdog
Society listed rough, smooth and
bearded types but farmers often
interbred dogs with different
coats and ear-carriage. The bob-
tail was also used as a drovers'
dog; I can remember an old
grazier on Salisbury Plain thirty
years ago telling me how the instinctive skills of the bobtails varied: some preferring to lead the
sheep, others to drive them as a
flock and some to guard a flank.
This behaviour occurred in young

untrained dogs.

Other bobtailed dogs, somewhat smaller than ours, are the
berger des Pyrenees, the Gos
D'Atura of Catalonia and the Pol-
ski owczarek nizinny or Polish
lowland sheepdog, although
some specimens in these breeds
which are born with tails can be
seen undocked. The Cao da Serra
de Aires from Portugal, known as
the 'monkey dog ' from its heavy
eyebrows, beard and moustache
and the goat-haired Pastore
Bergamasco or Bergamese sheepdog both feature the full tail, the
latter breed carrying it gaily when
working. This Portuguese dog,
the Schapendoes of Holland and
our own bearded collie are as-
tonishingly similar in appearance,
a significant fact if one day gene
pools need enlarging.

I understand that every
bearded collie registered in the
world can be traced back to just
twelve dogs, a small genetic base.
This fine breed will need wise
breeders if it is to retain its
characteristics, robustness and
virility. Already in Canada I've
seen the breed described as having set a record for 'the breed
ruined in the shortest possible
time'. It is surely vital to breed
every ancient breed true to its
heritage rather than for those
who see only cosmetic appeal.
The beardie should be a medium-
sized dog not a rival to the old
English sheepdog. The beardie
should be long-backed and its
eyes should be visible not con-

*Jimmy Dunford, still working
on Salisbury Plain, at 71, in 1937*

cealed. I like the phrase used in the outline description of the breed in *Our Dogs* of December 17th, 1898: 'The face should have a sharp, inquiring expression'.

Old English Sheepdogs of fifty years ago

Facial expressions can tell you a lot about dogs as well as people! Soppy-eyed dogs shouldn't be tolerated in a working breed and neither should excessively-heavy coats.

The Cumbrian sheep farmer Malcolm Ewart of Barkbeth Farm

near Bassenthwaite Lake works beardies on grazing stints on Skiddaw of around 3,000 feet. He has a waiting list for his pups, so highly are his dogs rated as workers. But his dogs do not feature the length of coat seen on show ring specimens in the breed. Show breeders may not want their dogs to work on Skiddaw but if they are true bearded collies they should be physically able to do so .

We should value the herding breeds for their unique service to man and respect their historical role and form by breeding dogs still able to carry out their original function – even if never required to do so. The longer-haired herd-

ing breeds have coats which can mask a score of faults and judges of these breeds have a more difficult task. Unsound movement is less easily screened from someone with an eye for dogs, being probably the worst fault in a working breed and such breeds demand more practised, more widely experienced and enlightened judges than the ornamental breeds. This particular group of herding dogs readily arouse our affection; it is even more important that they are afforded our respect, respect for

The Gos D'Atura or Catalan sheepdog

Cao Da Serra de Aires — the Portuguese Beardie

Shepherd and dog in 1864

their true type and correct conformation.

Writing on the dog in the 18th century, Oliver Goldsmith used these words: '...to man he looks in all his necessities with a speaking eye for assistance; exerts for him all the little service in his power with cheerfulness and pleasure; for him bears famine and fatigue with patience and resignation.' He could have been writing about the herding breeds; their 'little service in our power' should be reciprocated and their best interests served.

North-country cowherd (1901) with old type Beardie

The Pastoral Dogs of France

Only comparatively recently have we in Britain come to appreciate and then value the herding or herd-protecting breeds of France. But nowadays, with 136 bouviers des Flandres and 274 Briards registered with the Kennel Club in 1986 to reinforce the Pyrenean mountain dog, our acknowledgement of their many agreeable qualities is manifesting itself. It is claimed I know that the bouvier des Flandres (or drover's dog of Flanders) is Belgian but the breed developed when Flanders, a medieval principality spanning what is now Holland, France and Belgium, was French, although there was once Spanish influence there too. I always think of the bouvier des Ardennes, a breed reminiscent of the pumi of Hungary, as the Belgian drover's dog, although again the Ardennes region occupies what is now Belgium, Luxemburg and northern France.

Just as the bouvier des Ardennes looks like the pumi, all the French herding breeds resemble other European breeds too. The berger de Brie or briard is like the schafpudel of Germany, the berger de Beauce is similar to our own smooth collie, the berger de Picardie resembles our Smithfield sheepdog, the berger des Pyrenees looks like the Schapendoes of Holland, the Bergamese shepherd and our bearded collie, whilst the bouvier des Flandres has many similarities with our own drovers' dog, the old English sheepdog, also bob-tailed and able to feature a shaggy grey coat. Lesser known varieties like the berger des Pyrenees à face rasée or smooth-faced Pyrenean sheepdog, the berger du Langedoc or farou, the berger de Bresse, the berger de Savoie and the Labrit from Les Landes in the south-west indicate the way in which the various areas can produce their own types, rather as the Galway sheepdog, the Glenwherry collie, the Welsh hillman, the black and tan collie and the old Welsh grey existed in the British Isles.

These regional differences, based on a very similar model, can be seen too in the herding breeds of Holland and Belgium, with the wire, short and long-haired varieties of the Hollandse herdershond, the four varieties of Belgian shepherd dog and the owtcharka breeds further east. Essentially we have a 20-25 inch shepherd dog in a variety of coat-lengths and coat-colours fulfilling the same basic function. The mountain dogs illustrate the additional need for a much more substantial dog to repel wolves and human predators in the more isolated areas. But protection of their charges apart, the linking factor with all these breeds is sheep and to a lesser extent cattle, more particularly, man's trading in these grazing animals.

Domestic sheep were first taken to Europe by early neolithic farmers around seven thousand B.C. These early farmers also kept cattle and had a need to prevent both animals from wandering and protect them from predators. Tame dogs would have been invaluable allies in the attempt to meet these needs. When these farmers moved on to new pastures their cattle, sheepdogs moved with them.

Up to 1000 B.C. something like four-fifths of Europe north of the Alps and the Pyrenees was covered by dense forest and over the next two hundred years extensive clearance by farmers provided the basis for new growth through local trade, notably from the fairs dating from Charlemagne. This growth brought an unprecedented demand for good herding dogs, both to work the herds and get them to market. Bruges became the capital of medieval Flanders and was the chief European wool manufacturing town as well as its chief market; until its harbour silted up in the late 15th century it was the link between the Baltic, the North Sea and the Mediterranean. It would have been surprising therefore to find Flanders without really good sheep-driving dogs. In the south, Lyon played a key role in linking

A French shepherd with his Cur-dog

the inland market-towns with the ports further south. Again the need for dogs to drive the sheep and cattle was considerable.

In the sixteenth century Spain had three million sheep and exported them both overland and to her new territories. The main trade was overland to France in the north over the Pyrenees, with dogs playing a vital role in this trade. Two hundred and fifty years ago the Danes were sending 80,000 head of cattle a year to Germany by driving them overland using dogs. The routes taken by the various drovers with their herding dogs crossed every European boundary and it would be unwise to claim purity of descent for the different national breeds of today. Similarities appear therefore in the herding breeds of Belgium, Holland, Flanders, Alsace, southern France and the Iberian peninsula, with the Catalan and Portuguese sheepdogs for example strongly resembling the berger des Pyrenees. These breeds indicating in this way the classic time-honoured drovers' routes of southern Europe. Few breeds of dog developed in isolation from their function.

Against this background, the bouvier des Flandres became associated with the agricultural plain of Flanders and enjoyed a wide variety of names: vuilbaard (dirty beard), koe hund (cow dog) and toucheur de boeufs (cattle-mover or drover). When cattle and sheep were transported to market and ports by rail and truck, concern was expressed for the dogs of the local drovers,

rugged handsome dogs conforming to an identifiable type. In 1910 the bouvier was first exhibited as four varieties (e.g. the bouvier de Roulers) but in 1912 the growing band of enthusiasts combined forces to standardize these into one. Then the Great War played havoc with the breeding stock and it was left to a Belgian Army veterinary surgeon, Captain Darby, who by saving some good specimens founded the modern breed through his sire Ch. Nic de Sottegem.

By 1922, the breed club had agreed the desired type and drafted a breed standard. Since then the bouvier has become more a personal guard-dog, police or army dog than a pastoral breed but has remained essentially a working dog. The first American standard was approved in 1959, and revised in 1975 following the sensible Franco-Belgian agreement. With the breed type now agreed internationally, the bouvier is gaining in strength in many widely-separated countries on sheer merit. I am more than a little puzzled though why the colour chocolate-brown should be so disliked and severely punished in the breed; if an otherwise good pup emerges in this colour, why consign it to the bucket?

The berger de Brie has the same shoulder height of the bouvier but not the forequarter bulk. I get depressed when I read again the old fallacy of this breed originating in a barbet-beauceron cross, based on appearance presumably but denied entirely by history. The Briard has existed in its own right for as long as the Beauceron and belongs to a type which breeds true all over Europe. Of far greater interest is the observation that this breed-type appears wherever the Celts settled.

The most numerous of the French sheepdog breeds the Briard has, like many of the multi-

Picardy Sheepdog . . . probably the oldest of the French pastoral breeds and still very much a working breed

talented herding breeds, been used widely, as a police-dog, red-cross dog, sentry-dog and ammunition-carrier. Dogs like the Briard are alleged to have been utilised by Napoleon to drive live-stock during his Egyptian cam-paign; the Egyptian sheepdog of more modern times, the Armant, being coincidentally very like a Briard. The Marquis de Lafayette brought dogs of this type to north America to work with sheep. The Club Francais du Chien Berger de

Beauceron in classic role

Brie was not formed however until 1897, despite one of the breed being placed first in the class for sheepdogs at the first French dog show held in Paris over thirty years earlier. In the modern breed I have concern still about their temperament especially excessive shyness, having learned long ago the deceptive and unpredictable nature of this feature. But there seems to be a responsible breed club in Britain working to improve every aspect of the breed here.

The French herding breed which impresses me the most in that country however is the Beauceron, a strapping handsome dog with the majesty of the Akita and the alertness of the Dobermann. (I strongly suspect that Herr Dobermann resorted to Beauceron blood in the creation of his breed). Black and tan or harlequin and sometimes dubbed 'bas rouge' or red stockings because of its red-tan legs, the Beauceron is little known outside France but is attracting interest in the United States where a breed club has been formed and a stud-book opened. A big, robust, powerful, muscular but not heavy breed, 26 inches at the withers, very strong-minded and rather fierce in appearance, it is one of the few breeds whose strength of will you can sense and whilst it lacks the 'strong eye' of our working sheepdogs, its work with cattle is in the brusque no-nonsense style. They have been used by both the French army and the police and my French friends tell me they

were originally hunting dogs used on boar and stag, representing an ancient French type. The harlequin factor is found in hounds, as the Dunker hound, the Great Dane and the dachshund illustrate; the 'merling' of the Beauceron is more like the hound-colouration than that found in collies.

The Farou or berger du Languedoc, also called the berger de Camargue and chien de Larzac is probably a southern version of the Beauceron. The Labrit, probably getting its name from the town of that name in the south of France, (although some suggest it comes from de la Brie, since it is Briard-like and there was a tendency in the last century to call all French smooth-haired shepherd dogs chiens de Beauce and all coarse-haired dogs chiens de Brie) is probably more closely related to the Pyrenean sheepdogs. The berger de Bresse is almost certainly now lost to us and the berger de Savoie, Beaucheron-like but drop-eared, may too not have survived.

We have probably lost more types of herding-dog all over Europe than of any other group; the pastoral scene has changed dramatically in this century and the advent of the pedigree dog has seen human whim play its part too. But this group of dogs have given man supremely loyal and devoted service over many centuries and whether French in origin or British deserve our gratitude.

The Pastoral Breeds of Hungary

'What, o ye wild Carpathians, to me
Are your romantic eyries bold with pine?
Ye win my admirations not my love;
Your lofty valleys lure no dreams of mine.
Down where the prairies billow like a sea,
Here is my world, my home, my heart's true fame.
My eagle spirit soars, from chains released,
When I behold the un-horizoned plain.'

This extract from Petofi's poem *Az Alfold* – the Great Plain, gives a vivid image of the Hungarian landscape, even if it is now an image of the past. North Americans could identify it at once; the evocative phrases 'prairies billow like a sea' and 'the unhorizoned plain' perhaps reminding them of the scorching summers and freezing winter winds of their own prairie-lands. Such climatic extremes in Hungary made nomadic herdsmen, their sheep and cattle and their herding dogs, hardy, stoical ... and well-covered! The marauding packs of hungry wolves and the occasional bands of robbers called for vigilant herdsmen and powerful resolute dogs. It is not surprising therefore to find the Hungarian pastoral breeds mostly huge hairy dogs, well able to take care of themselves and their charges.

Near Debrecen is the renowned Hortobágy puszta covering over seventy five thousand dead flat acres, empty and barren. But the Hortobágy once held many villages and fertile land. Then after the Tartar invasion of the thirteenth century, villages were laid waste, crops destroyed and trees cut down for firewood, so that the cruel winds soon created near-desert conditions. For centuries the only inhabitants of the Hortobágy were shepherds and herdsman, weather-beaten nomads living in wheeled huts drawn by oxen. Their cattle, sheep and horses were never brought under a roof, summer or winter. Under such conditions, breeding stock of high value was developed; from such knowledgeable stockmen magnificent dogs were bred and proudly perpetuated down the years.

The name of Hungary in the native language is Magyarland, the Magyars, a primitive tribe related to the Finns and Estonians, coming over the Carpathian Mountains a thousand years ago. But throughout its history, Hungary has had to face the constant threat of invasion, from north, south, east and west. The Tartars or Mongols devastated the country six hundred years ago and after them came the Osmanli or Ottoman Turks; for 150 years a Turkish Pasha ruled in Buda.

In no country can breeds of dog be studied without reference to the history of that country. It is interesting therefore to hear the Hungarian gundog the Viszla being linked with the Yellow Turkish Hunting Dog, to note similarities between the Transylvanian Hound, the Finnish Hound (Suomenajokoira) the Black Forest Hound of Czechoslovakia (Slovensky Kopov) and the Russian Trail Hound (Guanchi) and to see the likeness between the Kuvasz, the strikingly-beautiful Hungarian herding breed and the Maremmas of the Abruzzi, the Tatra Shepherd Dog of Poland and the Pyrenean Mountain Dog. These latter breeds, huge white dogs of great composure and majesty, draw comment wherever they are seen. The powerful felt-coated Hungarian Komondor too has some

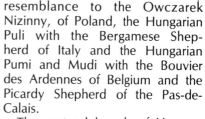

resemblance to the Owczarek Nizinny, of Poland, the Hungarian Puli with the Bergamese Shepherd of Italy and the Hungarian Pumi and Mudi with the Bouvier des Ardennes of Belgium and the Picardy Shepherd of the Pas-de-Calais.

The pastoral breeds of Hungary make up five most distinctive breeds, from the ivory-white grandeur of the extremely handsome Kuvasz, the highly-individual dry-spaghetti coated Komondor, the endearing natural scruffiness of the Pumi, the curly-coated Mudi which produces such enchanting puppies, to the strange corded-coated animated hearth-rug of a dog, the Puli. Doctor Pal Safkńy, one-time president of both the National Association of Hungarian Dog-breeders and the Federation Cynologique Internationale (F.C.I), the international Kennel Club, considers that the Hungarian breeds arrived in the Carpathian Basin during the Great Migration preceding the Magyars, the Huns and the Avars, then with the Magyars and later with the immigrating Pechenegs and Cumanians as their pastoral and hunting dogs. These dogs were bred by their fierce nomadic owners for their functional excellence, weedy specimens neither being tolerated by human owners nor spared by the demanding climate.

The selective breeding of Hungarian dogs was instigated in the second half of the nineteenth

The Kuvasz, from the same source as the Greek Sheepdog

century by Count István Szé-chenyi (1791 – 1860), statesman, writer, leading figure in the Hungarian Reform Movement and as the establisher of controlled horse breeding (and horse racing) in Hungary, a man who had a natural eye for a good dog. But selective breeding had for centuries been exercised too by the herdsmen, good stockmen who travelled great distances to get their bitches covered by worthy dogs. The pioneers of Hungarian sheepdog breeding. were three men: Géza Buzzi, Károly Monostori and Emil Raitsits, who selected those individual specimens which best represented the respective breeds and then conducted repeated planned breeding programmes.

The three small pastoral breeds: the Puli, the Pumi and the Mudi were bred basically for the same function, herding cattle and sheep. The two big kinds, the Komondor and the Kuvasz were essentially herd or flock-protectors rather than herders. Strictly speaking all five breeds should be called pastoral breeds, the three smaller ones should be called herding breeds and the two larger ones, shepherd dogs. The word sheepdog should denote a 'sheep-working breed' a 'strong-eyed' breed, like our Border Collie, which displays the highest form of pastoral dog-work. But inaccurate or loosely-applied nomenclature has long bedeviled dogdom.

The two 'big kinds' of these Hungarian breeds really are big dogs; the Kuvasz often weighing some 100 lbs and standing nearly 30 inches high, whilst the Komondor can weigh about 110 lbs. These two breeds are white coated whereas the Puli can be black, grey or pure white (but always of one solid colour), the Pumi is usually reddish black but also often dark and light grey and the Mudi is usually black, but can be white, or black with white, in scattered patches. But more varied than colour of coat in these breeds is the texture.

The huge but beautifully symmetrical Kuvasz has the thick medium length coat of the mountain dogs, the Pyrenean, the Estrela, the Bernese the Tibetan mastiff and the Charplaninatz of Yugoslavia. The powerful and well-draped Komondor, with the macaroni-looking felted coat and the Puli, with its distinctive corded coat remind me of the ancient water dogs, perpetuated today in our own Irish Water Spaniel and the corded poodle. Nick Waters, 'whiptail' fancier, has pointed out a number of similarities between his breed and the Afghan Hound. Now if you believe, as I do, that the waterdogs originated in China as 'liondogs' and were passed along the silk routes to the Mediterranean ports of Antioch and Tyre via the southern edge of the Gobi Desert and then Tashkent, Samarkand and Northern Parthia then it is tempting to speculate on a link. Afghanistan is what was Southern Parthia; the Mongols invading Hungary from the south came from the Tashkent area. Furthermore the Mudi with its black curly-coat is remarkably similar to the Dutch water-dog, the Wetterhoun, whilst the Pumi has a distinct Bedlington Terrier look about it. I say this because I consider the Bedlington's origin to be from a blend by gypsy breeders of the working terrier of the day and the Tweed Water Spaniel. The coat-texture of all these breeds follows the pattern of the ancient water-dogs and their descendant breeds.

But whether from water-dog stock or not, the Komondor, like the corded poodle, is a 'once-seen never-forgotten' breed, with their vast bulk, low head carriage, drooping tail, very shaggy or corded long white hairs tumbling fringe over the eyes and rounded

heads. The Komondor has been traced as a breed back to 1544; Amos Comenius wrote in 1673 of them as 'herd-guarders' and Ferenc Pethe in his *Natural History* of 1815 gave a very full description of their appearance and employment. Down the centuries few changes in the breed can be detected; some old drawings depict the breed with prick-ears but this was the result of ear-cropping not a different ear from today's dog. The Komondor Club of Hungary was formed in 1924 and ten years later, 972 were registered, as opposed to 1700 Kuvasz, 992 Puli and 293 Pumi. The Komondor is al-

The Puli

leged to be monogamous, preferring to have one mate, even if from a different breed. Both the Komondor and the Kuvasz have no signs of albinoism. Their skin is almost grey, probably from the ancient shepherd breeders finding that darker pigmentation was a sign of tougher skin.

Whereas the Kuvasz could be described as noble-looking and statuesque and the Komondor as having a ponderous dignity, the Pumi by contrast is terrier-like perpetually busy, investigative and quick to give tongue. But the Pumi is largely unknown in Britain, whilst the Puli makes

The Komondor

ground: 21 registrations in 1971, 52 in 1978, 64 in 1980, 72 in 1987; the Komondor struggles to become accepted: 5 registered in 1975, 18 in 1978, 1 in 1982, 12 in 1986, but to me most surprisingly the huge yet graceful Kuvasz has not become established. In America however this magnificent breed is favoured, the Hamralvi kennels of Dr and Mrs Z Alvi producing some quite outstanding specimens.

These pastoral breeds have been put to other uses too, the Mudi in boarhunting, the Komondor as a police-dog, the Pumi in deer hunting, the Kuvasz as a house/estate guard and the Puli as a water retriever. Indeed the Pullis proficiency in this role has

sometimes led to their being dubbed the 'Hungarian Water Dog', which rather supports my own theory as to their origin.

Not easily confused with other breeds of dog and prized over many centuries an working dogs, the Hungarian pastoral breeds make a highly individual and most distinctive contribution to the pastoral dogs of the world. 'Down where the prairies billow like a sea' was very much the working environment of these ancient breeds of dog for centuries and I only hope they are still valued in the homeland which nurtured them, for they are an essential element in the pastoral heritage of Hungary and well merit preservation.

The Mudi from Hungary

CHAPTER THREE

Scent Hounds

The Origin of the Hound

I believe the hounds came first, not of course looking like contemporary breeds of hound in conformation, but first in functional use for man. Buffon, I know, for one, argued that the sheepdogs came before them but I can find no logic in that. For to use sheepdogs primitive man had first to become a farmer of sorts yet man was a hunter-gatherer long long before he became a farmer. Although I acknowledge that in some places sheep were domesticated before dog. The sheepdog's instinct for rounding up numbers of sheep or singling one out for attention almost certainly developed from the hunting style of primitive wild dog and is still practised in the wild today. But before man kept animals of his own, he needed to fill his pot with the meat of wild animals and

what better ally than a tamed wild dog acting as a hound.

Such a canine ally could assist man to locate game in the first place, be used to drive the game towards precipices, pits or human hunters with their primitive weapons such as spears. Subsequently these domesticated dogs were to be trained to drive selected game into specially-constructed enclosures or into cleverly-positioned nets. In due course very fast game was hunted using very fast dogs, big game was hunted with big dogs or hunting mastiffs and feathered game hunted using dogs which could either silently (like a setter) or noisily (like a bark-pointer) indicate the location of the quarry. In time the tracking dogs became specialist hounds, able to hunt boar or hare, wild asses or deer, bison or elk. In Europe, the names of the early breeds in the hunting field indicate their function: bufalbeisser (buffalo-biter), barenbeisser (bear-biter) and bullenbeisser (wild bull-biter).

Much is made by breed-historians of the hounds of Egypt, Greece and Rome but there is ample evidence of hound-like dogs long before these times. In the mesolithic period, 9000 years ago, one or two species of larger animal provided the main source of meat in the human diet. In Europe these were red deer and wild boar, in north America the bison and in western Asia the gazelle and wild goat. One survey (Jarman 1972) carried out in 165 sites of late palaeolithic and mesolithic age throughout Europe revealed the meat-sources of the hunter-gatherers. 95 per cent of the sites indicated the presence of red deer, 60 per cent showed roe deer, 10 per cent revealed elk and chamois and a few had bison and reindeer. 20 per cent of the sites indicated the presence of dog. One of the earliest records of dog remains comes from the palaeolithic cave of Palegawra in what is now Iraq, some 12,000 years old. Canid re-

The Carian hound came from the same area as these houndlike Anatolian Shepherd dogs

mains found at Vlasac in Rumania date from c.5400 - 4600 B.C. and the other remains there indicate no other domesticated animals.

There were huge hefty hunting dogs throughout western Asia from well before 2000 B.C. and a variety of hunting dogs in ancient Egypt, their white antelope dog resembling our modern harriers in conformation. The Celts, the Greeks and the Romans greatly prized their hunting dogs and left

Apart from the ears, the Laconian hound resembled this Italian short-haired Segugio

descriptions of them. Hounds were extremely valuable as pot-fillers and were therefore extensively traded.

But well before 2000 B.C., the Sage Kings of the Yellow River valley in China, the Dravidians of the Indus valley in India and the Sumerians in the valleys of the Tigris and the Euphrates were, especially by European standards of that time, sophisticated hunters. Discoveries from near Ergani in Turkey dated from 9500 B.C. and from east Idaho in the United States dated from 9500 B.C. to 9000 B.C. prove the existence of

tracking dogs in cave settlements. Ivory carvings from Thebes, dating from 4400 to 4000 B.C., depict fast running hounds. The Phoenicians had hounds hunting both by speed and by stamina using scent. In Babylon powerful short-faced hounds were used to hunt wild asses and lions. The Assyrian kings, assisted by their keepers of hounds, hunted lions, wild bull and elephant. From 2500 B.C. onwards hunting with hounds was a favourite entertainment for noblemen in the Nile delta.

One scribe of the 19th dynasty described a pack of hounds, 200 of one type, 400 of another, stating that 'The red-tailed dog goes at night into the stalls of the hills. He is better than the long-faced dog, and he makes no delay in hunting...' In the Rig-Veda, an ancient Sanscrit record of Hindu mythology, we can find hound-like dogs described as 'broad of nostril and insatiable...'. In time the specialist hounds developed physically to suit their function, the 'long-faced' dogs needing a slashing capability in their jaws backed by excellent longsighted vision. The 'broad-nostrilled' wider-skulled looser-lipped dogs needed plenty of room for scenting capacity in both nose and lips where scent was tasted. As hounds became linked with human preferences in method of hunting and choice of quarry, so the breeds developed.

It is possible to find in Greek and Latin literature some sixty-five breed-types by name although some are merely synonyms. The Greeks had hound breeders who insisted on the importance of pure bloodlines. But not all their hounds were Greek in origin for the Greeks were a maritime people, with knowledge of the whole of the Mediterranean and the Black Sea. Pollux and Oppian referred to a breed coming from the Spanish peninsula as the Iberian; in Italy there was the Ausonian, discovered by Greeks settling in Naples, the Salentine, the Tuscan (a hunting dog which indicated concealed game not a ground scent seeking hound) and the Umbrian, able to run down game but not kill it.

Flavius Arrianus, in the second century A.D. described two Celtic breeds, the Segusiae (named after a tribe from a province which included what is now Lyons) with excellent noses, good cry but a tendency to dwell on the scent and the Vertragi (literally 'lots of foot'), rough-haired greyhound-like dogs. Claims have been made for the Segusiae being the prototype of our modern scenthounds . . . bloodhounds, foxhounds, bassets and harriers. But Arrian found nothing remarkable or noteworthy about them, merely explaining that they hunted in the same way as Cretan and Carian hounds. Xenophon records seeing gazehounds in Asia Minor. I suspect that the Greeks and Romans found the Celtic greyhound not a new breed but a variety of one of the oldest types in existence. In time the Greeks became aware of the hounds from the Rhineland called Sycambrians, the Pannonian hounds from what is now northern

Yugoslavia and the Sarmatian hounds from southern Russia.

From the north of the Himalayas came a ferocious breed of hounds known as Seres after the people of that name. From further south came the red-brindle Indian hounds, recommended by Xenophon for hunting deer and wild boar. From Persia in early

The Magnesian hound may have resembled the Rhodesian Ridgeback, without the Ridge marking.

B.C. came the Elymaean hounds (more precisely from the Gulf area), the fierce Carmanians, the savage mastiff-like Hyrcaneans (from the area where Tehran now is and probably more like today's broad-mouthed breeds than any Molossian) and the fighting hounds, the Medians. In Asia Minor were the Carians (from the area where the hound-like Anatolian shepherd dogs of today come from), esteemed by Arrian as tracking hounds, with good nose, pace and cry. The much bigger variety of the Carian, the

Magnesian, was a shield-bearer in war. And from the south of this region came the Lycaonian hounds, highly regarded for their admirable temperament.

In north Africa, Aristotle tells us that the Egyptians favoured the smaller sighthound type, comparable with the so-called Pharaoh hound and whippet of today. The Libyans had good hounds and the Cyrenean hounds were allegedly crossed with wolves, with lurcher-like all-purpose hunting dogs known to exist in central and southern Africa.

In ancient Greece, Epirus in the extreme north-west, produced the Acarnanians, which unusually for those times ran mute, the Athamanians, the Chaonians (from which came the legendary Laelaps) and the longer-eared Molossian hound. Since the cynologist Otto Keller produced his personal theory which linked the latter with the big mountain dogs of Tibet and then with the Tibetan wolf, mastiff and Great Dane researchers have had a field day. The Molossians of ancient Greece were in fact usually sheepdogs, sometimes shaggy-coated and often white. Xenophon referred to the Locrians as the powerful short-faced boar-hunting hounds. For me, the most important Greek hound was the Laconian, sometimes called the Spartan hound. This hound was good enough to be held in high esteem for many centuries, hence the Shakespearean reference — although the description there is not entirely accurate.

We have on record a great deal of information on the Laconian hound, a harrier-sized scenthound with small prick ears, free from throatiness or dewlap. It was more tucked-up than our scenthounds of today but not as much as the modern sighthounds; the contemporary Italian breed, the Segugio, ears apart, being the nearest modern equivalent. Tan and white or black and tan, bold and confident, built like a steeple-chaser, their fame spread wide and their blood was extensively utilised. Xenophon's chief delight was hunting hare with them.

Equally important however is the Cretan hound, a superb tracker in the mountains, with one variety the 'outrunners' running free, under the control of the huntsman's voice only, the first to do so in Europe until the end of the sixteenth century. The Cretan was subsequently crossed with the Laconian to produce the Metagon, so highly praised by Gratius but strangely by no other.

It could be that the stamina-packed Laconian of the Greeks was crossed with the skilled trackers, the Segusiae of the Celts, to found the subsequent scenthound types further north, the Norman hounds, St Huberts, the great white hounds of France and the grey hounds of St Louis. In time specialised functions led to specialist breeds; the Franks for example developing specialist hunting dogs to support their expert bersarii (for large game), veltrarii (for greyhounds), beverarici (for beavers and otters),

The Southern Hound from Youatt an engraving from The Dog *by Stonehenge (1867)*

falconers and wolf-hunters. In wolf-hunting, scenthounds and sighthounds were used in mutual support. Leashed scenthounds were usually employed to put the whole pack on the correct line, rather as 'tufters' do in stag-hunting to this day. Hunting with hounds became the obsession of noblemen all over the world, fortified by the medieval superstition that the strength and guile of animals passed on to man when he ate their flesh.

Parforce hunting relying on the strength of hounds may have been replaced by hunting cunning which relies on the unraveling of confused scent by skilful hounds and big game hunting with giant hounds may have lapsed. But the pursuit of game by man with hounds spans eleven thousand years and from such a heritage is likely to survive modern pressures just as the hounds themselves have adapted to each century. As perhaps the greatest hound breeder of modern times, the much-respected 'Ikey' Bell, once wrote on behalf of foxhounds:

> 'And don't think: "Man's a
>   hunter!"
> It's strictly a hound's game.
> Hunters we are by birthright;
> You are but one in name.'

This Istrian hound comes from the area where the Pannonian hound originated

Hunting by Scent

No scientist has ever satisfactorily explained the mysteries of scent in the hunting field. Scent is variously affected by the direction of the wind, heavy rain, freezing fog, high humidity, different crops, baking heat and the ground temperature. But no-one has confidently stipulated the conditions needed for good scenting; Alington once observed that 'scent is almost certain to be good between 3.30 and 4.30 after a warm October day, when the thermometer suddenly drops to near freezing point.' He then hastened to add: 'Under no other conditions would the writer care to back his opinion that scent will be good'! And even when humans are discussing the mysteries of scent in this way, they are talking about a dog's ability to detect scent not theirs, for man's sense of smell is quite abysmal in comparison. Dogs have remarkable powers of scent , some breeds more than others, some individuals excelling. For scenting powers are not just about a highly developed sense of smell but this capability backed by the use of the brain. It is the unravelling of different smells where the dog excels particularly with the extraordinary canine ability to follow the scent of one animal when a multitude of other, often more powerful, smells abound.

Reference is often made to the sweet scent of the hare and the rank smell of the fox, yet in similar atmosphere and ground conditions foothounds have had a field day whilst foxhounds nearby have had barely a serving scent and then only in covert. General Hutchinson in his classic *Dog Breaking* at the beginning of this century recalled a terrier in Scotland winning endless bets for his master through an unerring ability to indicate quite separately whether he was pointing snipe, woodcock, grouse, hare or duck. The terrier would give his master a distinct signal for each before it was sprung. His master would then announce the identity of the hidden game and win his wager. General Hutchinson also described a pointer which would point rabbits differently from other game by specially vibrating his tail. Some foxhounds have established a reputation for being able to track a fox down a road, one such being described in an old sporting magazine as a 'warranted macadamiser'. These prepotent road hunters pass on this skill to their offspring. Lord Henry Bentinck kept a detailed hound book, listing each hound's virtues and vices; against *Regulus, 1861* he noted: *Regulus for roads*. Of course the partnership between hound and huntsman is the determinant of success, a hound indicating correctly has to be believed! The use of the wind by foxes and the hare's wiles in discontinuing ground scent too add considerably to the challenge posed to the scent-hound.

But the challenge posed to the Master of Hounds lies in the performance of his scenthounds *as a pack*. A hundred years ago in

France, Comte Elie de Vezins wrote down his methods of blending the differing characteristics and varying abilities of individual hounds to build a comprehensive team which could hunt in style. He aimed to build this team around a leader or chien de tête backed by various types of chien de centre and then les chiens de chemin. The chien de tête was an individual with great ability and superior speed who naturally led the pack. His instinct was to drive on, follow the scent boldly and set a pace for the others to emulate. For a chien de tête scenting ability was more important than for any other type of hound. He was also expected to have a strong and resounding voice to rally the pack. Without superior stamina too he could not stay out in front. But no pack could tolerate two chiens de tête, the competition between them would disorganise the team work essential for success.

Comte de Vezins described the core of the pack, the chiens de centre in three types: chiens de centre pur who are not ambitious hounds but happy to hunt together and pursue the indicated line; chiens de centre avance who back the pack leader, push on boldly and keep the pack in contact with the natural leader, le chien de tête; chiens seconds number only two or three in a pack and support very closely the pack leader, driving on after him and replacing him if he makes a mistake.

The chien de chemin has the precious quality of Regulus 1861,

he can track on roads when other hounds cannot. He is a specialist with a precise capability and not every pack is fortunate to possess one. He must never speak falsely; it is often the practice to have two chiens de chemin so that one can confirm the work of the other. De Vezins also mentions the 'skirter' who hunts on a flank, is often brainier and unable to conform to pack discipline; such a hound is not good for the pack but has qualities of initiative which are better used elsewhere.

In her excellent book *Foxhounds* (Batsford 1981), Daphne Moore describes the merits and individual capabilities of famous foxhounds. It is interesting to keep de Vezin's hunting types in mind when reading her pen-pictures and many scenthound owners will notice such similarities of instinctive behaviour in their own hounds. We forget that in dogs as well as in humans, there are leaders, those who prefer to be lead, those content to be middle-of-the-roaders but try to keep up and those with special talents. A scenthound is not usually as quick to learn as a sheepdog, is not always prepared to allow humans to interfere with his nose-work and has to be stubborn in order to persist with a cold trail. We need to remember what our different breeds were developed for and prize both their breed-instincts and their individual talents before we pro-

The mixed blood of French hounds of the chase ensures a sustained performance

ceed to treat each too casually as just another dog.

It would be wrong however to think that foxhounds, harriers and beagles bred for the hunting field do not suffer from absurd human whim just as, say, bloodhounds and basset hounds do in the conformation showring. South Staffordshire Denmark (1922) won the Peterborough Doghound Championship in 1924 and I don't think I have ever seen a picture of an uglier, more physically faulty or less functional hound anywhere in the world as a show champion. But the 'fashion' in foxhounds at that time involved massive bone with forelegs like tree trunks, great width of chest with outstanding ribs which must have interfered with the elbow movement, heavy upright shoulders, knuckled-over knees and in-toeing feet. How on earth such a wretched creature could ever run down a superbly-constructed quarry like a fox is beyond me!

I am reminded of Denmark (1922) when I see contemporary show bloodhounds. Not because they exhibit the same anatomical deficiencies of Denmark but because, to me, they reflect rather forlornly breed-enthusiasm gone wrong. There simply is no historical accuracy in breeding bloodhounds with enormously-domed heads, grotesquely-sunken eyes

(previous page) Scenthounds are used in the continental shooting field

(right) Various scenthounds were used in the German Boarhunt

and absurdly over-endowed with loose skin. There is certainly no value in such exaggerations to the hound, whether he works or not. If you are neither breeding for historical correctness nor for the well-being of the dog then you are indulging in your own fancy and that is rarely connected with love and respect for animals.

The bloodhound is a very special scenthound and one deserving to be perpetuated as he was intended to be; for originally the bloodhound was the specialist lymmer or leash-hound, so gifted with scenting-powers that he was selected to lead the less able hounds to the track of the quarry, whether at the start of a hunt, after a trail had been lost or when wounded game had to be traced. If any breed is the king of the scenthounds it is the bloodhound. The demands made on the bloodhound when set to track one particular human are enormous; he has to ignore tempting animal smells, other human scent and a multitude of distractions. Hunting the clean boot is not the instinctive act of any hound but has become the specialist skill of the bloodhound. I am saddened to see German Shepherd Dogs being used for this in these times, but they are healthier, more robust, live longer, breed easier and take less time to train. Such pragmatic considerations are inevitable in a cost-effective age.

But it is good to see modern bloodhound fanciers keeping faith with the heritage of this great breed by trialing them over 'clean-boot' courses. The lymmers are an essential element in the lore of scenthounds. It would be good to see closer links between show bloodhounds and hunting bloodhounds; every owner of a bloodhound must surely ask himself at times, could my hound hunt a man?

In time the Otterhound breeders will face a similar dilemma; are their show hounds still capable of hunting? It is not a question of whether they do but whether they could. The foxhound doesn't feature in our conformation dog shows but in America an English Foxhound (as opposed to an American Foxhound, a different breed) won the Hound Group at the Westminster Show in 1984. The Welsh Foxhound whose blood was used to remould the English foxhound some 60 years ago into a less heavily-shouldered more active hound, the Fell Hound, with their fine tapering heads and excellent feet and the Trail Hounds, Cumbria's own breed, are scenthounds of immense stamina yet renowned scenting power. The Dumfrieshire black and tan foxhounds, magnificent canine athletes, whose blood was used with outstanding success to improve the working bloodhound, the Staghounds of Devon and Somerset and the Kerry Beagles of Southern Ireland are renowned throughout Europe as superb scenthounds. We have every reason to be proud of our scenthounds despite their mixed ancestry.

We have at times been rather arrogant in Western Europe about our own breeds. Sir John Buchanan-Jardine's so-called *Hounds of the World* published in the 1930s, mentioned 18 breeds of French hounds, 13 British and covered two or three breeds in the United States but no others. There are scenthounds in Scandinavia, Switzerland, Spain, Germany, Russia, Hungary, Finland, Brazil, Argentina, Poland, Italy, India and Czechoslovakia which have been acknowledged breeds for some time. Perhaps Sir John

. . . The challenge posed to the master of hounds lies in the performance of his scenthounds AS A PACK . . .

intended a second volume! We do however play down the incredible powers of scent in the domestic dog all over the world. These incredible powers, in which taste and smell virtually act as one, allied to remarkable stamina, makes the scenthounds of the world formidable hunters. We may not require our showdogs to trot ten miles to a meet, gallop for six hours and then walk ten miles back to kennels but we cannot claim to be breeding *hounds* unless we seek the anatomy which would allow this to happen. The heritage of the scenthound is a rich one and so worth preserving.

Death at Vincennes from The Book of Hours *of the Duke de Berry (Bibliothéque de Chantilly) showing big white hounds at a Boar-hound*

96 HERITAGE OF THE DOG

Hunting Mastiffs

'They are almost shaped as a greyhound of full shape, they have a great head, great lips and great ears, and with such, men help themselves well at the baiting of the bull and at hunting of the wild boar, for it is natural to them to hold fast, but they are so heavy and ugly, that if they be slain by the wild boar it is no great loss', so runs the translation by Edward, second Duke of York, put into modern English, of a part of Gaston de Foix's classic work *Le Livre de la Chasse,* written in 1388. The hounds so described by de Foix were the 'holding' or 'seizing' hounds, used to delay the quarry until the hunters could arrive with spear, arrow, club or hunting knife to dispatch the deer, wild boar or wild bull. In carrying out this function however, the dogs were often gored, sometimes to death, and specialist hounds were used, bred for their dash and remarkable courage but not so prized as the big white hunting dogs, the Alauntes.

Holding dogs or hunting mastiffs were used in very ancient times, by the Egyptians, Assyrians and Babylonians. Such dogs had to be immensely strong, especially in the jaw, almost recklessly brave and yet be athletic enough to perform in the chase; they had to be able to go on breathing whilst hanging on to a wild bull or stag and so developed as broad-mouthed, short-muzzled dogs, heavy, immensely powerful yet active. The Celts and the Teutons utilised such dogs and they were called the 'beissers', even more definitively as bullenbeissers, bufalbeissers or barenbeissers, as to whether they were employed against wild bull, buffalo or bears. The modern breeds of Boxer, Bullmastiff, Dogue de Bordeaux and Neapolitan Mastiff owe their origin to such dogs. The Bullenbeisser survived in Germany until the last century. These hefty brave determined dogs were often employed by butchers to control or even 'pin' difficult bulls, with the Rottweiler a surviving example to this day. Such breeds are characterised by having very powerful neck and shoulder development, strongly-constructed jaws and tremendous courage.

The 'running' mastiffs also needed courage but were considered far too valuable to be sacrificed at the kill, their fine powers of scent, great stamina and considerable determination needed to be preserved. Such dogs were once described as the 'hunting Alauntes', as opposed to the 'Alauntes of the butcheries', the holding dogs. The hunting alaunte had the conformation of a heftily-built greyhound but with more substantial bone-structure, a heavier, shorter-muzzled head and squarer jaw. A white coat was preferred, with black markings near the head and above the tail most favoured. It was allegedly ... 'better shaped and stronger for harm than any other beast.' The modern harlequin Great Dane would be the nearest surviving equivalent.

An intriguing breed, however, very much alive today and yet not known in this country and evidently a 'running mastiff', is the Dogo Argentino used for hunting big game in the Argentine pampas. Pure white, with a distinct Great Dane look about it, it quickly conjures up the mental picture of a hunting Alaunt of the 14th century in Europe.

These dogs were intended to hunt big animals such as the puma, jabali (wild boar), peccary (a small local wild pig) and the very large native foxes. Required to be silent in the chase, hold a good scent, have great dash and yet be athletic too, white bull terrier and bull mastiff blood was used to provide strength of jaw and courage, pointer and foxhound stock was utilised to produce the powers of scent and then Great Dane blood to produce size, substance and intelligence. It is alleged that the blood of the Cordoba Fighting Dog was introduced too, to imprint an element of reckless courage. One could imagine too use of the old type of Spanish Bull-

A continental Bullmastiff . . . living example of a holding breed

dog, the dogue de Burgos, the Spanish Mastiff (sometimes called Masti de Estremadura and often white coated) and the Pyrenean Mastiff (sometimes referred to as the Mastiff of Navarra, usually white-coated, often confused with the Pyrenean Mountain Dog, a quite different French breed).

The founders of this breed were Dr Antonio Nores Martinez, a professor at the National University of Cordoba and his brother, Dr Agustin Nores Martinez, who laid down a standard for the breed in 1928 in an attempt to standardize what had emerged as a distinct type of national hound. A similar breed is found in adjacent Brazil, the Fila Brasiliero, or Brazilian guard dog. Although not white and used more as a guard-dog than a scent hound, there is a clear running or hunting mastiff look about this breed, the most popular breed in Brazil, with 6,000 registered last year.

Believed to have been introduced from Spain and Portugal into Central America at the time of the Conquistadors and possessing the throatiness and heavy-headed look of the modern Burgos Pointer, this is a fierce breed, usually brindle and standing over two foot at the shoulder.

Similarly used as a guard dog, the Neapolitan Mastiff today provides a living example of Columella's description of the 'guard dog for the house' in Roman times: 'should be black or dark ... When night falls the dog, lost in the shadows, can attack without being seen. The head is so massive that it seems to be the most important part of the body', a feature perhaps not surprising in what was originally developed as a 'holding' breed. Equally massively-headed is the Dogue de Bordeaux, the Bordeaux Mastiff, claimed by scholars such as Kell and Tschudy as being derived from the Assyrian hunting mastiffs introduced into Gaul and Britain by the Phoenician traders. I rather support the theory, however, of M Boogazerdt, expressed when President of the Society of Bordeaux Mastiff Fanciers, that this breed is more recently traceable to the Burgos Mastiff from Spain. I know of one Scottish bull mastiff breeder who would like to use Bordeaux Mastiff blood with his British champion Bullmastiffs to get away from the pug-face so sadly prevalent in contemporary British bullmastiff specimens. The bullmastiff should have a short muzzle rather than no muzzle at all!

The bullmastiff, developed fairly recently by breeders such as Moseley from his Farcroft Kennels, through an admixture of bulldog and English mastiff blood, perpetuates the 'bullenbeisser' type from the more distant past. But of all the modern breeds of this type found in Europe, it could be argued that the Rhodesian Ridgeback represents most accurately the hunting mastiffs of ancient history. Neither broad-mouthed nor throaty from excessive dewlap, it nonetheless shows the same physical conformation as is illustrated by the Assyrian hounds, with their spiral collars for quick 'slipping', displayed in the British Museum. Significantly, both were used for hunting lions, in which agility as well as well as boldness must surely count.

I believe though that the seeking of such massive heads in modern specimens of the mastiff breeds is neither desirable nor historically correct. It leads to whelping problems and has become an unwelcome exaggeration. Our forefathers were often seeking to breed mastiffs the size of a calf but never quite so massively-headed. The sheer bulk and unnaturally heavy head of the modern English mastiff would not have given it much scope in the chase or indeed much mobility as an aggressive war dog. But whether heavy-headed or over-bestowed with dewlap, white or brindle, in southern Europe or South America, distributed by the Phoenicians orperfected by the, the Mastiff breeds have surprisingly survived, despite the lack of big game hunting since the advance of the sporting rifle and the end of their use by butchers

The Dogo Argentino — like a 14th century hunting Alaunt

all over Europe. I would now like to see them used much more widely as guard dogs, for their instinct to seize and hold their quarry still has much to offer to man.

At the turn of the century, Mr Burton of the Thorneywood Kennels used to give demonstrations with his night-dogs (Bullmastiffs) in which he would offer one pound to any person who could escape from a securely-muzzled night-dog. Spectators would be amazed to see how easily the dog could knock down its human quarry and detain it; after all those centuries of 'detaining' wild bulls and buffalo, perhaps humans don't present much of a problem, even to a muzzled dog. In these days of pitch invasions and street disorders, the long-suffering public could possibly be offered some solace with the discreet use of holding dogs, perhaps renamed the 'bully-beissers!'

Great Danes, contemporary examples of the ancient hunting Mastiffs

The Hare-hounds

A Triumph of Stamina Over Speed

'Now to speke of the hare how
all shall be wrought:
Whan she shall wyth hounds be
founden and sought.'

These words written in the 15th century by Dame Juliana Berners in her well-known *Boke of Huntyng* sum up rather neatly the hunting of the hare down the ages. For hares have been 'found' and then 'sought' by hounds for at least a thousand years. The reference to the hare in the feminine indicates at once the respect and affection all hare-hunters have had for this beautiful creature. Such affection has never been extended to say the fox or the boar. The hare has always been a highly respected quarry. The original plate of *Hare Hunting in the 17th Century* by Francis Barlow and W. Hollar depicting sixteen couples of harriers bore this inscription:
'The timorous hare, when
  started from her seat,
by bloody hounds, to save her
  life so sweet,
With Several Shifts, much terror and great payne,
Yet dyes she by their mouths,
  all proves but vayne.'
I know of no other inscription on a hunting scene which reveals such compassion, almost regret, about the fate of the quarry. No fox has ever earned such sympathy!

The scent-hounds used in hare-hunting were treated with sympathy too so that today the beagle and the basset hound have a gentler nature than say a foxhound or a staghound. This characteristic is shared by hare-hounds all over Europe: a soft look in the eye, a highly-boned almost finely-carved skull with ultra-fine leathers and a friendly nature. They are too remarkably similar in conformation, with the bassets displaying the leg-length preferred by the foot-hunters, the beagles relating to the terrain and the harriers being bred to be accompanied sometimes by mounted hunters. The coat colours too reveal the classic scent-hound markings of tricolour, black and tan, lemon and white, Gascony blue or mottled, with smooth-coated hounds being complemented by the shaggy Griffon coat.

The standard beagle is now an extremely popular show dog and pet with 900 being registered annually in the United Kingdom. In the United States the breed features in the top twenty most popular breeds registered with the A.K.C; in the 1940s and 50s it was second only to the Cocker Spaniel there. In the British showring however I do see some rather poor specimens, doghounds especially, too short in the back, sterns curling over the back, snipey muzzles and poor feet. A beagle is a running hound and many conformation show breeders would benefit from a visit to the Peterborough hound show and a sight of the Warwickshire, Wyre Forest, Ampleforth College or Newcastle and District's entries. No beagle from these packs would win at a hound show with a short-backed cobby build, this is entirely alien to the essential anatomy of a scent-hound able to gallop for miles and miles. I very much like the general appearance requirement in the beagle standard in North America: 'A miniature foxhound, solid and big for his inches, with the wear and tear look of the hound that can last in the chase and follow his quarry to the death.'

A typical beagle in the early 1800s was a barrel-chested, stockily-built, apple-headed animal and often crooked in front. It was not until halfway through Queen Victoria's reign that the delights of beagling began to appeal to a wider audience. The modern beagle almost certainly has harrier blood, introduced to produce a racier product, and through that blood, that of the foxhound too. The contemporary field or hunting beagle must be one of the hardiest of all canine breeds. That hardiness comes from years of selective breeding in pursuit of function without any lists of breed points. Masters of packs are free to breed the type of hound best suited to the country over which their particular pack has to perform . . . but they have to perform!

I have seen beagles in the hunting field exceeding sixteen inches at the shoulder and one or two no more than ten inches high. But a beagle around fifteen inches should be able to cope with the terrain in most English hunting countries. If beagling is to be a sporting pastime, it is important not to overmatch the hare. The rewards of beagling come mainly from watching the hounds unravelling the intricate lines of the hare as she goes through her extensive escape and evasion technique. If you just want to kill hares, a brace of lurchers will always be quicker and very much cheaper.

Beagling was officially established right at the end of the last century, with the founding of the Association of Masters of Harriers and Beagles. Just before that event there were eighteen packs; shortly after there were around fifty. Eighty five were listed eighty years later. It would be sad indeed if the beagles in the hunting field were to develop quite separately from those in the showring and I would like to see distinguished Peterborough beagle judges like Colonel John McLaren becoming involved on the show circuit. Either the beagle is perpetuated as a running hound, capable of catching its quarry through stamina and scenting powers or the breed in its true form will disappear.

In total contrast the harrier has never been a show breed yet to me the harrier is the perfect hound. Those I have seen in the past from the Cambridgeshire, the Cotley, the Wensleydale, and the Dart Vale and Haldon represent my ideal scent-hound. The Cambridgeshire have sent hounds to several places abroad, including Finland, where they sport a quite excellent scent-hound of their own (the 23 inch Finsk Stovare, a fine-looking tri-colour). The first time I saw a Hamilton Stovare in Sweden, I was at once reminded of the superbly-bred Cambridgeshire harriers of Betty Gingell. The Dart Vale and Haldon have sent hounds to the United States and New Zealand to hunt hares and to Jamaica to hunt agouti. The harrier has always been an all-rounder, many packs in Britain

The Hare Hound from Brittany — the Basset Fauve de Bretagne

hunting fox exclusively. The Dart Vale and Haldon hounds, perpetuating the West Country Harrier as opposed to the Studbrook harrier, have hunted fox and hare separately with two identical packs. Most admirers of the West Country Harrier respect the blood of the Quarme Harriers disbanded in 1939 from their Exford kennels. The Wensleydale harriers, hunting the valley of the River Ure in North Yorkshire are physically similar, especially in coat colour – white with grey or lemon markings. These 19–20 inch harriers excel at hunting through sheep foil and along trackways, with great drive and low scenting. The famed Quarme

Hare hunting (mid 1800s)
a Harrier pack at work

harrier bloodlines have been used to improve both foxhound and beagle packs; contemporary breeders of pedigree dogs must forever be mindful of the skilful *blending* of bloodlines vital both for the establishment of a functional breed of dog and for its faithful perpetuation.

The English Basset is perhaps a living testimony of this. If the basset hound in England becomes too low on the leg, too lavishly leathered and too massively boned for its function, then an outcross is essential, unless you are breeding purely for exaggerated characteristics. The tendency of the working basset to revert to the original 'carthorsey' hound of

the 1870s was confronted by Eric Morrison in the late 1940s and an outcross to the Studbook harrier resulted. The desired basset hound hunting tendencies, such as finer scenting powers, the deep bell-like voice and basic agility have been enhanced. I believe it is fair to say that the show basset is now out of step with its basset relatives elsewhere, the Fauve de Bretagne, the Griffon Vendeen, the Blue de Gascogne and the Artesien-Normand. None of these sister-breeds have the ultra-short legs, excessive leather-length or massive bone of the

A classical marked tri-colour Harrier of 50 years ago

show basset in England. When a basset hound enters a showring, steps on its own ears, performs a graceless somersault and is laughed at by the spectators, we are in effect insulting the integrity of an ancient hunting breed (as well as deeply offending the unfortunate hound involved!)

Hunting the hare around the world has led to some interesting observations and practices. In America, the Cotton-tail Rabbit which is hunted by their beagles, is with its short burst of hard running able to be used to demonstrate the capability of a pack at an

Petit Chien Bleu de Gascogne
. . . French Hare Hound

otherwise 'bench' hound show. These field trials gave the judge an opportunity to judge performance as well as conformation. I imagine however that the judges have a difficult task in this, since scenting conditions can vary throughout the day. The Swiss use hare-hounds to drive the hares in front of the guns. In France at the end of the last century, the Comte de Vezins who mastered the family pack of eight or ten couple of Gascon-Saintongeois hounds, blue-mottled or black and white, recorded that there were tree types of hound used for hare-hunting: the pure-blooded hound, the bri-quet — a harrier created from

more than one breed and the cross-bred hound or improved briquet. He favoured the latter, standing 19 or 20 inches, with a good voice, lightly-built, clean-coloured and able to hunt as well in the hills as on the plain.

The French have never hesitated to cross-breed in pursuit of field excellence, the Beagle-Harrier, the Anglo-French varieties and the Briquet Griffon-Vendeen illustrating this today. The Porcelaine was improved with the blood of the quaintly-named Billy and our own West Country Harrier. The Scandinavian breeds of hare hound also have a mixed origin, but the English Foxhound has been used in their development although the Hygenhund and the Drever have German hound blood behind them. The Spanish harrier (Sabueso Espanol Lebrero) and the Swiss hare-hounds show in their long leathers the influence of French hounds, but the Norwegian Dunker hound, descended from the Russian Harlequin hound is highly individual.

But whether harlequin or tricolour, hunted in packs or as a brace, used in chasse à tir or chase à courre, the hounds used to hunt the hare are prized the world over and have been so down the ages. The Laconian hound of Ancient Greece was the size of a large beagle or small harrier. Xenophon championed the back and tans and the tricolour. Here's to the next two thousand years of hare-hounds with a black saddle!

The Otterhound

Always a Rated Breed

'. . . it happens that the breed has become unusually savage and that they are constantly fighting in kennel. Indeed, instances are common enough of more than half being destroyed in a single night, in the bloody fight which has been commenced by perhaps a single couple . . .'

Such comments on Otterhounds were not rare fifty to one hundred years ago, the celebrated sportsman Captain L.C.R. Cameron writing in 1932 on Dreadful, an old dog-hound:

. . . 'But in kennels he was very troublesome, constantly starting fights in which the rest of the pack joined forces against him, so that he always came off worsted. He would obey no rate but mine . . .'

Yet this temperamental background shows very few modern signs as this old sporting breed survives the banning of otter-hunting and gains increasing strength in the show ring. Undeniably the oldest of organised British field sports with hounds hunting by scent, the Celts used rough-haired water-dogs and armed themselves with flint-headed spears. There are many references to the otter-hunting activities of Henry II and his son John and Edward II. It should be

Otterhound of today

remembered too whenever modern distaste for otter-hunting is expressed that fish once played a far more important role in the diet of the British, with fish-ponds equating to present-day trout-farms and fresh-water fishing forming an essential element in self-sufficiency among country people. The otter therefore posed a threat to their larders.

Much is made, when speculating on the origin of the Otterhound, of the blood of the *Southern Hound*, the Welsh Hound, The Bloodhound and, both in the 12th century and later in Victorian times, the infusion of Nivernais' Griffon and Vendeen Griffon blood, yet, to me surprisingly, little mention is made of 'water-dog' blood. I find it inconceivable that for hounds designed to work in water in days when water-dogs were an identifiable type of the functional dog world, that water-dog blood would not be utilised. If you have ever seen the Dumfriesshire pack in the water and also seen Barbets at work in the water in France then the resemblance is extraordinary. An examination of the web-feet, the shaggy coat and general conformation shows fascinating similarities. The Barbet is of course a surviving breed of water-dog, related to the poodle, the Portuguese and Spanish water-dogs and our Irish Water 'Spaniel'.

Amiable and boisterous, with the inquisitiveness of a Basset

Hound, the perseverance of a Bloodhound yet without the obstinacy of either, the modern Otterhound is becoming increasing rated as a companion dog, in spite of their old fearsome kennel reputation and allegedly bloodthirsty nature. But as with all working breeds 'gone pedigree', it is important to retain the correct breed-type; the harsh oily coat with the double, dense woolly undercoat, the big almost Newfoundland-like feet as opposed to the cat-foot of the foxhound, the perfectly symmetrical build and keen nose. The show-bench otterhound must look like

Staffordshire Otterhounds on the scent

a hound bred and developed to work in water and never become a soft-coated leggy Basset Hound. Some of course are still used in the field, for mink hunting in particular.

But the habits of mink and the nature of the animal give mink-hunting a different style altogether from otter-hunting. The moral objections too will continue especially from those considering that all hunting with dogs causes needless discomfort to the quarry and is therefore unacceptable. I hope the show ring quest for conformation will not bring false standards to this ancient hound, for so long part of the sporting heritage of Britain.

At the moment because the

show ring stock is coming from old working packs, there is just one type, unlike English Springer Spaniels and Golden Retrievers where bench and field dogs are so often quite dissimilar. The traditional 'typiness' is there too, with Culmstock Crafty, champion Otterhound bitch at the West of England Hound Show in 1980 being the same type as say Falconcrag Nugget in the show ring or that matter not at all that different from the famous Talisman of years gone by. Not surprisingly there was great concern for the future of the breed when otter-breeding was banned. But a com-

bination of enthusiasm among fanciers, assistance from the Kennel Club and the hunting world, together with commendable vision, led to the formation of the Otterhound Club. This was timely for pure-bred Otterhound was developed to hunt a long travelling animal not a hole to hole bunker with a short swim to ground like the mink. It is interesting that otterhounds utter a different cry when hunting mink, less melodious, more ferocious.

But Otterhounds have long been famed for their wonderful

The Otterhound of 50 years ago

music, if too noisy for some. With their great perseverance, huge stamina and very sensitive nose, Otterhounds have always been a highly individual breed.

In the show ring I have noticed some young hounds with shortish ears without the fold, upright shoulders and a lack of spirit or flourish. I do hope that the admirably intentioned fanciers in the breed will perpetuate the charac-

Bellman an Otterhound, an n *engraving from* The Dog *by Stonehenge (1867) now relegated, as a breed, to the show-ring*

ter of this hound, the substance (anything under 23 inches at the withers and 80 lbs is really too small), the range of coat colours – grey, brindle, black, red-fawn or lemon and white and the level, forward-facing open nostrils.

In 1576, in his celebrated *Booke of Hunting,* Turbervile wrote that . . . 'A good Otter hounde may prove an excellent buck-hound, if he be not old before he be entred.' Four hundred years later, the good Otterhound is still proving adaptable and versatile; an ancient breed so much part of our country heritage, now capable of changing to meet changing times.

The Talbot Hound (from the Shrewsbury MS in the British Museum)

The White Hound of the Talbots

'The Norman conquerors of England brought their hounds with them when they took possession of this country and there is evidence to show that the breed known as St Huberts or Talbots were the foundation stock of the breed afterwards known as southern hounds. The Count de Conteulx de Canteleu says that the St. Huberts were celebrated as far back as the eighth century, when they were known as Flemish hounds – St Hubert's Monastery, the home of the breed, being in the Ardennes. They were subdivided into two strains, the black and the white'... these words

from *Hounds in Old Days* by Gilbey (1913) give the modern researcher an excellent start when considering the origin of the so-called Talbot hound. We get an immediate impression of a white bloodhound-like dog brought here from Normandy. Sir John Buchanan-Jardine in his celebrated *Hounds of the World* (1937) describes the Talbot hound as the white variety of the St Hubert hound without excessive wrinkle or loose skin but stressed that it was the *Normanised* St Hubert that could be white. He stressed that it was medium sized and *low-set*.

Yet in the last century we had Blaine in his *Encyclopaedia of Rural Sports* describing the Talbot as of 'great size, long ears, formerly light-coloured now darkly-pied' and T.B. Johnson in his

Hunting Directory calling them of 'great size... 27 inches at the withers... dark tan in colour'. The latter scolds Somervile for calling them white in his poetic description in the early 18th century:

> . . . 'the bold Talbot kind
> Of these the prime, as white as Alpine snows;
> And great their use of old...'

Johnson also boldly states, recklessly risking the fury of the Celts, that 'All the ramifications of the hound which we at present possess sprung from one and the same source, namely the Talbot or old English bloodhound.'

So was the Talbot hound low-set and medium sized or of great size, around 27 inches at the withers? Even Sir John Buchanan-jardine, who had a deep knowledge of the ancestry of the hound wrote tentatively that... 'the white strain may possibly have had something in common with the 'Chien blanc du Roi' i.e. the 27 inch great white royal hounds of France. The subject is clouded too by the fact that Talbot was also a popular name for a hound as Chaucer indicates in his *Nonne's Preeste's Tale*:

'Ran Colle our dogge, and Talbot, and Gerlond;

And Malkin, with her distaf in hire hond' and that the expression 'St. Hubert's breed' has been loosely used to describe all hounds of the chase.

I suspect that the strongest connection between the low-set medium-sized bloodhound-like Talbots described by some and the great white hounds described by others lies in the colour white rather than in the blood. I believe that the Normanised white variety of the St Hubert came from different root-stock and had a different purpose in the hunting field from the taller white hounds favoured by the kings of France. Charles IX of France in his *La Chasse Royale* (c.1570) stated that all breeds of hounds descend from four breeds: Chien blanc du Roi, Chiens gris de St Louis, Chien de St Hubert and Chien fauve de Bretaigne. The first two named are believed to have been brought back from the crusades by French noblemen; the last two survive through the modern bloodhound and the chestnut hounds of Brittany.

George Turbervile in his *The Art of Venerie* (1575) also describes four distinct breeds of French hounds: the White, the Fallow, the Dun and the Black or St Huberts. Ten years later, Du Foilloux, writing in his *La Venerie* states that ... 'the hounds of St Hubert should generally be all black'. I believe however that black or mainly black was the favoured colour, associated with good scenting powers, rather than the only colour for a St Hubert hound.

In this way, Gervase Markham in his *Country Contentments* of 1611 considers that . . . 'the black hound, the black tanned, or he that is all liver hew'd, or the milk white, which is the true Talbots, are best for the string or line, for they do delight most in blood, and have a natural inclination to hunt dry foot; and of these the largest is ever best and most comely.' Although he does emphasise size, he is stressing mainly their prowess as lymmers or leashed scenthounds and in hunting a cold scent rather than hot-foot. He is not describing hard-running high-headed fast-moving hounds like the Great White hounds of France.

One hundred and fifty years later, around 1763, a writer calling himself 'Le Vernier de la Conterie' in his *Ecole de la Chasse* states that 'We have in Normandy two kinds of hounds of really pure breed; the one of grey or black and tan hounds, the other of white hounds.' He favoured the white ones for deer but complained of lack of pure blood because of crossing with English hounds. It was probably the outcrossing to good English hounds which led to the disappearance of the white Norman hound. Writing in 1858 the Comte le Conteulx de Canteleu considered that really good specimens of the Norman hound of absolutely pure blood were hardly to be found. And in 1875, H. de la Blanchere-Feroa wrote of the white Norman hounds as extinct and the coloured ones purest in England as bloodhounds. But the low-headed groundscent-seeking sometimes leashed Norman hounds, St Huberts and the big white royal hounds were essentially 'chiens courants' or running hounds. We must not forget that five hundred years ago man when hunting demanded specialist hounds particularly when hunting bigger quarry.

At the end of the fourteenth century, Gaston III, Comte de Foix, wrote a book on hunting in which he listed the five main breeds of sporting dogs. One of these he described as the 'alan gentil' (and separated then from 'chien courants') with a good specimen as lithe and trim as the greyhound but with a powerful, large, square head ... in other words, a hunting mastiff, strong enough to pull down large game. The coat could be rough or smooth but the colour should be all white with the exception of a few spots around the ears. Gaston de Foix wrote that 'a good alan must gallop on like a greyhound and when he has got up to the game he must let in his teeth and not let go ... these are they who by their strength and stature can do more harm than any other breed.' He was describing a 'holding dog' which hunted by sight not scent. Modern breeds like the harlequin Great Dane, the white bullterrier, the Dogo Argentino, the Rhodesian Ridgeback and the bullmastiff come from this mould.

In his *De Canibus - Dog and Hound in Antiquity* R.H.A. Merlen states that such dogs as the alan gentil 'may have been distantly related to the Mede, Hyrcanian and other Caspian breeds and so ultimately perhaps to the 'Indian' dogs of Aristotle's day.' Indeed, there is a remarkable likeness between the alan gentil and the white antelope dog depicted an artefacts in Ancient Egypt.

It is important to remember two points here, firstly that in those times pedigree breeding in our sense was not practised and that field excellence was the supreme goal; the blood of a proven hound, whatever its background was prized. Our distant ancestors never hesitated to crossbreed in pursuit of a better hunting performance. Secondly, all hounds perpetuate an instinctive style of hunting; some specialise in unravelling the mysteries of scent, others prefer to run down rather than track down their prey and there are those bred to bay or even physically hold the larger game until the hunters arrive to complete the kill. I believe that the Talbot hound was a tracking hound but acknowledge that inter-breeding with other hounds took place down the centuries to improve stock. The 'chiens blanc du Roi' exemplify this; their heritage is certainly mixed and not unromantic.

In 1470, the squire of Poitou presented Louis XI with a white hound called Souillard, which was passed on to Louis' daughter, Anne de Bourbon. Souillard was

Hanover Scenthound — a contemporary breed displaying the likely conformation of the Talbot Hound

mated to a famous bitch called Baude, producing 2 or 3 litters totalling 16 pups, 6 of which were supreme hounds and laid the foundation of the royal packs. In 1500 Louis XII had a white Italian pointer bitch mated to a white hound and produced the celebrated 'Greffier', a beautiful, white with lemon hound and a new line developed from this match. In 1560 Francois II was given a white hound bred in Scotland (Barmud) which was used as a stallion with the white bitches of the royal pack. Their offspring were described in 1585 by du Fouilloux as ... 'steadier among fresh deer than any other breed of hounds.'

In 1608 Henry IV sent a whole pack to James I of England for them to become the likely ancestors of the white staghounds found in the royal hounds as late as 1820. Subsequently, Louis XIV bred his big white hounds to be slower so he could keep up in his old age, by bringing in the blood of Norman hounds. This pack was dispersed in 1725 when Louis XV was presented with a pack of hounds crossed with English foxhounds.

The province of Poitou was considered to be the hone of French venery. In the 18th century, the Poitou hound, long in the back, sometimes 29 inches high, white or white and lemon and rather greyhound-like was the envy of every French sportsman, having a fast, dashing, impressively resolute style based on the use of air-scent and the eye. It was not the style of the plodding but persevering scenthound like the St Hubert. This Poitou hound is perpetuated to-day in the Chien de Billy and the Chien Porcelaine, possibly too in our light-coloured West Country harriers and fellhounds. The old lemon-pied staghounds which used to feature in this country, the big 28 inch hounds, perfect in tongue, found in the Epping, the Royal pack at Ascot and the Devon and Somerset, are sometimes said to have contained Talbot blood but I believe this comes from confusing the great white royal hounds of France with the low-set medium-sized white Norman hounds.

The name Talbot comes from the Talbot family of Alton (now the theme park Alton Towers), later the Earls of Shrewsbury and Talbot. The 6th Baron, Sir John Talbot, was created the Earl of Shrewsbury in 1442 and had strong associations with France. He was a famous fighting soldier with the very name Talbot becoming feared by Frenchmen.

His coat of arms features two white hounds, long-eared heavy-headed white scent-hounds. In the Shrewsbury manuscripts held in the British Museum, the Talbot hound depicted there is low-set, rather as Sir John Buchanan-Jardine described the breed. Public houses called the Talbot Inn often feature in sign showing a nondescript white hound or mottled hound. But the heraldic sign on the Talbot helmet depicts a black hound, with a further family heraldic sign displaying a mottled hound.

Perhaps Sir John Talbot when in

*The coat of arms of the Earls of
Shrewsbury and Talbot
showing a pair of white hounds*

Normandy in the 15th century saw the blacks, the liver-hued and the milk-whites but like Gervase Markham two centuries later, admired the latter and adopted them as the most suitable features for his subsequent coat of arms. The true Talbot hound should surely therefore be the long-eared, heavy-headed, low-set medium-sized white hound . . . as favoured by both Sir Johns.

The Origin of the Spotted Coach Dog

The claims down the years by some of the most widely quoted authorities on dogs over the origin of the breed registered as the Dalmatian have not only done the breed a great disservice but must also have misled many devotees of the breed over what their dogs were actually intended to do. Does the breed come from Dalmatia, Bengal, Denmark or the gypsy camps of Europe? Is it a pointing breed, a hound or a stable guard dog? Caius, Bewick, Buffon, Youatt, Stonehenge, Idstone, Vero Shaw . . . the immediate resorts of the overnight breed experts, are no help at all with this breed; if anything their words add up to a collection of misleading plagiarised inaccuracies. Yet here we have an ancient breed with, like the curly-coated retriever, an in-built protection against mongrelisation in its distinctive coat. I suspect too that the breed is clever enough to be used both as a hound and separately as a pointer and still find itself employed as a coach dog. After all, there are all shapes, sizes and coat-colours in the gundog and hound families, but nothing as individual as the Dalmatian, which breeds true . . . or gets found out!

My interest was first aroused by seeing illustrations of the patched and spotted ancient Egyptian pet dog which belonged to King Cheops or Khufu, the builder of the great Pyramid in 3700 B.C. This dog was nothing like a Dalmatian but showed the royal interest in a spotted dog. The dog of this time which did however very much resemble the Dalmatian was the White Antelope Dog, not in coat-colouring but in conformation. There was clearly a use for dogs of that construction, shape and size. Of far great interest, although much later in history, is the frescoe of a boarhunt from Tiryns preserved in the German Archaeological Institute in Athens. This shows three hounds after a fleeing boar, two brown and white and one black and white, not just black patched but with four groups of perfectly round black spots arranged in distinct patterns as though the artist wished to stress that the black spots were of significance. The brown and white hounds have random brown patches but the black patches on the black and white hound suggest very clearly that the black patches were made up of contiguous smaller black spots merging to form bigger black patches.

At that time there was in Ancient Greece, according to Xenophon, a hunting dog called the Cretan hound. The Cretan hound was light-boned, nimble, could run well in mountains and came in three varieties, the Cnossians — famed for their noses, the Workers — so keen they hunted by night and day and the Outrunners, who ran free under the huntsman's voice control only and, according to Aristotle, ran along instinctively beside the horses during a hunt, never preceding them and not lagging behind. Unlike some of the other hounds used by the Greeks in the Chase, the Outrunners were not dewlapped or flewed. Oppian and Xenophon recommended keeping them pure. They were used by the Cretans to hunt a four-horned antelope, as Aelian has recorded. These hounds were too special for use on hare-hunts, too valuable for use in killing the boar, biddable enough to be used as 'braches' as opposed to 'lymmers' i.e. they ran free, and hunted by sight and scent. Julius Pollux in his Onamasticon recom-

Dalmatians have always had a distinct hound look about them

mended that the colour of these hounds should be 'neither wholly white nor excessively black.' It should be noted that the Cretans were exceptional in hunting with hounds running free, both up to their time and for two centuries or so subsequently, such was the quality of their hounds and their training methods.

I am not suggesting for one moment that the Dalmatian existed in Ancient Greece but pointing out that there was a White Antelope Dog in Ancient Egypt which resembled the Dalmatian in size and shape; that the Greeks imported their fast hunting dogs from Egypt and crossed them with scent-hounds to give the latter greater speed and all round hunting capabilities; the Greeks pur-

sued the boar with black and white hounds, some of them spotted; there was a variety of the Cretan hound which instinctively ran alongside the horses in the hunt and, most unusually, ran free. This was a variety used to hunt the antelope.

Turning to the alleged Indian origin and the use of the term 'the Harrier of Bengal' by Buffon, a famous French naturalist but not an accurate source of research on dogs, I can find no trace anywhere of dogs marked like Dalmatians being indigenous to India. The only breeds I can detect there as being similar to the Dalmatian are the Poligar, found in the Rajapalayam or Chettinad, and the Chippiparai, used as a greyhound in the south. Both are white coated but with other colours occurring as spots, flecking or small patches, very muscular athletic dogs, superb long distance runners with good reliable noses. The Poligar has been used for pig-hunting for generations and has the same outline as the White Antelope Dog of Ancient Egypt; both this breed and the Chippiparai carry their tails rather as a Dalmatian does. There is a famous painting 'Shri Shahu Maharaj with dogs' which depicts two medium-sized hunting dogs accompanying a mounted hunter, they are white dogs with spotting or flecking. There is a reference in the Ayeen Akbari to a breed from Kabulistan which was believed to be a cross between a dog and a leopard but there is nothing to suggest that this alleged hybrid displayed the leopard's spots. The

Portuguese, as early as the 15th century, the British, the Dutch and other traders or colonists did of course visit India over the centuries and sometimes took dogs with them.

But any nation producing a breed of dog with such a remarkably distinctive coat-coloration would preserve it, prize it and trade with it. Could the classic Dalmatian coat have occurred only rarely and not breed true until comparatively recent times? The marbled coats of the hounds of Gascony and the blue and red roan of the spaniel/setter breeds were acknowledged long before the breed-name Dalmatian became known at the very end of the 18th century. Perhaps the Dalmatian coat, as in the black over white garb worn by officials in church, is the origin of the name but surely Border Collies would have first claim here. One of the problems in researching the breed in Britain is that from the end of the 16th century not one book on dogs was published for two hundred years but books on hunting in that period do provide some items of interest. When looking at old sporting prints however it is important to remember that on the Continent hounds have long been used in the *shooting* field. We should therefore never assume that a hound-like dog in a painting with a man with a firearm is a pointer in our sense of the word.

My own theory about the origin of the word Dalmatian is that it comes from a corruption of the terms for such running dogs in the 13th century i.e. hounds de mota (mote = a spot or blemish hence our word mottled — dappled with spots) or 'de meute de chiens' meaning 'of a pack of fallow hounds'. Dama is Latin for fallow deer, in French daim (m) or dain (f), in Italian daino. Canem daymerettum was one expression for the running hounds which hunted fallow deer, with both daymerettum and dama-chien sounding like Dalmatian.

In those times spelling varied even on the same page of books and 'mute de chiens' was some-times used for twelve running dogs and a 'lime-hounde'. In 1216 we can read in the *Close Rolls* of John, who maintained a vast hunt-ing establishment, reference to 'fifteen greyhounds and thirty-one Hounds "de mota".' They were also referred to as Moota Canum or Muta Canum. In 1213 we find reference to '114 "de mota" dogs and five greyhounds for hunting fallow deer in the park of Knappe' in a letter from King John to Roger de Neville. Henry III in a letter to the Sheriff of Oxford refers to sixteen 'de mota' dogs and one 'limarius' or leashed scenthound. Hounds for hunting stags were different from those for hunting fallow deer;

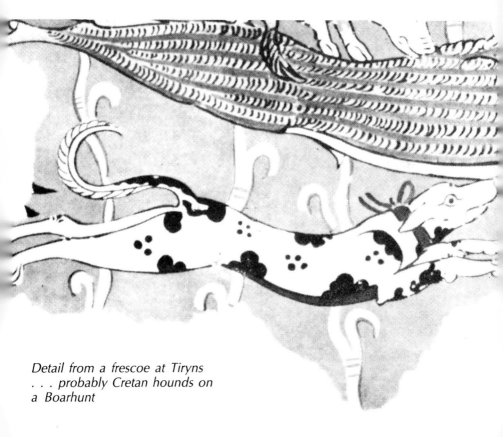

Detail from a frescoe at Tiryns . . . probably Cretan hounds on a Boarhunt

Henry III sent three men to hunt in the new forest with 'canibus cervericus et damericus', with deer being 'damos' or 'damas'. Edward III refers to hounds for hunting 'deymerettors', with fallow deer then being known by the name 'deyme' or 'desme'. Early in the 17th century Gervase Markham in his *Countrey Contentments* recommends for hunting deer . . . 'the white hound, or the white with black spots or the white with some few liver spots.'

James V of Scotland wrote to the Duke of Richmond requesting 'hounds which could ride behind men on horseback'. There are letters on record from Queen Margaret in the 16th century referring to hounds which 'will ride behind me one hors back'. Another letter from T. Magnus to the 'Quene of Scotts' mentions 'houndes of the beste kynde that woll behynde men upon horseback.' In Henry VIII's time there is reference to, in Latin, 'caunum nostrarum damorum vocatum bukhoundis.' It is the 'canum damorum' which is of great interest to Dalmatian researchers.

But what happened to these specialist fallow hounds, fleet-hounds or sharp-nosed hounds, as they were variously called? Firstly the hunting of fallow-deer became restricted, secondly the style of hunting changed and thirdly the coat-colouring of scent-hounds became almost standardised. The 'de mota' hounds, like the White Hounds of France, hunted *by sight* principally and went very fast once the lymmer or leashed tracker

had given them the right line. With the preference for 'hunting cunning' in which the unravelling of the scent by a pack of scent-hounds became the admired style of hunting, the days of the 'de-mota' hounds were numbered. No longer was speed the principal factor in the pursuit of game on horseback, the houndwork on the ground was all. Gervase Markham described in 1611 the hounds required for 'hunting cunning' and stressed the need for hounds 'not given to lie off or look for advantages', in other words solid scenthounds. Those scenthounds were later favoured in tricolour coats, often with a black saddle. The lemon-pied, blue-mottled or badger-pied markings were mainly retained in harrier packs, as the Hailsham and West Country packs exemplified.

So with fallow deer hunting reduced, running hounds with their heads up no longer being required and mainly white hounds not being sought, the 'de mota' dogs lost their role but, if my theory is correct retained their love of running with horses to become the coach-dogs we now know as Dalmatians.

A corruption, remembering that word of mouth was used much more as a means of communication in past centuries than in our contemporary world of books and wholescale literacy, of 'de mota' could so easily have sounded like 'Dalmatian' and then been written down as such. I believe, in similar vein, that epagneul comes from the old French verb 's'espanir', to sett or crouch, and not from espagnol as so many assume. There is no more evidence of Spaniels coming from Spain than there is of Dalmatians coming from Dalmatia.

I consider that the references to the Dalmatian as a 'Danish' dog comes from the ignorance of the writers concerned. It is much more likely that le grand Danois meant the Great Dane, le Danois meant a hound like the Dunker Hound or Russian Harlequin Hound and le petit Danois re- ferred to the Harlequin Pinscher. The harlequin factor genetically is very different from the spotting and flecking in gundogs and hounds. It is also possible that 'dainois' meaning of a fallow-doe in French was mistaken for 'danois' meaning of Denmark.

Despite having studied dogs in some thirty different countries, I have only come across one breed which has reminded me of the Dalmatian and that is the Porcelaine of France, although the Ariegeois in its white coat with small black markings randomly spread over a light mottling is of interest. The Porcelaine is de-

The Porcelaine — note the mottling on ears and underparts

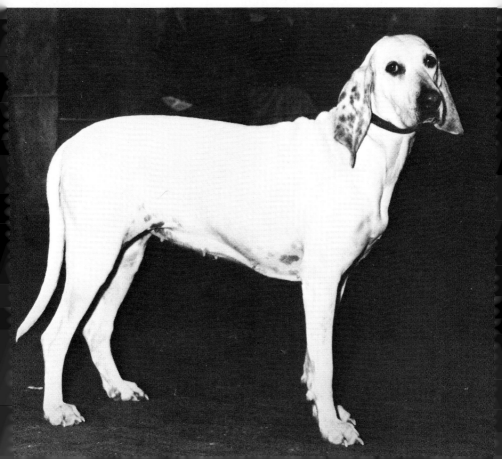

scended from the renowned Royal White hounds and the breed name comes from the quiet dignity of their character, a look of high breeding and quality but especially from the translucent look of their extremely fine almost elastic skin and black mottled coat. The mottling shows through the coat to give a blue glazed look which I've seen too in Dalmatians. The orange spots on the Porcelaine, which is a harehound, never form a blanket or saddle but are well spaced and super-imposed over black spotting on the skin. The liver and black spotting of the Dalmatian is very similar; most of the early prints depicting Dalmatians showed the longer ear of the

French hounds. There was a breed called the Bleu de Foudras which was blue mottled but I understand that they disappeared in the 18th century.

Clifford Hubbard, thirty years ago, linked the Dalmatian with the 'Istrian Braque' or pointer, Istria or Istra being near Dalmatia. I don't know of an Istrian pointer but only of an Istrian Hound (Istrski Gonic) which has a smooth or wire coat and is a hare or fox hound, but does look like a pointer. For me however the Dalmatian is more likely to have been a Western European fallowdeerhound, a descendent of the 'de mota' dog or 'deymerettors' of over a housand years ago in the mould of the Cretan 'outrunners'. If I am correct, this would be a fitting ancestry for a breed of great charm and considerable distinction.

A fine specimen from Holland — is the Dalmatian the 'Damachien' of 700 years ago?

CHAPTER FOUR

Sight Hounds

The Sight-hounds

Hunting by Sheer Speed

Hounds make up a very large group of the dog family and down the ages have traditionally been divided into those which follow game by sight and those which do so by scent. This may be a convenient way of separating the quite different styles of hunting conducted by the two divisions but it has led to all sorts of absurd assumptions. It would be more accurate and much better sense to divide them into the same two sections but describe one as hunting principally using their stamina and the other as mainly using their speed. For all hounds hunt by scent *and* sight. There are plenty of recorded instances in which greyhounds and whippets have been able to course rabbits or hares despite being blind or nearly so. Salukis in the desert track their game and then use

their speed once their keen eyes have located their quarry. Foxhounds don't use their noses when their eyes can see 'charlie.' And with dogs' eyesight not being their greatest asset yet with a sense of smell at least one hundred times more effective than ours, it would be remarkable for a group of hounds to elect to hunt *entirely* using their sight.

Rather as spaniels, retrievers and pointers complement one another in the shooting field, so too do the two types of hounds in the hunting field. the hounds hunting principally by scent were predominant in wooded and hilly country, those hunting principally by using their speed were able to operate more effectively in open country. But scent-hounds and sight-hounds were often used together, the former being used to 'spring' the quarry for the latter to chase and catch. This was often the style adopted at wolf-hunts in Czarist Russia. At the famous

Perchino hunting box the Archduke Nicolai Nikolaevich hunted with 120 to 150 Borzois, 15 English greyhounds and two packs of 120 scent-hounds. Sight-hounds have also been worked extensively with the hawk and a pointing dog.

Coursing was for centuries the sport of kings all over the world and strong claims have been put forward, by Jesse and others, to link the 'grey' of greyhound with grehund, the noble, great or prize-hound. Many have claimed a derivation from Greek-hound. The fallible Dr Caius proposed that its origin was in the Latin *gradus* . . . 'being absolutely the best of the gentle kinde of houndes.' Baillie Grohman considered the word came from Crech or greg, Celtic for dog. But it may well have come from grey, the common nickname for a badger, from the common colouring of badger and greyhound. But whatever the derivation, the greyhound and his relatives in different coats and varying sizes has long been famed the world over as a pot-filler. From the coursing hounds of nobility to the lurchers of the lowly the ability to catch game through speed has long been admired.

From the Afghan hound and the Saluki to the Podengo of Portugal and the Ibizan hound of the Balearics, from the Galgo of Spain to the Agar of Hungary, from the Rampur and Mudhol hounds of India to the Tasy of Central Asia, hounds which utilise speed to catch their prey have long been prized by man. It would be wrong however to describe a lurcher as a sight-hound, for its hunts by stealth and, like the Pharoah hound and the Portuguese Podengo, uses its scenting powers to full effect before catching its quarry by sheer speed. It is their speed in the chase, rather than their hunting by eye, which links this international group of hounds.

Such hounds were known to the ancient Egyptians, Greeks and Romans. Otto Keller, a noted cynologist at the beginning of this century who had no doubt about the multiple origin of the dog considered that the greyhound type came from the Abyssinian wolf. But the sport of coursing was introduced into the ancient world by the Celts some time before the second century after Christ. The hounds used were the Vertragi from the Celtic word ver, an intensive and trag which meant foot. So taken entirely the word Vertragi means animals with 'lots of foot' or plenty of leg. The same word appears again later in Old French as veltre, which meant greyhound. The two Celtic breeds, the Vertragi and the Sequsiae have sometimes been referred to as one because Arrian calls them both Celtic hounds. But an accurate translation indicates that the slow tracking hounds were the Segusiae and the swift and graceful gazehounds were the Vertragi. Incidentally even the best part of two thousand years ago, Arrian was stressing the need for the shoulder-blades in the greyhound to stand apart. I see greyhounds in the show ring with their shoulder-blades touching and wonder how they could ever hunt. They may never be asked to do so, but to be a proper greyhound they really must have the physique of a hunting dog. Pedigree greyhound fanciers would find it rewarding to view Mick the Miller, the phenomenal racing greyhound, now preserved in the Natural History Museum. No touching shoulder-blades (or excessive angulation of the hind legs) on this superbly fast dog!

The conformation of any dog which hunts at great speed is eternal, the long lean head, good

*Borzoi, Deerhound and
Lurcher of 50 years ago*

length of back, strong but light bone and hard-muscled legs being as essential now as in Arrian's time. And whilst it may be more difficult to judge physical points in the case of say an Afghan hound, the sight-hound physique must surely be perpetuated however ornamental such a breed may become. I was depressed recently by seeing some Pharoah hounds at a show. I first saw these dogs in Gozo nearly thirty years ago. The rabbits of Gozo have nothing to fear from the Pharoah hounds I saw in that show ring!

I can see no point at all in breeding pedigree dogs to a desired peak of physical perfection if the physique produced in so

doing does not allow the breed concerned to carry out its original purpose. What is the sense in becoming fascinated by a breed and working to promote it if at the same time you are actually changing your breed? You cannot be proud of the origin of your breed if you do not remain true to that origin. Pedigree sight-hounds must be able to hunt at speed. Using the coursing greyhound as a standard sample, with a shoulder height of 26 inches and a weight of 70 lbs, the two key elements in a sprinting dog's anatomy, girth of chest and loins must be commensurate with that height and weight. Without appropriate heart and lung room and the necessary muscular power such a canine athlete not function.

The girth of chest of such an animal would need to be 26 to 31 inches and the girth of loin from 18 to 24 inches. Great strength of loin is mandatory in a gazehound. But how many show ring sight-hounds could produce comparable girth and loin dimensions? The early (unapproved) standard of the Pharoah hound actually

A superbly constructed and highly successful racing Greyhound sporting the classic 'Irish' coat-colour combination: Westmead Poncho

used these expressions: flat-muscled body, narrow thorax — not as deep as the greyhound, exceptionally long hind-limbs, ribs flat; no wonder the Pharoahs I saw were poorly constructed. Yet in its 'general appearance' the breed is described as 'belonging to the original species of greyhound.' Whatever would Arrian think of such words?

In his *Cynegeticus,* written around 150 A.D., Arrian gave this advice: 'Now I myself shall tell by what means you should judge the fast and well-bred ones . . . First,

Sighthound — like hunting dogs of the middle ages

then, let them stand long from head to stern . . . Let them have light and well-knit heads . . . Let the neck be long, rounded and supple . . . Broad breasts are better than narrow; and let them have shoulder blades standing apart and not fastened together . . . loins that are broad, strong not fleshy, but solid with sinew . . . flanks pliant . . . Rounded and fine feet are the strongest.' Not a bad basis for a sight-hound's breed standard and written nearly two thousand years ago!

But however old or new the breed standards, there can only be one test for any hound which hunts using speed: Can it run? And having run fast two or three

times, it is still fit enough and physically sound enough to go again? Most coursing men know the famous tale of *Snowball and the Hare* which inspired Sir Walter Scott to write a poem eulogising 'Fleet Snowball'. The actual course lasted four miles, included forty or fifty turns of the hare, and it took Snowball and the hare twice up and down a hill a mile high. How many contemporary pedigree sight-hounds could match such a feat of fast sustained running?

Whilst Master McGrath will probably go down in history as the best greyhound ever bred, many old coursing experts considered that Bed of Stone the dark fawn bitch who won the Waterloo Cup in 1872 presented the perfect picture of breed points. Such a model should be studied by all those who have the best long-term interests of their sight-hounds at heart. Our ancestors handed on to us these superb functional animals and we owe it to their memory to perpetuate their handiwork for those who come after us. The hounds which hunt by speed form a unique component in the canine family. They are superb canine athletes which deserve to be conserved in the physical form evolved in the hard conditions of the hunting fields over many centuries. These are not ornamental creatures fit only to conform to some passing obsession with handsome appearance but an irreplaceable element in the rich heritage of the domestic dog. We simply must preserve them as *running* dogs.

Coursing: the sport of kings all over the ancient world

The Herited of our Fathers

'Saluki Racing, Sunday, August 31st at 2 pm, Ford's Greyhound Track, Blindley Heath, Surrey' . . . the advertisement simply leapt out of the paper to seize my attention. Saluki Racing . . . I looked out the train window, speeding away from London, and my mind drifted back to Arabia nearly thirty long years ago. I remembered the leggy puppies cared for by the Bedouin women, the very best hounds carried across the Sheik's personal camels on longer treks, but most of all, *the chase.* In the wide open spaces of the Arabian desert, the Saluki seems to fly over the ground rather than run, their highly individual racing action creating the illusion of their not touching the ground at all. Not as fast as our greyhound as a coursing dog in this country and probably too proud and independent to be trained formally for track racing, the Saluki has much greater stamina; in Arabia and North Africa often having a run of three miles after a single gazelle, separated from the herd. Hare and gazelle in particular are their true quarry but they have been used to course any creature providing a run, even the big jackals of Syria.

Salukis are sometimes run in conjunction with the sakr falcon — those generally used being larger

Lt. Col. Walter Stirling with a Gazelle-hound Damascus 1917

and more powerful than the peregrine, although slower in flight. The falcon is taught to go for the head of the gazelle and slow it down, by being fed lumps of meat tied to the head of tame gazelle. But the real test to challenge the best and fittest hounds is coursing the gazelle without the help of the falcon, the hounds often being used in two couples, one to tire the prey and the other brace to settle the issue. The art in hunting gazelle in this way being to isolate one from the herd, since another gazelle will often help one of its kind tiring in the chase by diverting the hounds on a different track.

Brigadier-General F. F. Lance, who with the Hon Florence Amherst did so much to pioneer the breed in Britain, records seeing a large smooth Saluki in India, 30 inches at the shoulder, kill a black Indian antelope, larger than a springbok, a full grown male not a doe in young, single-handed. The more mountainous and rocky countries produce the taller and heavier varieties than say Iraq or Arabia. Mesopotamia used to produce the lighter-coloured hounds, the dark colours came from the Syrian hill districts — sometimes a most distinctive black and tan, whilst the fawns and reds came from further south. But I always look at their feet first rather than their colour or stature. For a hound to run flat out over the baking unyielding rocky terrain of their native countries, they must have remarkably tough feet; tight, strong and big enough to cope with small rocks but compact enough not to slow the hound in the 'gallop'. The gallop is all-important, the Bedouin sometimes put a wide strap around the Saluki's loins so they don't gorge themselves and are kept 'light in the loin'.

Mohammedans abhor dogs but revere hounds and you only have to look at their horses to recall that Arabs are skilled at breeding. They are inordinately proud of their coursing hounds; in Arabic, one expression stressing their vital role . . . 'my hound is my butcher: he makes me independent of imports *and* importers'.

Possibly the most ancient sporting dog, the Saluki-type is known from Morocco to the steppes and from the Sudan to Afghanistan.

Fifty years ago, Joseph B. Thomas the American authority on Borzois listed nineteen distinct varieties of Saluki/Borzoi type gazehounds, nine of them Asiatic including the Persian, Arabian, Sudanese and the Turkoman Borzoi. With the Sloughi now being introduced into Britain as a separate breed – unfortunately recognised as such by the F.C.I. (the International Kennel Club) it might be simpler to call the Saluki, the Persian Greyhound and the Sloughi, the Arabian Greyhound – not for accuracy but for clarity. The confusion is deep-

A young Sloughi

ened by the fact that the Saluki can be called the Saluqi and the Slughi; but the Sloughi is markedly different in type! The Sloughi is sometimes confused with the smooth Saluki, the latter still being rather unusual in Britain. Deborah Copperthwaite of Al Caliphs Salukis has Elke, the first smooth Saluki to win a Junior Warrant and good enough to be only the fourth Saluki to gain the J.W. whilst still a puppy. The Sloughi, mainly found in Morocco although there are very few pure strains left there now, was brought to Europe by the Moors;

The Saluki — grace, elegance with sheer speed

the Galgo or Spanish greyhound being a descendant. With a broader skull, a more powerful muzzle and smaller feet than the Saluki, the Sloughi has distinctive black 'spectacles' around the eyes and a noticeably deeper chest. Prick-eared Sloughis were used by British officers in Palestine in the 1920s, believed to have been purchased in Upper Egypt. They were not as fast as the standard Saluki but considered to be superior at tackling game. Arabs used to crop their hounds' ears and so I am suspicious of the 'prick-ears' described.

A French tapestry of Richard the Lionheart shows Salukis in his entourage, they are widely travelled as well as being most ancient;

one of the best of the breed I have ever seen was the International Champion Schiram Ibicus at the Oslo show. But they have great versatility too. They hunt using scent but keep the head up, until the quarry is spotted and then they hunt by sight.

They have been known to point to quail and partridge and stand steady until the bird was flushed. They will stalk a desert partridge or even a bustard, 'spring' it into sudden flight and with speed and agility often catch it in the air — launching themselves many feet into the air from full gallop. Perhaps English partridges are in for a surprise! I am surprised however that Salukis have not been used with the falcon in Britain, they excel at marking game. The Saluki is an ideal companion (when trained to do so) for those who exercise horses, he can keep up at a full gallop and only then really comes alive.

The desert tribes of the Sahara call the Saluki, Barake, or 'Specially Blessed'. When a Saluki changes hands it is as a prestige gift rather than in return for money. In the Libyan desert, the Saluki is called 'El Hor', the Noble One, the tribesmen saying of him 'Are not these the herited of our fathers, and shall not we to our sons bequeath them?' Would that our own ancient native breeds be so revered!

A brace of Salukis of 60 years ago

Hunting Dogs of the Mediterranean

Whilst northern European man was still living in caves in a very primitive stage of development, the golden valley of the Nile was teeming with the activities of a relatively advanced civilisation, the land was tilled and irrigated, great temples built and speech preserved by a form of writing in signs and pictures. From this picture-writing we have been able to learn a great deal about the hunting dogs of Ancient Egypt, many of the pictures depicting hounds or hunting dogs very much like the Basenji, Saluki and Great Dane of today. For several thousand years before Christ, when the Khufu Dog and Bahakaa, the white hound of An-tefa II, were so prized, the countryside, flora and fauna of Egypt was vastly different from today. Lush vegetation in which game abounded was the order of the day and it is quite incorrect to depict ancient Egypt in stark desert conditions, as some modern breed historians do.

The naturalist, Keller, considers that all greyhounds descended from a common source and identifies Ethiopia as the seat of its formative years. This theory develops to show the greyhound spreading first to Egypt and from there to Europe and Asia during the Pharaonic period and thence evolving into different breeds and regional varieties. Another expert, Kallmeyer Belin, considers Assyria as the geographical area of origin for the greyhound, relying on the pictorial representations discovered there by archaeologists reaching back 7,000 years. Certainly, two thousand years before Christ, in Babylon, Phoenicia and both lower and upper Egypt, hunting dogs built like modern greyhounds but usually with high-carried curling tails and bat-ears, were utilised by man in the fertile valleys of the Tigris, the Euphrates and the Nile. In the subsequent commercial development and climatic changes in these areas, the Basenji-type hunting dogs disappeared but were retained in the upper Nile, the Sudan and across the trade routes to the Congo. Called variously the Congo terrier, Bongo, Nyam-Nyam and Zande dogs, they have been linked in skull formation, ear and tail carriage and coat and colour inheritance with the hunting dogs of Ancient Egypt, as Professor Thomas Noack's writings for the Zoological Society have shown. A barkless hunting-dog, the Basenji does however have a coat, unlike the African hair-less dogs and so-called Abyssinian 'sand-terriers', introduced into Britain some sixty years ago.

Buffon has claimed that all breeds have either preserved their primitive characteristics or not, according to their environment, the role given to them by man, the climatic conditions and, in particular, their degree of isolation. The contrast between the Basenji, for example, and more developed breeds from more developed areas, like the Spanish Galgo and the Hungarian Greyhound - which could easily be mistaken for English racing greyhounds, rather proving this point. Yet the Pharaoh Hound, the Ibizan Hound and the Sicilian equivalent, Cirneco Dell' Etna, all retain the classic head of ancient Egyptian hunting dogs. The Phoenicians conducted a thriving trade in hunting dogs built like greyhounds which they obtained first in North Africa and then in Asia and which they brought to Greece, the Greek islands, then to Sicily, Malta and Gozo, Spain and Southern Italy. Today, the Italian short-haired Segugio displays a physical conformation between the sight and the scent-hounds, especially in skull structure, the long ears and the tucked-up loins. Hunting fox, hare and rabbit, but prepared to take on wild boar as well, the Segugio hunt in pairs, using scent and then sight, displaying lurcher-like cleverness in the chase. The scent-hound ears make a marked contrast with the greyhound-like skull but the 22 inch height and the shoulders matches the Sicilian equivalent, Cirneco Dell' Etna, which hunts mute and is used on feathered game as well as fur. Aelian, in his *De Natura Animalium,* records this latter breed as being in Sicily, especially around Adrano, since prehistoric times.

The Pharaoh Hound, a very similar breed if a little taller, now increasingly popular as a show-dog in Britain (33 were registered with the Kennel Club in 1988) I remem-

ber more as the rabbit dog of Gozo. Looking like a cross between a Manchester Terrier and a Whippet but nearly always tan, they were being used by the young sportsmen on Gozo when visited the island in the mid 1950s. A similar hunting dog is found in the Canaries but still retains the tell-tale curly tail. They are used there in small packs to drive wild rabbits out of stone walls for their owners' guns. Bigger still yet anatomically almost a twin is the Ibizan hound from the Balearic Islands, sometimes known abroad as the Mallorquin (from Majorca), the Charneque (or Charnique) and the Podenco Ibicenco, again a combination of scent-hound and sight-hound yet also a natural retriever.

The distinctive physical feature of the Mediterranean hunting dogs is their prominent upstanding Anubis-like bat ears. No British hunting dog, let alone a sighthound, displays this feature, as our deerhounds, whippets, foxhounds, beagles and all our gundog breeds aptly demonstrate. This is in spite of the fact that such a feature invariably devotes enhanced hearing, as the Scandinavian hunting dogs, the Norwegian and Swedish Elkhounds, the Finnish Spitz and nearly every type of wild dog, the fox and the wolf exemplify. The Australian Dingo has quite remarkable hearing – and prick-ears of great size. The Mediterranean hunting dogs, like the

Cirneco Dell'Etna . . . the Lurcher of Sicily

dingo, have outstanding ears and outstanding hearing, with ultra-sensitive highly mobile ears which react to sound like directional signal-collecting radar receivers. I suspect that prick ears are the natural shape for all dogs and that in pursuit of breed conformity we may have impaired one of dog's most important senses. I have seen increasing numbers of lurchers with prick-ears in recent years, perhaps showing collie-cross blood but maybe Ibizan or Pharaoh Hound blood too.

I have noticed too that the rabbit dogs in Malta and Gozo, as well as the Portuguese Podengos, nearly always have dry noses. I have never believed that a dry-nosed dog is a sick dog but have found that gundogs with dry noses are never the best followers of scent. Centuries ago, hunting dogs were bred excessively 'lippy' so that the scent of game could be 'tasted' as well as 'sniffed'; wet lips and a wet nose were believed to help medieval hounds.

But just as pedigree dog breeders pursue fashion in dogs' ears, so too do they in the colour of dogs' eyes. Dark eyes are considered highly desirable in nearly all pedigree breeds of dog and yet the keenest-eyed working dogs I come across are invariably light-eyed, as are many of the Mediterranean hunting breeds. Light-eyed dogs too seem to retain their sight much longer than their darker-eyed brethren. Hazel-eyed or amber-eyed gun dogs, like the Chesapeake Bay Retriever, are usually the best markers of fallen feathered game too. I always find that perfect oval eyes are the healthiest, yet round eyes are actually desired in some pedigree breeds. The long-established and much prized hunting dogs of the Mediterranean littoral have perfect oval eyes, with no trace of the sagging lower lid which causes such problems for many of the scent hound breeds, related to the Bloodhound and the Basset Hound. The cruel winds and the

(left) The small variety of the Portuguese Hound — used as a hunting terrier

(right) The large Portuguese Hound (Portugues Podengo)

gritty dust found in the Mediterranean areas would soon give considerable discomfort to any hunting dogs with sagging eyelids used there.

The hunters who developed this group of dogs could not afford the luxury of evolving separately and utilising individually the specialised dogs of their Northern European counterparts, the setters, pointers, harriers, beagles, terriers or deerhounds, their hunting dogs performed all these functions. But the sheer variety of roles led, in the Portuguese Podengo for example, to a small variety which acted like terriers, beagles and spaniels, a medium variety which was used as a har-

rier and a large variety which performed both as watchdog and hound. In this breed too the coat varies between the smooth or the rough, the latter predictably predominating in the mountains and further north. The Ibizan Hound too features the smooth and wirehaired coats and has in addition a pointing instinct in some specimens which is of historic interest.

In his celebrated masterpiece on the pointer, William Arkwright makes reference to the 'renowned partridge-dogs of Gorga . . . the famous breed that existed here for three centuries – the Gorgas – so called from the little coast town of that name near Denia . . . much lighter than the

old cylindrical Navarrese dog. They were noted for their gentleness and fineness of nose . . .' Denia is on the Spanish mainland across from the Balearic Islands, where the Ibizan Hound comes from. Anyone seeing an Ibizan Hound 'point' a partridge could be forgiven for identifying an English pointer at work. Could the light-boned fine-nosed gentle natured hunting dogs of Ibiza and Majorca be linked with the similarly-described Gorga partridge-dogs on the nearest stretch of mainland from Spain, a country which produced many fore-runners of Northern European pointers? Now there's an intriguing thought!

The Pharoah hound

The Wolf Hounds

*'This Dog hath so himself
Subdu'd
That Hunger cannot make him
rude,
And his behaviour doth confess
True Courage dwells with Gen-
tleness.
With sternest Wolves he does
engage
And acts on them successful
rage.'*

These words of Katherine Phi-
lips written in 1664 on the Irish
Greyhound, nowadays known as
the Irish Wolfhound, convey the
timeless admiration for the noble
nature of a huge brave hound, an-
gry in the chase but gentle in response. And a wolfhound had to
produce a 'successful rage' to engage a wolf, a savage powerful
creature well able to defend itself
and capable of weighing a hun-
dredweight. Wherever wolves
were found and livestock (or even
human travellers) had to be defended, the big shepherd dogs
like the German, Belgian and
Dutch varieties or the even bigger
mountain dogs, like the Estrela,
Pyrenean, Maremma and Kuvasz
were utilised. Whenever an offen-
sive had to be mounted however,
faster but similarly-sized hounds
were used, with the Russian wolfhounds inspiring Turgenev and
Tolstoi by their heroic endeav-
ours.

Although the Russian wolfhound is known to kennel clubs
around the world as the borzoi,
the word means light, swift, agile
and was used rather as greyhound
used in England, levrier in France
and windhund in Germany. The
borzoi was more commonly used
for fox and hare coursing and the
Russians used to refer to Asiatic
borzoi, Polish borzoi and Crimean or Tartar borzoi, the latter
more like a Saluki than a pedigree
Russian borzoi of today. The Scottish greyhound (deerhound) was
used against wolves and other
prey, coursing hounds having
long been used in a variety of
ways. It is easy to forget when
looking at all the modern pedigree breeds that their ancestors
did not breed true to type and
were judged on sheer performance not desired conformation
to a standard. Behind the modern
Russian borzoi, there are barrel-
chested Caucasian borzoi, long
curly-haired Courland borzoi and
bigger-boned Crimean dogs. Behind the Irish Wolfhound there
are at least three distinct types;
one hundred years ago Fitzinger
identified: '. . . The Irish
Greyhound, next to the Indian
and Russian Greyhound, is the
largest specimen of the
greyhound type, combining the
speed of the Greyhound with the
size of the Mastiff' . . . (adding
that this type was nearly extinct).
'The second type is the Irish coursing dog, a cross between the
Irish Greyhound and the Mastiff
or ban-dog. He is shorter in the
neck with a coarser skull, broader
chest, and heavily flewed lips.'
The third variety he described as a
cross between the Irish
greyhound and the shepherd
dog, being low on the leg and

having a shaggy coat.

The Indian Wolf has been hunted by the shaggy-coated Bangara Mastiff (more usually employed as a herding dog), the smoother-coated Shikari dog of Kumaon, the Great Dane-like Sindh hound, the greyhound-like Vaghari dog, the beautiful ivory-coated Rajapalayam and the Dobermann-shaped Patti of Tamilnad. But as in other countries where the wolf no longer poses a threat, such breeds are mostly no longer preserved today. The Irish wolfhound was all but lost to us too in the latter half of the last century. Then in 1863 an English-man, Captain George Augustus Graham, a breeder of Deer-hounds, noted that some of his stock threw back to the larger type of Irish Wolfhound. He obtained dogs of the Kilfane and Bal-lytobin strains, the only pure Wolfhound blood existing in Ireland at that time, interbred these with Glengarry Deerhounds which had Irish Wolfhound blood in their own ancestry and in due course produced and then sta-bilised the type of Irish Wolf-hound which he believed to be

Wolf hunt 1873

historically correct.

Modern Irish Wolfhound fanciers must be careful to breed a functional animal; massive bone and a heavy gait is foreign to a coursing hound, as the springy gait of the Deerhound illustrates. It is difficult to see how a breed club can justify an Irish Wolfhound with legs like tree-trunks when a russian wolfhound has limbs like a greyhound. The standard of the Irish Wolfhound

A wolf hunt of 1734 (Oudry); specialist wolfhounds are not involved, only coarse scenthounds

states that it should . . . 'not be quite so heavy or massive as the Great Dane, but more so than the Deerhound, which in general type he should otherwise resemble.' The vast majority of Irish Wolfhounds I see nowadays are heavier in build than many Great Danes and more like the latter in a shaggy coat than the Deerhound. The minimum height of an Irish Wolfhound dog is 31 inches and the minimum weight is 120 lbs. A Scottish Deerhound dog should be from 30 inches tall and from 85 lbs. in weight and a Great Dane dog should be from 30 inches and 120 lbs. On these desired size cri-

teria I would have thought it inevitable that Irish Wolfhound
breeders would end up producing a dog more like a Great Dane
in substance than a Deerhound in
their efforts to reach the height-
weight ratio set out in their own
standard. To me a height from 31
inches should never produce a
correctly-constructed coursing
hound weighing any more than
100 lbs. The height-weight ratio
for a Russian Wolfhound dog is 28
inches and from 75 to 105 lbs.

The graceful athletic build of
the Russian dog has drawn widespread admiration; Charles Darwin described them as an "em-
bodiment of symmetry and
beauty." Undoubtedly the coat of
the modern pedigree borzoi en-
hances its physical appearance
but as with gundogs like the
Weimaraner, the Vizsla and the
German pointer and other gazehounds like the Ibizan hound,
there were varieties of coat in the
borzoi too. The Hunter's Calen-
dar and Reference Book published in Moscow in 1892 divided
the borzoi into four groups: First,
Russian or Psovoy Borzoi, of more
or less long coat; second, Asiatic,
with pendant ears; third, Hortoy,
smooth-coated and fourth; the
Brudastoy, stiff-coated or wire-
haired. But whether the hounds
were sleek or brittle-haired, coursing in Russia before the Revolution was what foxhunting was to
Britain and parforce hunting was
to France. As Leo Tolstoi recorded
in *War and Peace*: 'Fifty-four coursing hounds were taken with six
mounted horse-men and keepers
of hounds. Apart from the Master

and his guests, another eight
huntsmen took part, with more
than forty hounds. In the end
there were one hundred and
thirty hounds and twenty horse-
men in the field.' Tsar Peter II
kept a pack consisting of 200 coursing hounds and over 420
greyhounds. Prince Somzonov of
Smolensk had 1,000 hounds at his
hunting box and he called himself
Russia's Prime Huntsman.

Better known was the hunt with
the Perchino hounds near Tula on
the river Upa, where Archduke
Nicolai Nikolaevich established a
hunting box in 1887 and hunted
with two packs of 120 parforce
hounds, 120 to 150 Borzois and 15
English grey-hounds. All the hunt
servants were mounted, mainly
on Kabardine horses, half-bloods
from Central Asia, while the hunting party used English half or
three quarter thoroughbreds
which were greys of dappled
whites. Both horses and hounds
were kept in cold stables to ensure sufficient hardiness for winter wolf hunts.

Usually 20 leashes of Borzois
were taken to a hunt, each consisting of two males and a bitch. The
hunting season was summer coursing (June to early August) for
hare and fox, then summer training for borzois in August consisting of 20 kilometres walking and
trotting with the hunt horses, followed by advanced training on
captive wolves in early September
then the wolf-coursing season
from mid-September to the end
of October. Hunting from sledges
sometimes took place from October with mounted beaters putting

up the wolves, which were often fed to keep them in hunting areas. In the Perchino game reserve between 1887 and 1913, 681 wolves were killed, as well as 743 foxes, 4,630 brown hares and 4,026 white hares. Borzois obtained the biggest proportion of this bag. I know of a Scottish farmer who to this day uses a brace of borzoi on the hill foxes raiding his lambing fields. The Borzoi is still important for the Russian fur-trade for it catches foxes without mauling them and spoiling their pelts.

Coursing with borzois in Tsarist Russia called for a high standard of horsemanship and superbly-trained hounds. Each mounted handler rode with his three hounds on long leashes, slipping the hounds whenever a wolf was either put up by the extended line of mounted "beaters" or flushed out of the woods by scent hounds. Many of us would find it difficult enough to control three borzois on short leashes whilst dismounted!

Huge shaggy-coated hunting dogs were used by the Celts in their central European homeland in the 8th century B.C. and these accompanied them on their migrations to Britain, Ireland and Northern Spain from the 5th to the 1st century B.C. There are many references to these hounds down the ages, from Consul Quintus Aurelius Symmachus recording in 391 A.D. that seven were sent to Rome to fight in the arenas, to Nicholas Cox's *'Gentleman's Recreation'* of 1675 in which he wrote: 'Although we have no wolves in England at the

The Albanian Wolfhound

present, yet it is certain that heretofore we had routs of them, as they have to this very day in Ireland; and in that country are bred a race of greyhounds which are commonly called wolfdogs. Now in these greyhounds of that nation there is an incredible force and boldness, so that they are in great estimation, and much sought after in foreign parts, so that the King of Poland makes use of them in his hunting by great beasts by force.'

It is claimed that Captain Graham used borzoi blood when re-creating the Irish wolfhound in the last century. Could not the King of Poland in the 17th century have bred his Irish 'greyhounds' or wolfdogs with his own stock? If so, there could be Irish wolfhound blood behind some borzois, for the hunting-mad nobility of Europe had little respect for pedigrees only a high regard for field prowess. Whilst speculating it interests me, knowing that the Celts took their huge hunting dogs to Spain with them that the modern so-called Spanish mastiff is a huge brindle thick-coated dog. And many of the hunting dogs portrayed by Velasquez have a distinct deerhound look about them. But whether Celtic or Russian, exported to Poland or Rome, the courage and steadfastness of the wolfhounds has long been acclaimed: 'Gentle when stroked, fierce when provoked' is an apt summary of their virtues.

With such a Deerhound, the Irish Wolfhound was recreated

The Humble Whippet

Graceful, gentle-natured and beautifully-mannered, with a smooth coat that needs no attention and the ability to curl up almost unseen in any household chair, the Whippet has long been valued as a companion dog. The pedigree Whippet has steadily increased in popularity in the last fifty years, with 111 registered with the Kennel Club in 1942, 76 in 1952, 1903 in 1962 and 2003 in 1972. But the Whippet is above all a working dog, a functional animal, a hunter's companion.

At 16 yards a second, the Whippet is for its size probably the swiftest of all animals. Some years ago, a lecture at the Royal Institution on the Dimensions of Animals and Their Muscular Dynamics, Professor A V Hill pointed out that a small animal conducts each of its movements quicker than a large one, with muscles having a higher intrinsic speed and being able proportionately to develop more power. The maximum speeds of the racehorse, greyhound and whippet are apparently in the ratio 124:110:110 but their weight relationship is in the ratio 6,000:300:100. The larger animal however can maintain pace for longer periods. Professor Hill suggested that up a steep hill the speed of a racehorse, greyhound and whippet would be in reverse order to that on the flat. It is generally held that a Whippet's best performance is over a furlong on the flat, when the Whippet can capitalise on its ability to provide the maximum oxygen supply per unit weight of muscle.

This dainty unobtrusive rather gentle-natured little hound, with its almost timid manner and obviously sparse build, hardly hints at this kind of aggressive athleticism yet few rabbits underestimate them – twice! And it is as a rabbit-dog that the humble Whippet has earned his keep and his reputation, in the mining villages of the North East, in the Black Country and amongst Lancashire Mill workers. Speed is not the sole distinctive feature of the little racer however. No other breed of dog can combine the variations of coat-colour, height and weight found in the Whippet. From jet-black to pure white, through shades of blue, grey and grey-brindle, from red to fawn and with part-white combinations of these, the Whippet provides an infinite range for those seeking variety in colour with shades as varied as their owners' preferences. For just as Grattius, writing in the last century BC, declared 'Choose the greyhound pied with black and white: he runs more swift than thought or winged light', and Oppian later wrote that black and white in combination led to 'overheating' whilst Edward, second Duke of York, stated in 1406 that 'the best hue is rede fallow, with a black moselle', so too do whippet-fanciers relate excellence directly to coat colour. Black combined with white chest and face markings has often been favoured in the coursing field, with whole brindle the preference of many race-minded miners in the North-East of England.

Show ring specimens are usually around 18 inches high and 21lbs weight but racing whippets have been successful from 15 to 21 inches and from 16 to 25lbs. A Durham miner once told me that sixty or seventy years ago, his grandfather favoured an 8lb whippet . . . 'so's it could fit in y'overcoat pocket'! But whether 8lbs or 18, the Whippet is not the delicate fragile creature which it appears to the uninitiated; pound for pound this is one of the most deadly killers of furred game, producing the physical power from a lightboned superbly muscled physique which results in 200 yards being covered in some 12 seconds. Yet a Whippet in full flight gives no impression of great power, more sheer graceful swiftness and sleek silky-smooth sprinting, rather as Ovid described:

'Scarcely had we let him off from hand,
But that where Laelaps was we could not understand;
The print remained of his feet upon the parched sand,
But he was clearly out of sight Was never dart I trow,
Nor pellet from enforced sling, nor shaft from Cretish bow,
That flew more swift than he did run.'

No one has satisfactorily explained the origin of the word 'whippet'; I suspect it is a deriva-tive of 'whappet' an old English word used to describe any small yelping cur. It is not correct however to trace the origin of the breed through references to the word 'whappet' in early writings. Breed historians speak of the whippet being developed in the 19th century from greyhound, Italian Greyhound and terrier stock. But small greyhounds have been favoured throughout recorded history and the emergence of the whippet merely exemplified this in the last century. I can't see North Country miners having much access to Italian Greyhounds – the ornamental pets of the nobility. If any cross were needed to install gameness then I could see the blood of the Old English White terrier being used. Now extinct , the latter had many whippet-like qualities, both in conformation and temperament.

The very strong whippet-racing centres were Lancashire, the North-East, the Eastern Counties, the Potteries and the West Riding of Yorkshire with the Airedale track featuring electric judges even in the 1920s. Handicapping was by height or weight, 4 yards to the inch or 2 feet per pound with physical limits varying from area to area. In Durham in 1958 there was a height limit of 21 inches, at Grantham and Nottinghamshire in 1961 a weight limit of 28lbs and at Worcester in 1962 a weight limit of 26lbs. In Northumberland and the Potteries, bigger dogs, 25-35 lbs, were favoured in the 1940s but the size of winning dogs was always varied; Comedian, a 21 lb fawn dog was a great racing winner in the early 1900s and Wild Irishman a regular winner around 1910 was 12 1/2 lb.

The breed gained pedigree status with the Kennel Club in 1890 and was then featured at the Darlington Show in a 'snap dogs' class, for the breed has borne many names, 'snap dog', 'rag dog', 'lightning rag dog' and 'race dog' among them. For any four-legged animal to move at 16 yards a second and cover 200 yards in 12 seconds, whether to race like lightning to snap at a waving rag or to course a rabbit, requires superb athleticism based on a beautifully-constructed sprinter's physique. Not surprisingly a great deal has been written about the physical points or conformation in the breed.

Sound movement in front is rooted in the setting of the shoulder blade which, for the shoulder to be well laid back, must be long and slanting. If the shoulder blade is too short then the shoulder cannot be correctly positioned, and only when the shoulder is soundly constructed can

A German Whippet

the force of violent exercise like racing over uneven ground or hurdling be properly absorbed. The neck line must be clean and graceful; a dog with upright shoulders looks short-necked and the neck itself badly set, the dog will have stilted front movement and will be lacking the long low stride with the feet well in front of the body.

Correct movement behind is similarly based in the pelvis – the set or slope of the pelvis. This affects the position of the hip joints – the hinge of the rear propelling power, power derived partly from the angulation of the upper and lower thighs at the stifle. With insufficient angulation the dog cannot gallop freely or be fully agile. This correct angulation of course must be supported by strong muscular development on both the upper and lower thighs and low-placed hocks.

But the sound movement is nothing without lung and heart room, backed by a determined spirit, the latter usually detected in the eye of the dog. The chest, even on such a lean dog, must be broad; none of that 'both front legs coming out of the same hole' which has so ruined the show fox terrier. The brisket must come down to the elbows with good 'galloping space' behind, i.e. a long-coupled body. The eyes must be bright, alert and keen when in the field, if gentle in repose. Stanley Wilkin of the 'Tip-tree' whippets once had a blind whippet which ran with the others and was often in at the kill. It tried hard to get in body contact with another running dog but mainly seemed to manage on its powers of scent and hearing.

Whippets are surprisingly robust dogs and usually have no health problems. Racing whippets sometimes suffer injuries from bend racing, caused by leaning in towards the inner fence in order to counteract centrifugal force. This usually takes the form of instant or fatigue fractures of the carpal bones, ruptures of the triceps muscles or of the inner superficial flexor tendon. Show ring whippets do seem more prone to kidney problems than is desirable in a working breed. These are hardly vintage years for show ring whippets in Britain; movement is disappointing, far too many of the dogs are too short in the loin and few breeders seem to understand what is really important in a functional breed. This too is one of the most difficult breeds to judge in the show ring. Registrations have slipped from 1,676 in 1980 and 1,417 in 1981, to 1,247 in 1982.

There are some talented whippet breeders in Sweden, with 30 – 40 dogs featuring in classes there. The breed is favoured in Canada, with the Stampede City Whippet Club well to the fore; whippet racing is commendably much encouraged amongst the show dogs to ensure an all round functional dog being perpetuated. In the United States, despite some neglect of the solid colours and a mania for 'pigmentation', often at

(previous page) A racing Whippet ready for the off

the expense of soundness, the breed is more popular than ever, with bigger more robust dogs being bred. A year ago, controversy raged there over the so-called 'long-haired' whippets being bred by Walter A. Wheeler, Junior: the American Whippet Club predictably formed an investigative sub-committee which equally predictably sought the disqualification of these dogs. The committee concluded that the Wheeler Whippet was . . . 'an emerging but separate breed of coated miniature sight hound notwithstanding the fact that all or a major part of its primal blood-

lines may have come from the documented Whippet genetic pool.' It was recommended that a separate stud book should be set up with a view to separate recognition of these long-haired whippets being sought.

Owners of small lurchers in Great Britain may hardly know whether to laugh or cry when they read of such goings-on. In the international show-dog world we now have smooth-coated Salukis recognised as a separate breed called sloughis, long-haired Weimaraners allowed undocked tails but not the smooth-haired variety, long-haired and smooth-haired Dachshunds both with undocked tails, smooth and rough-coated St Bernards recognised as one breed but smooth

The Whippet features a wide variety of coat colours

and rough-coated Collies recognised as two. How would today's canine authorities have registered an Irish Setter litter of two hundred years ago, which might well have included lemon and white pups and the odd smooth-coated one. No one seems interested in whether the Wheeler Whippets are sound sporting dogs, just whether or not they conform to the 'standard'; cynics might question the right of humans to set standards for dogs at all! I must admit however that a whippet for me, from a throwback or a misalliance, should have a short-haired coat. But whether long-haired 'sports' or smooth-coated 'standards', confusion in the show ring or clarity in the coursing world, the whippet remains a game little breed. Did not Bert Gripton, when terrier-man to the Albrighton thirty or so years ago, have one that went to ground to fox and badger! The dual-purpose Whippets of the Laguna Kennels of Mrs D. U. McKay, the racing whippets of Major Coates, the Goodad and Karryon Kennels and the coursing whippets of such as Group Captain Whittingham have long kept the small greyhound flag flying, praise be to them all.

Whippets — a group from the continent

A Judgement on the Lurcher

For a thousand years in Britain the humbler hunters have had their own hound, with pride in its performance never in its pure-breeding, yet purpose-bred in the pursuit of hunting excellence with as much dedication as any fox-hound, setter or spaniel. Long associated with gypsies, poachers and country characters, the lowly lurcher has survived the campaigns of rural police forces, watchful gamekeepers and wary land-owners and still fills the pot of many a working class household. But today the lurcher-fancier is classless; regimental ties and cavalry-twill trousers feature at the Lambourn lurcher show just as much as moleskin, denim and mufflers. The phenomenal rise in Lurcher Shows in Britain in the last twenty years indicates the interest in these extraordinary hunting dogs of such mixed heritage.

But what is a lurcher? If you look around at a lurcher show it is soon apparent that the event would be better labelled 'any variety, sporting dog', for the height, weight, coat and colour is essentially anything but uniform. For a lurcher *must* be a crossbred dog — fast enough to catch a hare, crafty enough not to get caught doing so, silent at all times and able to endure the cold and wet, as well as withstand the odd encounter with barbed wire. Purists would say it really must be a collie cross greyhound to be truly a lurcher but deerhound, whippet, saluki, Bedlington terrier and Staffordshire Bull terrier blood have all been used over the years to instil gameness, a more protective coat or more stamina.

It is common to find the less diligent researchers linking the 'tumbler', quaintly described by a number of sixteenth century writers, with the lurcher. Correspondents contributing to country sports magazines on the subject of lurchers often sign themselves 'tumbler'. But the tumbler was the decoy dog, a very different animal. Dr Caius, for all his learning, knew little about dogs and yet has over the years become much quoted as some kind of authority. But even he mentioned the 'Thevishe Dog or Stealer, that is a poaching dog'. His lengthy and extraordinary description of the 'tumbler' is in effect an exaggerated description of the antics of a decoy dog. I know of no lurcher which hunts by 'dissembling friendship and pretending favour'. The decoy dog lives on today in the Nova Scotia Duck Tolling Dog and the Kooik erhondje of Holland, one luring the inquisitive ducks to within range of the hunters' rifles, the other enticing them along ever-narrowing little waterways until they are netted. We have lost such as the 'ginger 'coy dog' of East Anglia, referred to by writers such as the late James Wentworth Day. But whereas the red decoy dog is perpetuated as distinct breeds, the lurcher was and ever shall be a nondescript dog. As

Stonehenge described them over a hundred years ago: 'A poacher possessing such an animal seldom keeps him long, every keeper being on the look-out, and putting a charge of shot into him on the first opportunity; and as these must occur of necessity, the poacher does not often attempt to rear the dog which would suit him best, but contents himself with one which will not so much attract the notice of those who watch him.' And although it is unrewarding to conduct scholarly research into what down the ages has been the farm labourer's dog rather than the squire's, Taplin for example being understandably thoroughly confused, Stonehenge has managed to convey the essential ordinariness, the vital anonymity and the fundamental lack of distinct type in what has long been a cross-bred purely functional hound traditionally used for illegal hunting.

This variation in type manifests itself in to-day's lurcher shows with classes for rough-haired and smooth-haired dogs and those over and under 26 inches at the withers. Some breeders swear by the long-haired Saluki cross and others by Bedlington blood; some fanciers favour a stiff-coated dog and others the smooth-coated variety; a minority prize the Smithfield blood from the old drovers' dogs and there are always the bizarre crosses such as Airedale cross Whippet or Bearded Sheepdog cross Dobermann pinscher. I have beard Kennel Club judges scoff at the whole business of even attempting to judge such wide variations at a show but lurchers are usually judged by results. Lurcher show judges anyway are hardly conformist characters, like Moses Aaron-Smith, a gamekeeper from Derbyshire, born in a gypsy waggon of pure bred Romany stock or Ted Walsh, a retired Army colonel and expert on coursing or Martin Knoweldon, a commercial artist specialising in depicting sighthounds in full stride.

A measure of organisation has been introduced into recent lurcher activities with the institution of the National Lurcher Racing Club, organised in regional branches but lurchers shouldn't just be fast dogs, but clever hunting dogs, able to use ground and air scent, track its quarry as well as course it. And how can anybody really organise such diverse characters as gypsies, miners, forestry workers, schoolmasters, navvies and cavalry officers! Diversity of type characterises their owners as well as the dogs.

Books on lurchers sometimes refer to lurcher types in other countries, like the Banjara greyhound, the Portuguese Podengo and the Italian Segugio. But this overlooks the unique ability of the lurcher of Britain, a combination of coursing greyhound, retriever, tracker, pointer and watchdog. It would be more correct to describe the word lurcher itself as indicating a role rather than a type of dog. For it really doesn't matter if a lurcher

Warreners at Barnham, Suffolk, early this century

is 20 or 26 inches at the shoulder, rough-coated or smooth, black or tan, prick-eared or drop-eared, provided it is biddable and can run.

One Sunday last summer I spent a few hours at the Indoor Terrier and Lurcher Show of a local hunt and then went on to spend some time at a 25 class members' sanction show of the local kennel association. What struck me most of all in comparing the two was the approach of the judges in both arenas. The show dog judge examined and studied twenty different breeds of pedigree dog without recourse once to breed classifications or scale of points. I envied him for his extraordinary memory. The judge at the Terrier and Lurcher show however surprised me just as much, for he made no attempt whatsoever to place hands on the dogs or study their movement and dismissed half one Lurcher class in only a few minutes. Either I had not appreciated his sheer genius and instinctive 'feel' for working dogs or he was wasting the time of good-hearted lurcher owners who had travelled a long way to be there.

I believe that it is possible to judge lurchers more precisely than this sort of cursory glance,

The black merle Lurchers bred by my namesake, poultry farmer David Hancock, are much respected

without ever spoiling the sheer fun and country atmosphere of these shows. Of course, unlike pedigree show dogs, the ultimate test will always be 'in the field', in the chase, working. But I suspect that some Lurchers succeed in spite of their anatomy, and that the judging at such shows should be more thorough.

It is possible to judge these purely functional dogs much more effectively; if we are going to judge them at all let's do it properly. A hound which hunts using its speed must have some basic physical suitability. Immense keenness for work will al-ways come first but the physique to exploit that keenness comes close second. A Lurcher must have a long strong muzzle with powerful level jaws, how else can it catch, kill and carry. The nose should be good-sized with well-opened nostrils — for despite old-fashioned theories, gaze-hounds hunt using scent as well as sight. The eyes should be fairly prominent and set slightly oblique to the side of the head. One eye should look away to the right and one to the left so that like any good rangefinder, both can be used at long distance. It is likely however that at close range only one eye is used at a time. The neck should be long but symmetrically so, muscular and really

Lurchers with strong Greyhound breeding

firm. Length of neck does not improve 'pick up'; flexibility in the 'swoop' comes from the placement of the shoulder-blades.

A Lurcher must have well laid back sloping shoulders; I always apply the 'two fingers width' test to the space between the shoulder blades of a standing dog. The Lurcher's back should hint at suppleness and power, be slightly arched in the lumbar region yet have a mainly level topline. The chest should be deep from the withers to point of elbow but be fairly flat with the under-part of the brisket fairly broad across. The ribs should be well-separated with good heart and lung room, with space between the last rib and the hindlegs to allow a full stride. At full stretch the impress of a hare's hindfeet is implanted in front of that of the fore-feet; the Lurcher should have the same capability. There must also be freedom of suspension in the ribcage or thorax in the way it is 'cradled' by the scapulae – the Lurcher needs to utilise this when hurdling a farm-gate or turning at speed.

The hindquarters must be powerfully constructed if they are to propel the dog forward in the chase, but symmetry and balance fore and aft is the key to any ability on the turn. Any sight-hound depends upfront on good long arms and fore-arms and in the hindlegs wide and muscular thighs and second thighs, length of stifle and good angulation. The feet must be really compact with well-knuckled toes and short claws, naturally worn from working. Many expert greyhound buyers have been known to look at the tail first, declining any sign of coarseness and looking for the tail of a rat, long and whip-like with little hair. Smooth-coated Lurchers are sometimes victims however of too little hair. I am not advocating a shaggy Wolf-hound coat but see advantages in a wirehaired or Bedlington-style coat. The twisty linty texture of the Bedlington coat gives excellent waterproofing without 'holding the wet'. The last, but far from the least, point to judge in a Lurcher is the alert eager expression in the eye – if the dog isn't keen, the physique is wasted. I would look out for this single characteristic, call it 'hunting spirit' if you like, before taking any closer look.

I shall remember all my life the gypsies and their dogs from my boyhood in Somerset and one lurcher bitch in particular. She was sent out to hunt and always came back empty-handed. Then when darkness fell she was sent out again to collect the booty from deep in a hedgerow where she had been taught to hide it. Now that is a lurcher at work . . . Speed and brains!

CHAPTER FIVE

Gundog Breeds

The Development of the Setters

'A Norfolk for the farmer
(or the parson if he shoots)
For picking up his driven birds
And finding in the roots.

A collie for the shepherd
And the cowman in his byre.
But, over all the common curs,
A setter for the squire.'

All over Europe the setting breeds have long been favoured by the landed gentry and associated with the nobility; the higher-headed pointers and setters too have long been regarded as the aristocrats of the gundog world. But just as aristocratic families have inter-bred across the national bound-aries so too have their dogs, the setters of Western Europe amongst them.

A setting dog is featured in the Falconry Tapestry, woven in the 1400s at Tournai. In 1563 Lord Warwick wrote to his brother the Earl of Leicester from Le Havre: 'I thank you for sending me so fine a horse. In return, I send you the best Setter in France . . .' It is too limiting to think of setters in the British Isles developing from the land spaniel as a purely British-bred achievement. Sportsmen seek good dogs anywhere and ev-erywhere with national bound-aries having no relevance for them. Setters were depicted in paintings on the Continent long before they featured in paintings produced here.

Yet time and time again British writers on dogs in the 19th cen-tury saw the excellent gundog breeds which were then being stabilised in Britain through wholly British eyes. The much quoted Stonehenge recorded: 'The setter is commonly sup-posed to be the old spaniel, either crossed with the pointer or his setting powers educated by long attention to the breed . . . I believe it came to pass that the English setter imitated the pointer;' Youatt wrote: 'The setter is evidently the large spaniel improved to his peculiar size and beauty . . .' going on to repeat the old story of the Duke of Northumberland being in 1535 the first man to break-in systematically the setting-dog. Half a century later, Drury, closer to the mark, considered that 'The setter is probably the oldest, and certainly the most elegant and beautiful of our gundogs. The ability to 'set' or 'crouch' at game was one developed in certain dogs by our sporting ancestors in the days when the hawk and falcon performed the offices of the modern gun.'

The setting spaniel was known all over Europe in the Middle Ages, but then the words referred to what we now call setters or epagneuls. Of course, our modern breeds of setter have developed in their own way throughout the last two or three centuries but the setting-dog is an established European type of sporting dog, evolving into separate breeds through local needs and preferences.

Espee de Selincourt, writing at the end of the 17th century and making early use of the genetic term gundogs (chiens de l'arquebuse) separated the spaniels

A French Épagneul of a century ago

from the braques. He defined setting-dogs (chiens couchans) as 'braques that stop at the scent (arretant tout) and hunt with the nose high . . . The spaniels are for the falcons (oyseaux) hunting with the nose low, and follow by the track.' But before the use of firearms in the field of hunting fur and feather, the net was the most common device with the huge nets being drawn over both setting dog and the area containing the game being indicated. I am inclined to believe that the earliest sporting dogs other than hounds of the chase were the dogs 'da rete' (of the net) and the waterdogs which would retrieve arrows and duck. The 'oysel' dogs of the 16th century were much more setter-like than anything else. It could be that the expression chiens d'arret or stop-dogs is a corruption of 'da rete'.

In these days of pedigree dog breeding with distinct breeds being favoured for what they look like rather than what they do, it is easy to forget that within the lifetime of our older sportsmen it was expected that a setter litter would contain reds, blacks, black and tans, white and reds, white and blacks and tricolour puppies, rather as still happens with 'langhaars'. In due course certain colours or colour combinations were favoured by some breeders: the liver and whites of the Prouds at Featherstone Castle Laidlaw at Edmond Castle and Grisdale at Naworth Castle; The Earl of Southesk's and Lord Lovat's tricolours; the lemon and whites of the Earl of Seafield; Lord Os-

sulton's jet blacks; the milk-whites of Llanidloes and the black and whites of Mr Lort of King's Norton, for example. It was said that the coats of the black and tans were coarser and more wiry than the other strains and they were long in the leg, looser in the loin, heavier headed and longer in the back. To this day some black and tans feature a most collie-like tail.

With the advent of dog shows and the registration of breeds with the Kennel Club, the setter colours were stabilised into three distinct breeds, English, Irish and Gordon and in time the Belton colouration dominated the English setter as did the whole-coloured red the Irish and the black and tan the Gordon. But it is good to see the Red and White Irish setter being favoured more nowadays and a white and black Gordon starring in the field. Richardson writing in the last century in his *Dogs their Origin and Varieties* described the Irish Setter as 'of a yellow or dun colour.' In the early nineteenth century there were far more kennels of black and tan setters in the midland counties of England than in the whole of Scotland.

But as with so many breeds of sporting dog, prominent sporting families promoted certain strains to give us the breeds we have today: the fourth Duke of Gordon (1743–1827), the O'Connors and the Earl of Enniskillen and the great setter-men of England, Laverack and Llewellin. It is often overlooked that both the 4th and the 5th Dukes of Gordon preferred tricoloured dogs; the Gordon Castle dogs were described in the 1860s as 'black-and-white tans.' But when the Kennel Club was founded in 1873 the breed was officially classified as the Black and Tan Setter. The breed was well to the fore at the first trial held in 1865, first, second and third prizes being won by black and tans. There was great variety in the breed at this time, with a decidedly bloodhoundy look in some and a collie-look conformation in others. Uniform quality was established by Robert Chap-

man in his Heather Kennels at Glenboig around 1875, producing a racier setter without losing substance or character. From the early 1900s, Isaac Sharpe of Keith, Banffshire, took up the lead; his Stylish Ranger winning the Kennel Club Derby in 1901. His early stock was from the Heather Kennel but in 1908 he acquired the remaining Gordon Castle dogs, despite the English setter blood introduced into them. Isaac Sharpe maintained that the Gordons were 'more easily trained than any other breed of setter.'

Less easily trained by some, the Irish Setter was championed by the Mahons of Castlegar, the Earl of Enniskillen and Jason Hazzard of Timasks, County Fermanagh in

The English Setter . . . long famed for sheer style

the early nineteenth century, to be followed by Moore, Oliver, McCarthy, O'Keefe and Sir John Blunden of Castle Blunden, County Kilkenny. Moore bred Ch. Palmerston, a 64 lb. dog, but sold him as a field failure. The Rev. R. O'Callaghan owned and bred many field and bench celebrities, including the fine-looking bitch Ch. Aveline. Sir Humphrey de Trafford at the end of the last century bred and owned some 26 F.T. and bench champions.

The early development of the English Setter is dominated by two famous names, with a third, also associated with Shropshire carrying on their foundation work.

Edward Laverack who was born in Keswick in 1798 and died at Whitchurch, Shropshire in 1877 and Richard Purcell Llewellin, born in 1840 and who died in 1925 and is buried at Stapleton in Shropshire are justly revered as being the master-breeders who developed the English Setter into a magnificent sporting breed in the last century. But in the field trial world, William Humphrey of Minsterley Shropshire, born in 1883 and who died in 1963, made undeniably the biggest impact of the three, in breeding and running the 'Llewellin' strain of English Setters; his grandson Christopher Sorenson of Lydbury North, Shropshire, perpetuates his stock to this day.

Laverack bought his first English Setters in 1825, the dog Ponto and the bitch Old Moll, both blue Beltons, from the Rev A. Harrison of Carlisle, who bred them from his own stock, a pure strain maintained from strongly constructed family estate dogs over 35 years. Laverack therefore had an established line to perpetuate, which he did for 52 years, giving 87 of continuous line breeding. He was a little reticent about his breeding methods but certainly used both Irish and Gordon Setter blood and his curly-coated specimens probably had old Welsh Setter blood too. Laverack's dogs were often well beaten at field trials but he was quite content with them provided they worked hard and made the day's bag of game a high one. With four or five dogs and guns, backed by reloaders, he would bag up to 1,000 brace of grouse in a single day, he claimed, on the best of his rentings. 'I have run my dogs of this breed for three weeks daily, from 9 a.m. to 7 p.m. and others possessing the same blood have done the same', he once wrote. Despite his age when dog shows became organised, he made up two show champions and in the period 1861 – 1892, eleven champions were 100 per cent Laverack-bred and of 25 champions made up only three had no Laverack breeding behind them.

The Laverack Setter was kept going as pure stock up to 1913 by Mr H.C. Hartley, with Dashing Fan born that year. Just over 200 were registered with the Kennel Club and it would be hard to find a blue Belton pedigree that does not go back to dogs of pure Laverack breeding. The first dual champion, Countess and her brilliant FT winning sister Nellie, both bred by Laverack, formed the nucleus of what later became known as the Llewellin Setter. Laverack's absorbing book on the Setter was dedicated to R.L1. Purcell Llewellin . . . 'who has endeavoured and is still endeavouring, by sparing neither expense nor trouble to bring to perfection the "Setter."'

Llewellin established in his strain of setters the greatest Field Trial winning record of all breeds of pointing dogs in the world in the 80 years from 1880 to 1960. His dogs were first of all a mixture of Gordon, probably Llanidloes Setter, a big milk-white curly-coated variety and the powerfully-made 'Old English Setter', a black and white variety. Later he used red

The Setter of the mid 19th century with less fringe and feathering

and white Irish Setter bitches such as Carrie, eventually modifying the resulting progeny with pure Laveracks. According to the official ruling of the American Field Dog Stud Book, the true Llewellin is the result of breeding entirely to any of the following three lines: Barclay Field's Duke and the Laveracks, Armstrong's Kate and the Laveracks and Statter's Rhoebe and the Laveracks. But it is not always acknowledged that Rhoebe, the greatest Field Trial winner-producing dam of all time, came from a sire who was the great grandson of a Gordon Setter and a dam half Gordon and half Southesk Setter, (a strapping black, white and tan strain from Forfarshire).

When Llewellin died in 1925 he left his dogs to his house-keeper, from whom William Humphrey subsequently purchased them.

Humphrey had owned Llewellins before this date but agreed not to run them in trials until Llewellin's death. William Humphrey saw his first field trial as a boy of nine in 1892 and won his first stakes two years later at the age of eleven winning his last stake in the spring of 1963, he set up the longest record of trial successes since field trials started in 1865. He so approved the Llewellin strain of English Setters that over 55 years he imported back from the United States 33 dogs and bitches previously exported. In 1941 he bought Mr H.C. Hartley's dogs when the latter died. Mr Hartley went into the Llewellin strain in 1876 and had a much admired kennel of both Laverack and Llewellin blood but was not interested in field trials or dogs shows, breeding for his own field purposes.

For field purposes in this decade we have Bob Truman's FT Ch. Freebirch Vincent, a black and white Gordon, Robin Wylie's FT Ch. Maningo of Auchintoul, a stylish English, George Burgess's FT Ch. Spinnigloch Raven of Crafnant, another Gordon, and the impressive Irish Setter FT Ch. Red Fergus, owned and handled by Mr P.J. McCabe flying the setter flag . . . aristocratic dogs in style but still valued for their field worth.

Setter backed by a Pointer

Britain's Pointer

The ability of the domestic dog to indicate unseen game by standing in a frozen posture staring hard at it has been utilised since ancient times. The ancient Greeks identified a breed of dog in Italy called the Tuscan which was covered with shaggy hair and would actually point to where the hare lay hidden, perhaps the ancestor of the Spinone. Wolves have been known to display the same capability however and many non-sporting breeds of dog have also demonstrated this instinctive trait. This scenting skill, translated through the classic pointer stance, has been of great benefit in the shooting field, especially in the days when 'walked up' as opposed to driven game was the favoured style.

The pointing dog was utilised all over Western Europe in the first half of the second millennium A.D., with distinctive types, some later being developed into distinct breeds, being stabilised in Southern Germany (the Weimaraner), in Spain (the Navarro), in France (the Braque varieties) and Italy (the Bracco), as well as in Britain and Portugal. A pointer is a type of short-haired (usually) hound-like bird-dog, not a breed.

I do not believe that the English Pointer originated in Spain or indeed that 'pointers' sprang from there, as is frequently claimed. Of course the Spanish Pointers brought home to Britain by British officers after their years of duty in Spain, after the Treaty of Utrecht early in the 18th century, had some influence on pointing dogs in the British Isles. But why should the British Army which served all over Continental Europe before and after this date not have come home with other pointing dogs too? I believe far too much has been made of this minute part of pointer history in Britain.

Espee de Selincourt, writing in 1683, who made perhaps the earliest reference to gundogs (chiens de l'arquebuse) also defined setting-dogs (chiens couchans) as 'braques that stop at the scent (arrêtant tout) and hunt with the nose high'. In the sixteenth century the Italian braque was called the 'cane da rete' — the dog of the net; the French, being great admirers of the Italian dogs, soon transmitting this into 'chien d'arret or stop-dog, in literal translation.

The French use the term 'chien d'arrêt' to embrace both epagneuls and braques; 'epagneul' is believed to come from an old French verb s'espanir, to flatten or 'set' and 'braque' from an equally old verb braquer, to aim. The words Brague and Pointer therefore have the same functional derivation. The Braque Français, or French Pointer, is an ancient breed, according to the French . . . ' undoubtedly the oldest breed of pointer in the world. It has been the origin of nearly all the continental and British short-haired setters.' No concession to any Spanish origin here! The infrequently seen German Poodle-Pointer undoubtedly has French Braque blood, as well as that of the Wurttemburg Braque. The Auvergne Pointer has the blood of the Old Pyrenean Braque and the Gascony Pointer. The German Short-haired Pointer however is admitted to have both English and Spanish Pointer blood.

William Arkwright in his book on the Pointer quotes from a most interesting letter from the U.S. Vice Consul in Valencia in 1900: 'In this part of Spain there are no pure-bred sporting native dogs of any kind. The famous breed that existed here for three centuries – the Gorgas – so called from the little coast town of that name . . . are now extinct or so crossed with inferior breeds as to be indistinguishable. They were very nearly pure white, and much lighter than the old cylindrical Navarrese dog. They were noted for their gentleness and fineness of nose . . . Tradition says they were of foreign origin, the first pair being presented by an Italian prince . . .'

Drury in his *British Dogs* of 1903 notes that the first record of the pointer in Great Britain is the Tillemans' painting of the Duke of Kingston with his kennel of pointers in 1725, commenting that the latter were the 'same elegant Franco-Italian type as the pointing dogs painted by Oudry and Desportes at the end of the 17th century'. Arkwright himself wrote that . . . 'the French were the chief admirers of the Italian braque . . . And after a time, though the heavier type of their own and the

Navarrese braque still survived, it was quite eclipsed by the beautiful and racing-like Italian dog with which Louis XIV and Louis XV filled their kennels'.

Rawdon Lee accepts that the French had their own pointers before the Spanish Pointer was introduced into Britain at the beginning of the 18th century, 'pointers far removed from the imported Spanish dog in appearance, were not at all uncommon in England and they could easily have been brought over from France'. The French have of course long maintained a smaller breed of pointing dog, the Braque Franças de petite taille. Richardson, writing in 1847 describes seeing Italian pointers in Scotland, only about a foot high, but remarkably staunch with superb noses. In his *The Art of Shooting Flying* of 1767, Page remarks . . . 'Pointers. – As nothing has yet been published on these dogs . . . I am inclined to think that they were originally brought from other countries, though now very common in England.' I am inclined to think they were originally brought from other countries too, France, Italy and Spain, with distinctive types from each country of previous development. The modern English Pointer is much more like the French Braque St Germain than the old Navarro and Burgos pointers from Spain and the modern Bracco Italiano. I do not agree with Stonehenge's conclusion in 1867 that . . . 'they (the modern English Pointers) are descended from the Spanish pointer in all his purity' but I do take note of his comment that 'The trace of the foxhound in these heavier specimens of the modern pointer is very slight if any; . . .'

A number of eminent British sportsmen experimented with the foxhound cross in the late 18th century, notably Colonel Thornton, to produce his celebrated dog Dash and much has been made of this by many writers, few of whom mentioned the greyhound blood in Thornton's foxhounds. Sydenham Edwards writing in 1800 stated that 'the lightest

English Pointers were once much more hound-like

and gayest of the Spanish pointers were judiciously crossed with Foxhound to procure courage and fleetness'. This 'judicious crossing' also produced footscenting, giving tongue, scimitarlike over-furnished tails, overknuckled knees and uneven coats. Colonel Thornton's 'Dash' was much used at stud but not with success. Perhaps because of this, pointers enthusiasts are inclined to play down the infusion of foxhound blood in their breed. But the celebrated Colonel Peter Hawkes, in his 1820 diary, mourned the loss of the best dog . . . 'I have ever had, ever saw, or ever heard of,' a pointer with . . .

'a cross of foxhound.' Famous pointer men such as Mr Edge of Strelly. The Rev Mr Houlden, Mr Moore of Appleby, Sir Tatton Sykes of Yorkshire, the Earls of Sefton and Derby and Sir Richard Sutton, all staunch fox hunting men, were known to have crossed their pointers with foxhounds. The pedigrees of all the top pointers in the 19th century were linked with the kennels of distinguished foxhound breeders. The dog we know today is lithe, clean-limbed, fast and stylish, able to quarter ground well (and silently!) and hunt for air scent with the head held high. If hound blood manifests itself today then it is by way of the sighthound conformation rather the scent-hound.

Arkwright's pointers had considerable influence in the making of today's pointer; his all-black Pointer coming from the greyhound cross and a large number of today's dogs, in Europe, America and the Far East exhibit the tucked-up loin, the tighter lips and low set tail from his greyhound blood. The English Pointer has the eye and the eyesight of a gaze-hound, certainly no trace of the sunken eye of the scent-hound breeds. In temperament too, the Pointer has more in common with the cool, aloof, reserved, rather aristocratic greyhound than the gregarious, much more extrovert and certainly noisier foxhound.

No other breed has the sheer style of the Pointer

Greyhounds too were often used in medieval falconry with the 'setting-dogs', rather as the saluki is in the desert to this day.

Professor J.M. Beazley has traced the origin of our modern English pointers back to seven discrete families and shown how these original family groups led to the emergence of two main lines of descendants from 1840 to 1980.

The four names usually accepted as having laid the foundation for the modern pointer are: Whitehouse's Hamlet, Garth's Drake, Brocton's Bounce (allegedly 1/8 foxhound) and Statter's Major. Early fanciers were led by the aristocracy: the Duke of Kingston, the Earl of Lauderdale, the Earl of Derby, Lord Mexborough, Lord Lichfield and the Earl of Sefton.

The famous Isle of Arran strain owned by the Duke of Hamilton was established in the 18th century and maintained by his descendant Lady Jean Fforde. The first field trial champion pointer was Sir Richard Garth's Drake, born in 1868, described as 'a rather gaunt dog with immense depth of girth, long shoulders, long haunches and a benevolent quiet countenance.' He was 25 inches at the shoulder, 36 inches from nose to root of tail and 22½ inches around the loin. Other early field performers were Whitehouse's Hamlet, Price's Bang and Wagg, Brockton's Bounce and Salter's Mike and Romp. William Arkwright had Tap and Barmaid. Henry Sawtell bred and owned the field trial and bench champion Faskally Brag, a prolific sire. Isaac Sharp with his 'Stylish' prefix was acknowledged as the best trainer of pointers in Britain.

Arkwright's most influential dog was probably Aldin Fluke, carrying the blood of Hamlet, Drake, Bounce and Major, and perpetuated to this day in the Steadmans' Mallwyd and Maessydds and Egglestons' Pennines. But Arkwright's lesser known contemporary Dr. Salter was a pillar in the breed throughout his long life, with his pointers being based very much on the Devonshire line of Bulled and Price. More recently the dogs of Lord Rank, Joe Dub, Lady Auckland, Oliver Watney and Alun Roberts have excelled, with the latter's Segontium Kennel influencing many of today's strains. In Ireland John Nash of Limerick has imported Italian and Finnish blood to make his Monruad kennels widely respected and Michael Eaby, Seamus O'Donnell and Sean Dennehy have made notable contributions. Winning dogs in recent Pointer and Setter Championship Stakes have included Lagopus Everest from County Meath and Irish Pete from County Antrim.

With over twice as many German pointers now registered, our English pointer is under the greatest threat in its history. The purists may wince but its survival here may depend on its use as an all-rounder, as it does on the Continent. It would be a small price to pay for the perpetuation of an elegant, stylish, distinctive and historic breed.

Continental sporting dogs:
Hounds or Pointers?

PORTRAIT OF THE ARTIST, WITH TWO POINTERS
Sketch in oils by Ben Marshall, 1767-1835

*English Pointers were originally
expected to retrieve as well*

The HPR Breeds

The Continental All-rounders

Pointing dogs have been known on the mainland of Europe since the 13th century, Latini writing in 1260: . . . 'others are brachs with falling ears, which know of beasts and birds by their scent,' and Albertus Magnus recording in 1280: . . . 'they get to find the partridge by scent and thus . . . they point . . . at the . . . birds.' But the Romans too made reference to a shaggy-haired dog called the Tuscan which would indicate unseen game, such a dog being of great value to hunters of any century, before and after the invention of firearms. In the 16th century Heresbach was writing: 'Spanish dogs, zealous for their masters and of commendable sagacity, are chiefly used for finding partridges and hares.' Early in the 17th century, the naturalist Gesner noted that '. . . We Germans and the French call these dogs quail-dogs . . . the Italians call them net-dogs' . . . He referred to such dogs as vorstehhund, literally, dog that stands before.

In the 18th century, Tanzer was writing that 'The best way to take partridges, as is done by princes and nobles, is to shoot the birds neatly, with a pointing dog; or take them by a pointing dog and nets. The sort of dog that is used is white and brown marked, or white and speckled' . . . At this time there were distinct types of pointer in Spain, a hefty scent-hound type believed to have been introduced from Italy from the thirteenth century, and the smaller swifter type favoured to the north in Central Europe. In due course this latter type came through in many different regions as far apart as Weimar and Hungary, Poitou and Compiegne, Auvergne and Belgium. Setter-like dogs were favoured in Brittany, Picardy, Munster, Friesland and Drente. Coarse-haired pointing-dogs were favoured in Piedmont, Lombardy, Hesse and Slovenia. In Hungary and Germany, pointing-dogs were produced in smooth, coarse and long-haired varieties to give us the Vizslas and the various pointer types from Germany of today. According to Wenze, the Vizsla was known in the region of the kings of the House of Arpad (11th to 14th centuries) but was used as an all-purpose hunting dog until the late 19th century. At that time the German pointer was being standardised through Hector I and Waldin, a whole-coloured brown dog. The Weimaraner, like the Vizsla, was initially used as a multi-purpose hunting dog, for tracking deer and boar, for example.

The coarse-haired dogs are usually referred to as pointing griffons and have a reputation for greater hardiness and determination. Some authorities believe that the Italian coarse-haired pointing griffon, the Spinone, is the oldest form of this type of dog. Certainly the Spinone was known throughout the Piedmont, in Venetia, Istria, Dalmatia and as far as the Danube, leading some to suppose the breed came from the East. The cynologist Tale records that one hundred years ago, roan-coloured spinones were well known in Lombardy and Venetia, usually with longer and noticeably silkier, almost setter-like hair. Another researcher, Tschudy, ascribes the origin of all pointing breeds to the Roman era when Greek traders and others from the western Adriatic coast brought coarse-haired quail-dogs to be developed subsequently by sporting fanciers in what is now southern Italy.

Whatever its origin, the Spin-one is remarkably similar to the Hungarian coarse-haired griffon, the drotszoruvizsla, the Czech coarse-haired griffon, cesky fousek, and the French equivalent, griffon d'arret à poil dur, better known as the Korthals griffon. Edward Karel Korthals was a talented breeder of gundogs and although Dutch-born, lived in Germany in the household of the Prince of Solms, developing his own griffon variety between 1870 and 1890. Believed to have used French griffon blood and Barbet (the ancient breed of duck-dog) stock, Korthals' great achieve-

The French Pointer (this is the bigger variety) is very much like the German type

ment was in not bringing in hound blood, the cause of many of the temperamental disadvantages of hound/pointer crossbreeds.

Korthals lived in Biebesheim and hunted in the marshy area where the Rhine and the Main meet opposite Mainz; he was after both a rough shooters' and a wildfowlers' gundog. In the early 1870s he began with seven roughhaired dogs, obtained in Germany, France and Holland. After many generations of extensive selective breeding, and greatly encouraged by Baron von Gingins,

who played a leading role in the organisation of the German Kennel club, Korthals produced a number of fine looking dogs, with bright intelligent eyes, a hard waterproof coat, superb stamina and great hunting skill. The Baron introduced these griffons to influential German sportsmen and after Korthal's death in 1894, took over the breeding of his stock and further promoted this hardy sporting breed. Since then, the blood of this griffon has been used again and again in the breeding of German wire-haired pointers to produce a broader genetic base. Nowadays this breed is called simply the griffon because, on the continent its reputation is such as not to need an

Small Münsterländer at work

identifying adjective.

Another griffon variety is named after the breeder, this time a French one, Emmanuel Boulet. An industrialist from Northern France, Boulet was advised by the great canine authority of that time, Leon Vernier and after only ten years of trial crosses did he produce two magnificent pointing dogs Marco and Myra, winners of many international competitions and the foundation-stock of all of today's soft-coated griffons. The Boulet griffon probably has rather lost the field prowess of its ancestors but retains the unusual 'dead-leaf' colour which Boulet discovered would best blend with the vegetation of his favourite shooting ground, the forests of Londe.

About that time, at the end of the last century, the Germans developed the quaintly-named Pudelpointer, in the customary Continental quest for an all-round general hunting dog, able to operate in wood and marshland, quarter ground and indicate game, flush and then retrieve. With a shorter harder coat, the Pudelpointer was created when Altmeister V. Zedlitz arranged an experimental crossing between a forester's black poodle and Kaiser Wilhelm II's best English Pointer, Tell. In time the requisite proportion of pointer to poodle blood was ascertained, three quarter pointer to one quarter poodle, and the new breed stabilised. More recently, the breed has rather lost its distinct identity, with technically perfect Pudelpointers appearing but having the pedigrees of German wire-haired Pointers. The latter, usually referred to as the Drahthaar, was developed by German hunters seeking a more spirited, more overtly aggressive dog for use in hunting bigger and more dangerous game. The Drahthaar, with its tough approach, resolute nature and wire-haired protective coat had no superior in the forests. It may be that Airedale blood gave this breed their extra character both in water and against aggressive quarry such as wild boar.

Continental breeders have never hesitated to cross-breed or out-cross in the pursuit of excellence in the field. The great sporting dog fancier, Alan de Lamothe once advising: 'the breeding of the wire-haired Pointer and its enormous success in the field should be a lesson to those who regard the secondary and conventional characteristics as immutable dogma. They are in danger of forgetting that our hunting dogs belong to working breeds, not the category of domestic pets.'

The Deutscher Stichelhaariger Vorstehhund, or Stichelhaar, is more often than not confused with the Drahthaar, the wire-haired variety of German griffon. But the Stichelhaar (stichel is our work 'stickle' as in stickle-back) or 'bristle-haired' or rough haired pointer is quite separate, distinguished physically by the scrubbing-brush nature of the coat and the unique whickers; indeed the breed was once dubbed the Hessischen Rauhbart, literally the rough-beard from Hesse. The Stichelhaar was known as far back as the 16th century but was not widely acknowledged until the breed was developed by a German cattle breeder from Frankfurt called Bontant, around 1870. The old Wurttemberg Braque was utilised to improve the old stock, as well as, some say, the old cattle dog from southern Germany, an ancient breed related to the Rottweiler but more resembling the Bouvier des Flandres or the Riesenschnauzer.

The setter-like Continental breeds, like the Langhaar, the two sizes of Munsterlander, the French epagneuls and the two

German Wire-haired Pointer retrieving

Dutch gundogs, the Stabyhoun and the Drentse Patrijshond, were little known in Britain until comparatively recently, more because of our preference for specialisation than any lack of field merit. Now the bigger Munsterlander is attracting interest, with around 100 being registered annually. The German short-haired pointer has numerically already overtaken our own pointer; in 1986 twice as many Weimaraners were registered here as our pointer. I suspect that the Brittany will find similar popularity in a few years.

Continental pointing breeds are sometimes accused of lacking style but I cannot see anyone accusing the solid liver G.S.P. bitch

Andesheim Utrice or the parti-coloured G.W.P. bitch Wittekind Blanche of that failing. It should be remembered that such dogs are retrieving pointers rather than retrievers which point. I would always prefer to see the pointing breeds retain the full tail, for this alone can give a more stylish and symmetrical impression, but I accept their need to work in dense cover where a full length tail would suffer damage. I suspect that the main problem in the United Kingdom with the field performance of the pointing griffons is not so much a lack of style or low nose work of the dogs but the lack of familiarity of their handlers with the control and em-ployment of breeds which find, hold on point, and then retrieve game. This is a comment not a criticism, for I have nothing but admiration for pioneers in any field. The fact is that the pointing griffons are not only here to stay but are already finding more appeal than our native pointers. Much as I admire the German pointers, and I predict that the G.W.P. will one day overtake the G.S.P. here, I would love to see a gifted British trainer/handler take on a Korthals griffon and run him here. But I was most interested to

A tricolour Brittany

learn that Mrs Durman-Walter, owner of Wittekind Blanche, a winner of many F.T. awards, has written: . . . 'no other dog has ever slotted into the niche of falconry and shooting so perfectly as the G.W.P. . . . we have trained Springers, Labs, English Setters, Irish Setters, G.S.P.s, Munster-landers, Vizslas and can say quite categorically that the superior H.P.R. are the wirehairs.' We all owe a debt to Major Wilkinson, Godfrey Gallia, Bill Warner, Mrs Mills de Hoog and the Durman-Walters for introducing these fine gundogs to Britain.

My concern for the future of the Weimaraners and the Vizsla in Britain is that their sheer hand-someness and considerable cosmetic appeal will make them increasingly attractive to the showring fanciers and pet-market. But all the H.P.R. breeds have their particular appeal and pose a new challenge to the gun-dog trainer in Britain, for their training is not as easy as the expression 'all-rounder' would have some believe. I support Michael Brander's words in his quite excellent *The Roughshooter's Dog*: 'The work that the general purpose dog is expected to perform, if he is to do it efficiently, is more complex than that of the specialist dog. Correspondingly the training must be expected to take longer. Even with a general purpose breed there is more to training than simply taking the dog out with the gun.' Wise words indeed!

The Drentse Patrijshond

Origin of the Retriever

The history of the breeds of the domestic dog is festooned with legend, bedecked with myths and buried in supposition. Even renowned writers such as A. Croxton Smith, C.L.B. Hubbard and Harding Cox have helped to perpetuate some of the more unlikely 'facts'. Croxton Smith attributed the origin of the Golden Retriever to a troupe of performing Russian circus-dogs, on the flimsiest of true evidence, later proved to be quite untrue, but repeated to this day in inadequately researched books on dogs. Hubbard placed the Pug in the Mastiff family, again on the skimpiest of true evidence a fact refuted by an examination of any pug skull. He also repeated the legend of the Romans having a formal appointee for procuring British mastiffs for the amphi-theatres of Rome, through confusion between the descriptions 'Procurator Cynegii' and 'Procurator Gynaecii' – Administrator of the Imperial Weaving Works! Even the celebrated Stonehenge initiated a quite absurd story – that the Mastiff is indigenous to Britain and that the Romans were astonished at seeing this new (sic) breed of dog. And if you read any account of the origin of the Newfoundland dog – the father of our retrievers, you will find a similar baseless story – that the breed is descended from Pyrenean Mountain Dogs taken to Newfoundland by Basque fisherman.

Croxton Smith in his *About our Dogs* writes 'In the absence of any evidence to show they were natives of the island, we are forced to the conclusion that in all probability they were of European extraction. *Several writers* go to the length of saying that they came from Spain, which strengthens my belief, formed from reading these statements, that the Pyrenean Mountain Dogs had something to do with them, though I am at a loss to explain how they became black.' I can quite understand his being at such a loss, since Pyrenean Mountain Dogs are never black. Writing in *The Book of the Dog* edited by Brian Vesey-Fitzegerald, Philokuon writes . . . 'I should think a reasonable supposition is that Newfoundlands sprang from what we now call Pyrenean Mountain Dogs . . . though I cannot say how the whole black came from animals that are white . . .' That sounds anything but a reasonable supposition! So far we have black dogs coming from white ancestors and fisherman taking Mountain Dogs across the Atlantic Ocean. In his *Dogs of Today*, Harding Cox plays it close to the chest: 'The origin of the Newfoundland is uncertain', he writes abruptly. Uncertain it may be but there is some useful evidence available, as I discovered in the Maritime Museum in Lisbon and the national museums in Ottawa and Halifax, Nova Scotia.

What has this magnificent breed inherited from its ancestor breeds? Newfoundlands are distinguished by their physical strength, flat dense coarse-haired oily-to-the-touch water-resistant coats, great love of water and immense skill as a swimmer, web-feet and broad, massive skulls, with a strongly developed occipital bone and a definite 'stop'. Stories abound of the Newfoundland saving children from drowning, swimming through raging seas to take lines to stricken ships and helping their fisherman owners with their heavy nets on the beach. The breed also had a reputation as a draught-dog, pulling

The Stabyhoun — the Dutch gundog, resembling the Landseer Newfoundland

carts or carrying loads like a pack horse. These are indisputable facts and have clear relevance when researching the origin of the breed.

Who could have brought the likely ancestors of the breed to Newfoundland? We know of course that the British and the French colonised the eastern seaboard of North America. We also know that the Scandinavians, especially Norwegians, Dutch and Portuguese traders regularly visited the area and that Indians used sled-dogs extensively all over North America, huskies of various kinds, very similar to the Spitz breeds of Scandinavia, especially the Elkhound, a breed known to the Vikings. Now what

are the links between these two sets of facts, the inherited characteristics of the Newfoundland dog and the likely ancestor-breeds.

Dealing with the Husky link to start with. Many of the old prints off Newfoundlands show unmistakeable evidence of a Husky ancestor. We can discover that the main land Husky is a dog of great power, long in the back, broad in the skull, short in the muzzle, with a harsh-haired coat, flat to the body - almost invariably a mixture of black and white. The husky is a draught dog, developed to pull sledges and carry loads. Web-feet however feature neither in the husky nor, for that matter, in the Pyrenean Mountain Dog; it is a feature of spaniel or water dog breeds. The surviving pure-bred water-dog is found in Portugal – with the following characteristics: a massive head with a well-defined occiput and a definite 'stop', a coarse-haired, lank coat with the following colours, all-black, black with white or brown with white. The Portuguese Water Dog is famous for swimming between fishing boats with a line, retrieving lost lines from the sea and hauling fishermen's nets on the beach. It is most significant that of all dog breeds only the Newfoundland and Portuguese Water dog have web-feet at the foetus stage. It is of interest too that the Newfoundland and the Husky have strikingly similar skulls.

Idstone has quoted a article written in 1919 stating that back in the eighteenth century Newfoundlands were large rough-coated liver and white dogs. French Spaniels (and many other Continental Gundogs) are invariably white with brown markings, have thick wavy coats and a broad skull with well-marked 'stop' and a marked occipital protuberance. The French Spaniel, physically similar to the Stabyhoun and the German Münsterländer, has a great love of water and is a big strapping dog, often two feet at the shoulder.

Ben Marshall's well known painting of a Newfoundland of 1811 depicts a leggy, curly-coated dog, with a most spaniel-like head, which is black and white. The nearest modern equivalent to this dog as depicted would be the Wetterhoun from Holland, an age-old water retriever, unchanged through two centuries; our own Clumber Spaniel, imported from France, has a similar head conformation. The Barbet, the ancient French water-dog, rough-coated and strongly-made, ancestor of so many water-retrievers, has, like the Wetterhound and the Portuguese Water Dog long been favoured by fishing communities and coastal hunters.

I believe that when fishing communities from Europe established settlements in Newfoundland two or three hundred years ago, they would be quite likely to have taken their 'water-dogges' with them. For water-dogs, clipped and shorn, rather as the Portuguese Water Dogs are now, were well known all over the Continent and in England, as Gervase Markham has testified, in the seventeenth century. In time, to combat the extreme climate, it would be quite likely that these dogs would be crossed with dogs, like huskies, well able to withstand the near-Arctic winter. The North-American Indians used a huge black 'wolf-dog' as a draught animal, long before Europeans made settlements there; this breed I include under the general term 'huskies'.

Water-dogs, Continental Spaniels and Huskies could be blended so effectively to produce a breed like the Newfoundland. It

Ben Marshall's 1811 Newfoundland displaying the water-dog coat

would be likely to have a great love of water, be a draught-dog, have a thick oily coat, a heavy old-fashioned spaniel's head and web-feet. It would have been black or black and white, brown or brown and white. The modern Newfoundland, although not brown *and* white, would answer that description (red-brown and white puppies have cropped up in Newfoundland litters in the past however, and Sydnham Edward's *Cynographia Britannica* of 1800 shows one featuring golden-yellow and white). And breeds descended from the Newfoundland, the Labrador, the Curly-, Flat-coated and Golden Retrievers and the Chesapeake Bay Retriever

(which also has web-feet) are either all-black or all-a shade of brown, with superb water-resistant coats.

You can also read of the Tibetan Mastiff as an ancestor of the Newfoundland and hence of our modern retrievers. In the nineteenth century the Tibetan Mastiff (and there were but a few of them in England) was used to develop the English Newfoundland, but by this time the development of the retriever was taking place quite separately.

I doubt very much too if the Pyrenean Mountain Dog gets a look in at all. One of the idiosyncrasies of the Pyrenean Mountain Dog is the double dew-claw on the hindlegs. This has never, to my knowledge, manifested it-

self in the Newfoundland. It is however known in several sheep-dog breeds such as the Briard. Mountain Dogs are often grouped with the mastiff family for classification purposes. The Pyrenean Mountain Dog however is almost certainly related to similar large white herding breeds found all over Europe, the Maremmas in Italy, the Kuvasz in Hungary and the Owtcharka in Poland. The Pyrenean Mastiff is a separate breed. But physical similarities between the Pyrenean Mountain Dog, the St Bernard

Billy, *a St John's or lesser Labrador dog — black retrievers were much prized in the mid 19th century*

and the Newfoundland are there – but it should be remembered that the St Bernard was 'recreated' at one stage using both Pyrenean Mountain Dog and Newfoundland stock. I believe that the Newfoundland is descended from Water Dogs, Continental Spaniels and Husky stock –

but what a splendid ancestry for our modern retrievers.

Big Spitz dogs, like this Husky, were known in Newfoundland before the European dogs arrived

The Labrador Retriever

The Sporting Breed of the Century

'The year 1903 was memorable in the history of Labradors, which had hitherto been little known except among a few select sporting families . . . I must admit that before 1903 I had never seen one, and the majority of doggy people had to confess to a similar ignorance . . . Then in that year a class was provided or them at the Kennel Club Show at the Crystal Palace . . . there were fourteen exhibits, of which the Hon. A Holland Hibbert (afterwards Lord Knutsford) had entered six. He won all the prizes . . .' This extract from Arthur Croxton-Smith's *Dogs since 1900,* published in 1950, sets the scene admirably for any account of the quite astonishing rise of the Labrador retriever over the last 80 or so years. In the thirties, the breed won Best in Show at Crufts three times, a remarkable feat for a breed developed in the sporting field and never originally intended to be judged on appearance and one only matched by cocker spaniels. In 1912 there were 281, in 1922 916 and by the 1950s there were some 4,000 registered, then in the last few years well over 15,000 a year, so that in 1985 and 1986 the Labrador was the second most popular pedigree breed in the United Kingdom. Only the German Shepherd Dog can match this meteoric rise and the sheer versatility of both breeds is greatly valued.

By 1908 Labradors were beginning to assert themselves in the shooting field. In that year, of the 106 dogs entered for field trials, sixty two were flat-coats, thirty nine Labradors, three curlies and two inter-bred retrievers. The flat-coats won 2 firsts, 5 seconds, 8 thirds and 3 fourths; the Labradors won 6 firsts, 2 seconds, one third and one fourth. Three years later, the flat-coats won 2 firsts, five seconds, one third and 2 fourths; Labradors won 13 firsts, eleven seconds, 13 thirds and 6 fourths. Two years on again, and the difference was even more notable, Labradors winning 20 firsts, 17 seconds, 19 thirds and 10 fourths, whereas flat-coats won one first, 2 seconds, 3 thirds and 1 fourth . . . and the Labrador retriever has never looked back.

Although our breeds of retriever were not developed until comparatively recently, the use of dogs as retrievers by sportsmen is over a thousand years old. 'Traine him to fetch whatsoever you shall throw from you . . . anything whatsoever that is portable; then you shall use him to fetch round cogell stones, and flints, which are troublesome in a Dogges mouth, and lastly Iron, Steele, Money and all kinds of metal, which being cold in his teeth, slippery and ill to take up, a Dogge will be loth to fetch, but you must not desist or let him taste food till he will as familiarly bring and carry them as anything else whatsoever.' So advised Gervase Markham early in the seventeenth century on the subject of training a 'Water Dogge' to retrieve. Half a century earlier, the much quoted Dr Caius, identified the curly-coated Water Dogge as 'bringing our Boultes and Arrowes out of the Water, which otherwise we could hardly recover, and often they restor to us our Shaftes which we thought never to see, touch or handle again.' Such water-dogs were utilised too on the continent; in *The Sketch Book of Jean de Tournes* published in France in 1556, we see illustrated 'The Great Water Dogge', a big black shaggy-headed dog swimming out to retrieve a duck from a lake.

Not surprisingly such dogs were favoured by the sea-going fraternity, the fishermen, sailors and traders. The dogs were trained to retrieve lines lost overboard and used as couriers between ships, in the Spanish Armada for example. In time such dogs featured in the settlements established along the eastern sea-board of the New World by British, Portugese, Dutch and French traders. Water-dogs exist today in those countries, the Barbet in France, the Wetterhoun in Holland, the Portuguese Water Dog and the incorrectly-named Irish Water 'Spaniel' in the British Isles.

It is significant that once the eastern sea-board of North America had been colonised, the Newfoundland, often greatly varying in type became in time *the* ship's dog, finding its way by this means to England, principally through the ports of Poole and Bristol. The long-maintained Labrador Fish-

eries Patrol manned by British naval officers in the early 19th century no doubt also resulted in sporting officers bringing good dogs home with them.

It is important to remember too that the modern Newfoundland is appreciably different from the Newfoundland of say 1811, as Ben Marshall's painting of that year shows – the curly coat and high tail in particular. The Newfoundlands in Sydenham Edwards' *Cynographia Brittanica* of 1800, too illustrate this high tail, as well as prick-ears and the yellow coat-colour factor.

The inheritance of coat-colour in the ancient water-dogges in the Newfoundland, the modern Portugese Water Dog, the Duck-toller and the modern Retrievers – Labrador, Flat-coat, Curly-coat, Golden, Chesapeake Bay and Irish Water is strikingly similar, as indeed is the types of coat found in the breeds. The Newfoundland, once known as the Great Retriever but nowadays bred to look like a heavy mountain dog, has a mixed origin and probably combines the blood of big black Indian draught dogs, ships-dogs like the ancient and traditional 'water-dogges' and continental epagneul breeds like the Staby-houn. The breed was favoured, perhaps romantically, in England as a heavy-coated water-rescue dog. But the early importations could be white, black or part-coloured, thick coated or smooth coated. The latter were sometimes referred to as lesser Newfoundlands or St John's retrievers. No sportsman wants a dog that is too heavy for field use; the instinct to retrieve, a love of water and a weather-proof coat were the attractive attributes of the early dog-imports from Newfoundland.

Retrievers as a *recognised breed* of sporting dogs are only in the region of one hundred and twenty years old, almost certainly starting in the 1850s, allegedly as a result of a cross between the Newfoundland dog and the Setter. But retrieving both arrows or bolts and shot-game by dogs, especially water dogs, is centuries old. It certainly didn't start when prominent sportsmen started to use specialist retrievers and stopped the training of pointing/setting breeds to retrieve, a very British practice. The early retrievers were a mixed bunch and varied from one noble family to another, with liver-coloured ones being favoured in Norfolk, for example, probably related to the type we now call the curly-coated retriever.

In his *Dog-Breaking* of 1876, the eminent General Hutchinson confirmed the 19th century view with these words: 'From education there are good retrievers of many breeds, but it is usually allowed that, as a general rule, the best land retrievers are bred from a cross between the Setter and the Newfoundland, or the strong Spaniel and the Newfoundland . . . the far slighter dog reared by the settlers on the coast, a dog that is quite as fond of water as of land . . .'

As far as the early development of the Labrador-type is concerned, I have my doubts about the influence of the setter and the spaniel. I say this for two reasons. Firstly, some fifty years ago the American veterinary surgeon Leon Whitney crossed a Newfoundland with a hound to produce offspring very similar to the Labrador. I have always found the latter to possess more hound-like characteristics than setter-like ones Secondly there exists in Portugal a breed known as the Cao de Castro Laboreiro, used nowadays as a herding breed but very much like the dogs depicted by Velasquez, the 17th century Spanish painter, his painting of Ferdinand of Austria for example — which showed his subject carrying a fire-arm ready for the shooting field with a Labrador-like dog. This Portuguese breed even in its modern form is remarkably Labrador-like, even displaying the characteristic otter-tail. Both Spain and Portugal took an active role in the early development of Newfoundland. Hound blood has sometimes been resorted to in attempts to improve field performance in the gundog breeds. Colonel Thornton's foxhound cross pointers are well documented in the 18th century, the harrier cross retriever used by Wentworth Day was an outstanding dog and I understand foxhound blood was used with Labradors in the north of England just after the last war, although principally to improve appearance. The head and movement of the Labrador do have distinct hound-like features. It has been argued however that the higher tail carriage of the hound is often accompanied by an un-desired un-Labrador-like aggression.

Stonehenge writing in 1860 commented that: 'Many well known sportsmen now possess their own breed of dogs, used for retrieving on land and water, but there is no established breed. Good retrievers are to be found in all breeds. Thirty years ago, William Evans, now head keeper to Lord Fitzwilliam, had a famous retriever by a Bloodhound of the late Lord Ducie's out of a Mastiff.' Cartwright took foxhounds and bloodhounds with him to Newfoundland in 1770; there is a record too in the notes of a traveller there in the 19th century of 'good dogs kept by settlers on the coast

Newfoundland cross hound progeny produced by Whitney in America

with smooth and short coats, able to stay free of ice.' In his, *The Dog* of 1854, William Youatt recorded: 'Some of the true Newfoundland dogs have been brought to Europe and been used as retrievers. They are principally valuable for the fearless manner in which they will penetrate the thickest cover. They are comparatively small but muscular, strong, and generally black. A larger variety has been bred . . . but is admired on account of his stature and beauty . . .' From these accounts can be seen not only the mixed ancestry of the breed but also the greater suitability for sportsmen of the smaller, smoother-coated type. This is reinforced by Idstone's words in his *The Dog* of 1872: 'There is the smooth-coated dog of the same family . . . I mean as short in the hair as a mastiff . . . the flat, the shaggy and the

smooth-coated are sometimes found in one litter . . .': going on to describe how a smooth-coated dog 'tracked his game like a Bloodhound . . . has a lighter eye . . . the best of all breeds for boating; they can stand all weathers . . .'

Against such a heritage it is hardly surprising if the modern breed sometimes displays the characteristics of its ancestor breeds, in the colour of the eye, the texture of the coat, the type of head, the topline and the tail-carriage. A few years ago a Swedish breeder was commenting on mis-marked puppies, brindling, chocolate with tan and black and fawn occurring. The 'brindle-legged retriever' was referred to by several writers at the turn of the century. A reader's letter to a sporting paper a few years ago asked where the old 'power-house' Labradors had gone, stating that exceptionally her bitch was 23 inches at the shoulder and just over 70 lbs. At the 1903 Kennel Club show, the Labrador winning first prize was the Hon. A. Holland-Hibbert's Sentry. He was 23 inches at the shoulder and weighed 65 lbs.

Just over thirty years ago, Mr H.S. Lloyd the famous breeder of cocker spaniels was quoted as saying 'Labradors are not what they used to be.' Earlier this year Gabriel Benson was writing 'The future of the working Labrador has never looked better than it does today . . .' Ten years ago yellow eyes were called into question; ninety years ago General Hutchinson considered their pos-

sessors to be the best markers of game. Complaints have been made throughout this decade of 'Rotweiler heads' cropping up in the breed and mean eyes becoming prevalent, unlike the soft-eyed retriever look which is essential in the breed. Coming from such a rich genetic background, it would be astonishing if diversions from the desired type didn't crop up quite regularly.

My own concern about the breed would be threefold. I wonder if we aren't losing the true yellowcoat and producing too pale cream a dog nowadays. The richer colour is so much more attractive and the coat-colour seems to bring a closer-lying more weather-proof coat with it. Secondly, I can foresee working tests becoming an expanded, all-year, more and more popular activity, perhaps producing champions of their own, but also producing retrievers with great speed, if less initiative and determination, not so suitable for the ordinary shooting man's purpose. But perhaps most important of all, the deserved popularity of the breed has led to over-breeding, in-breeding and unwise breeding with congenital diseases being perpetuated.

Entropion (inward-turned eyelids), hip dysplasia, progressive retinal atrophy (PRA), hereditary cataract, retinal dysplasia, haemophilia A and osteochondritis dissecans (OCD) (abnormal cartilage disturbance) have all occurred in the breed,, although not to such a worrying degree as in some other breeds. Vigilance, sound breeding programmes, morality amongst breeders, breed clubs acting in the best interests of the dogs and veterinary guidance will be demanded if these diseases are to be eradicated. Labradors breed without difficulty and have large litters; with the advent of pedigree breeding the gene-pool is closed and this alone may create future problems in the breed, as with all other popular purebred dogs.

But the standard of dog at the top of the field-trial side today is high, even if there are far too many poor dogs at the other end.

A curly-coated Yellow Labrador from pure-bred stock

Many knowledgable judges rate highly John Halstead's F.T. Ch. Breeze of Drakeshead who recently successfully defended its Retriever Championship, beating 26 other Labradors, 5 goldens and a flat-coat. It is reassuring to know that the current top field-trial dogs are also worked regularly – professional field-trailing dogs dedicated to competition work cannot be entirely good for the breed. I fear not just a showring-working gap widening but in future a working, showring and working-test division which could see breeders developing yet another type of retriever. It was so reassuring when F.T. Ch. Holdgate Willie won a first prize at Crufts in the early 70s.

It is probably true to say that all Labradors will work, will be aroused by the scent of game and respond instinctively. But it is really *how* they will work which is important. For a retriever to excel at marking, game-finding, water-work and have the physique to sustain its performance throughout a long day in the shooting field combines good breeding with sound training. Without the breeding, the handling becomes more difficult; it is fair to say that most modern Labrador breeders are unaware of the working requirements in their dogs. Yet the Bailey's F.T. Ch Gunstock Lisleholme Black Gun won 28 trial awards and came from almost entirely show-ring stock, with only one F.T. Champion behind her, and that five generations back. But show ring breeders producing short-backed, narrow-fronted; gormless dogs give future handlers in the field almost insurmountable problems.

Good breeding can produce dogs with a higher level of instinctive behaviour, such as casting themselves so as to have the wind coming to them when searching for a fallen bird. It was interesting when using the breed to track terrorists in the Malayan jungle to note how some dogs adapted and reacted far better than others in the breed. Retriever instincts and the physique to enable those instincts to be exercised are much more likely to come from carefully-bred stock down many generations. The tendency to run to flesh and become ponderous is ever-present;

it is worth looking at Holland-Hibbert's Munden Single, preserved in the National History Museum and Gwen Broadley's Sandylands type to see the authentic size and weight ratios in the breed. The great dual champion Knaith Banjo and his descendant Foxhanger Mascot were marvellous examples of sound balanced construction. Time and time again an examination of the pedigree of proven dogs shows the best kennel-names behind them.

All field trial Labradors can be traced back by male descent to Malmesbury's Tramp, Netherby Boatswain, Malmesbury's Sweep, Ilderten Ben, Bright and Buccleuch Bachelor, with Tramp perhaps having he greatest influence. His descendant Munden Sixty had the most influence in Lord Knutsford's kennel and in many others too. Lord Knutsford, over 50 years, bred for good looks and good work right until his death in 1935 and is revered for his foundation work in the breed. From the end of the first world war until the start of the second, the second great name in Labrador breeding is Lorna, Countess Howe with her Banchory kennel prefix. She produced the best dual-purpose dogs known in the breed, with her Banchory Bolo and Balmuts Jock quite outstanding. Lady Hill-Wood's Hiwood Chance is perhaps a rival to Jock.

Most yellows can be traced back to Major Radclyffe's dog Neptune. Major Radclyffe, with Major and Mrs Wormald making the greatest contribution to the development of the yellows between the wars, represents an important family in the breed. His father-in-law, a Dorset squire, Mr C.J. Radclyffe having had the vision to identify potential retriever talent in the ship's dogs coming into Poole in the late 19th century. Mrs A.M. Radclyffe still maintains a fine strain of Labradors in Dorset, using the Zelston prefix. Other dual purpose breeders in the last thirty years have been Dr T.S. Acheson with the Ballyduff prefix, Mrs. R.G. Williams (Mansergh), N.D. Robinson (Mallardhurn) and the Johnsons (Reanacre). Major Peacock (Greatwood) rarely bred but with his keen judgement of a dog produced seven field trial champions including three winners of the Championship, assisted by

The Portuguese dog, so Labrador-like in conformation. The Portuguese were early colonists in Newfoundland

the Chudleys of the Harpersbrook kennels. Another who rarely bred but had a shrewd eye for a dog was Mr F. Bell, whose F.T. Ch. Grousadee with J. Annard's F.T. Ch. Glenhead Zuider have had great influence in the breed from the 1950s onwards. Just about every field trial dog now features Zuider in his pedigree.

Andrew Wylie's Pinehawk kennels produced splendid workers from 1946 onwards, with, from the 1950s onwards, Lawrence Taylor (Galley-wood) and Harcourt-Wood (Glenfarg), having breeding importance. Dick Male trained and handled the Galleywood dogs before moving on to Charles William's Berrystead kennel to continue his great record. Other kennels of note are R.N. Burton (Brachenbank), D.F. Cock (Roffey) and G.M. Benson (Holdgate). Leading sires at the beginning of this decade were David Garbutt's 1981 F.T. Ch. Pocklington Glen and, second in the 1982 event, F.T. Ch. Green-

wood Timothy of Holdgate. But they don't come much better than John Halstead's F.T. Ch. Breeze of Drakeshead of today's dogs.

The Labrador matures faster than the other retriever breeds and can absorb instruction far younger. The Labrador excels at the close hunting of small areas, perhaps its hound blood manifesting itself in contrast with the setter blood of the Flat coat which has a higher head and a wider pattern. Labradors are quick to learn to respond to signals, realising the help this provides in their work; they are a highly co-operative breed. 'Idstone' summed up the value of such dogs in these rather picturesque words: '. . . it is a luxury to have a dog of some kind, trained expert as a detective, and always at your heel for an emergency, taught to restrain his natural love of chasing, and to sit . . . watching for the flip of your finger, to follow you as you put him on 'the foot' . . .'

The Labrador retriever has only been on 'the foot' as a bred for less than a century but is already our premier retriever, our most popular gundog and a highly versatile canine worker, whether guiding the blind, searching for drugs, tracking criminals or collecting shot game. We owe a great debt to those who had the vision to spot the potential in such willing and capable dogs.

The Labrador Retriever (a study from the 1930s)

Curly-coated Retriever

Whenever I think of this breed the words of that great sportsman and writer James Wentworth-Day come easily to mind . . . 'There is nothing feminine about a retriever. He is utterly masculine, whether he is the old English curly-coat, the toughest of them all . . .' The toughest of them all, what a tribute from such a distinguished gun-dog man!

Favoured by the informed and championed by the knowledgeable, the curly-coated retriever has hardly changed in 100 years as a breed and in 400 as a breed-type in Britain, Gervase Markham in 1621 recording: 'First, for the colour of the best Water Dogge, all be it some which are curious in all things will ascribe more excellency to one colour than to another as the Blacks to be the best and hardest: the liver hued swiftest in swimming . . . and his hairs in general would be long and curled . . .'

The aptly-named coat is its most distinguishing feature, with short tight curls with a crisp feel to the touch, the classic curly-coat of the ancient 'water-dogges', illustrated also in the Portugese water dog, the Wetterhoun of Holland and our own mis-named Irish water spaniel. The Tweed water spaniel and the Llanidloes Welsh setter, now both lost to us, also featured this tight, densely-curled, waterproof coat. L.P.C. Astley, writing in 1907, likened to curly's coat to the close fitting tightly-curled beautiful head of hair of many of the African people, opining that this was the only 'true and proper one . . . of which every knot is solid and inseparable. A coat of this quality is not capable of improvement by any methods of grooming, for the simple reason that its natural condition is itself perfect. The little locks should be so close together as to be impervious to water and all parts of the body should be evenly covered with them, including the tail and legs. A bad class of coat and one that readily yields to the faker's art is the thin open curl which, by careful manipulation, can be greatly improved.'

There are only two recognised colours, black and liver, both self-colours. The liver coloured dogs, were particularly favoured in Norfolk at one time, Norfolk fishermen and bargemen often having a liver curly about — to retrieve lost lines or swim to the shore with a line, the traditional tasks for the 'water-dogge' in many European countries and in Canada. These dogs are tremendously powerful swimmers, famed for their hardiness and prowess in water.

Ordinary grooming methods aren't much use with the curly, and on no account should a brush and comb be used. The coat needs to be dampened regularly with water and then rubbed with a flat, bare hand in a circular movement, which cleanses and tightens the curls. The tail, ears and legs are usually tidied up for the show-ring. The prominent white patch on the breast — as in the Portugese water dog, is not desired but a few white hairs on the chest of an otherwise good dog is allowable – as in the Newfoundland. The Newfoundland depicted by Ben Marshall in his well-known picture of 1811 is black with white and densely curled in coat. Stonehenge writing on retrievers in 1859 stated that 'the colour is almost always black with very little white; indeed, most people would reject a retriever of this kind, if accidentally of any other colour. The coat is slightly curly but not very long, and the legs are not much feathered.' Eight years later the same writer added . . . 'the face of a curly retriever should be clean; his hind legs from the hock downward free of feather; the re-mainder of his body covered with short crisp curls.'

Idstone writing in the same period had this to say of the famous curly Jet: 'He was a mass of black, crisp, short curls, except his face and forehead, which were as smooth as the setter's, which he generally stood next to in the rank, with his champion card above him, barking a husky and, as I think, high-bred welcome to all who passed by.'

This distinctive coat, always an in-built protection against any 'mongrelisation' in the breed, and the individual character, are the hallmarks of the breed. Serious-minded, dour to some, but always commanding respect, the fortitude and durability of the breed has long been admired by the wildfowling community.

This valuable combination of physical toughness and mental stoicism, allied with great hardiness and considerable strength, combined with intelligence, pace and an excellent nose, makes a really top-class gundog. As a worker he is responsive, willing to work, fearless and has huge reserves of stamina. Good on runners and an excellent marker, the curly is a dog that thinks about a problem and for this is sometimes accused, unfairly, of lacking speed and being more difficult to train than the other retriever breeds. This facet of his make-up should be treasured not scorned, encouraged not over-handled;

A Standard Poodle in working trim

speed and dash are not the foremost requirements of a wildfowler's dog.

It must be remembered that the curly is a slow maturing dog, continuing to develop until three years old. This and the fact that the curly has a very definite mind of his own and wants to do things his way, means that if you want quick results and a blindly-obedient dog, look somewhere else! Firmness, gentleness, endless patience and a respect for the innate character of the dog are the essentials in training a curly. Get inside the mind of a curly and

think as he does and in time you will have a trained dog to be proud of. I admire and respect this breed because of the inherent characteristics they display; I don't want them to be a Labrador with a curly-coat but have their own distinct identity.

The great versatility of this breed is not always appreciated. Diane Bush is having success with her dog Kizzy in obedience circles, Mary Solomon is training her dog Ebony Ambassador very successfully in working trials' activities, Derek Freeman as breeding manager for the Guide Dogs for the Blind recognised their merits over twenty years ago and several curlies are involved in the P.A.T. (Pro-Dogs Active Therapy) campaign in which dogs contribute to the treatment of handi-

The curly-coated Retriever, our surviving English water dog — this is the 1900 specimen

capped or disturbed patients. Lynn Hull of Hunter's Lodge Kennels in Somerset has in just a few days seen her curlies perform in the shooting field, successfully compete in the show ring, complete the local agility course, carry out a track or area search and then bring comfort to the inmates of the local old people's home as formal social workers. How many breeds are that versatile?

I was interested to discover that the guide dog trainers value the breed for its staidness, steadiness, calming influence, persevering nature, natural curiosity and genuine enjoyment of life. Mr Freeman was impressed by their phlegmatic stoicism and

rather serene view of life; in an effort to produce a faster maturer dog for guide dog training the curly was crossed with the Labrador and of the 31 pups in training, 28 made guide dogs. The resultant wire-haired coat being easily managed by a blind owner.

Distinctive in appearance, individual in character and robust both in physique and approach to life, the curly-coated retriever has always been a performer in the field rather than a poseur in the show-ring. Never a match for the sheer handsomeness of the flat-coat, the field trials dash of the Labrador or the effusive friendliness of the golden retriever, the 'curly' is the gundog for the 'loner' — the solitary sportsman, rather than the business-like syndicate. Admirable rather than adorable, highly independent and not, as in so many gundog breeds — constantly demanding attention from its owner, the curly, rather like the Chesapeake steadily earns your respect by his patient stoicism in the cold and wet, his reliable steadfastness in difficult circumstances and his fussless determination in conditions which would make other breeds turn back; the wildfowler's dog of dogs. The best watchdog of our native gundog breeds, with an unusually strong low-toned bark, the largest retriever, very much a man's dog and ideally a one-man dog, the curly has been described as the aristocrat of the retriever world — proud, at times aloof but

The Wetterhoun — so like our curly-coated Retriever

never lacking individuality, always conveying an impression of strength with quality.

With no incidence of the congenital diseases which plague our renowned labradors and sunny-natured golden retrievers, unique among retrieving breeds in outline, height and astrakhan coat, the curly has a magnificent air of self-assurance and is very much 'his own dog'.

In his classic *Dog Breaking*

The Portuguese Water Dog — another 'curly'

General Hutchinson wrote, at the turn of the century, of a famous retriever with close curly hair, in glowing terms . . . 'Indeed his superiority over all competitors in his neighbourhood was so generally admitted that his master was hardly ever asked to shoot at any place without a special invitation being sent to Ben . . . No winged pheasant fell to the ground and no hare went off wounded but there was heard, Ben, Ben . . . He retrieved with singular zeal and pertinacity.' . . . a very special breed for individuals amongst sportsmen.

The Golden Retriever

A Willing Charmer

Golden retriever owners could make a fair claim I believe to possess the dog breed with the greatest charm, the nicest nature and the one free of any kind of malice. Stimulating great affection from the general public and inspiring the ad-men has however brought what is to me an undesirable excess of popularity, with the relegation of far too many of the breed to the hearth. But the breed undoubtedly comes from impeccable working stock, bred by skilful knowledgeable men, with an enviable blend of blood for use in the shooting field.

As with so many pedigree breeds, the breed history of the golden retriever has suffered at the hands of well-meaning but fanciful devotees ever eager to romanticize their chosen dogs. We have stories of a troupe of circus dogs being their ancestors, then 'Russian retrievers' brought back from the Crimea and no doubt crafty market-traders teasing the gullible by offering good-looking golden-haired pups as Turkish hunting-dogs or Slovenian setters. Glamorised fiction apart, our sporting ancestors never hesitated to utilise the blood of a good dog, whether a clever circus performer or a battlefield stray. The question for breed researchers is always how significant in the development of the breed as we know it today are the various ingredients of the past.

Ever since retrievers were bred in pursuit of a specialist function, golden, liver, bronze, chocolate or yellow puppies have appeared in litters as part of the genetic equation of the more-favoured blacks. Yellow labradors, bronze Newfoundlands, liver flat-coats and chocolate labradors are with us today but blacks were preferred by 19th century sportsmen, a fact reflected by the preponderance of black in retriever breeds with other colour options.

Behind our modern retriever breeds lie the ancient water-dogs, exemplified today by the Barbet in France, the whiptail in Ireland and our own curly. They were characterised by their liver or black coloration and the unique texture of their coats. The Newfoundland, sometimes called the Great Retriever and a water-dog par excellence, produces black, black and white or Landseer, bronze and more rarely red offspring. Those depicted by Sydenham Edwards in the 18th century clearly displayed the yellow factor.

The most famous founding strain in the golden retriever dynasty is that of Lord Tweedmouth in the middle of the last century and so well researched by Elma Stonex thirty years ago. He bought his first yellow retriever at Brighton, a dog called Nous, which was bred by the Earl of Chichester. Two years later he obtained Belle, a Tweed Water Spaniel and a year later the Nous-Belle coupling produced four medium-gold pups with profuse wavy coats. One bitch pup went to the 5th Earl of Ilchester to found his Melbury strain, with black retrievers being freely used on the yellow. Lord Tweedmouth retained one bitch pup, Cowslip. He was familiar with the line-breeding techniques used by the hound fraternity and kept meticulous kennel records from 1835 – 1890. His last two yellow puppies to be recorded, Prim and Rose, were born in 1889. Their sire, on his sire's side, was a grandson of Cowslip through a mating between her and a red setter. Their sire was, on his dam's side, her great-grandson through her earlier mating to a Tweed Water Spaniel. Cowslip was herself of

Judging at the Golden Retriever show near Pangbourne in June 1937

course half Tweed Water Spaniel. Lord Tweedmouth used two further outcrosses, a black retriever as a mate for Cowslip's daughter in 1877 and ten years later another black retriever sire, a full brother to flat-coat Champion Moonstone, the sire of Prim and Rose's dam, who herself was a black from a litter of ten blacks.

A sandy-coloured or light tan bloodhound is known to have been used around 1890, although this is not recorded. Lord Tweedmouth died in 1894 and neither his successor nor the 5th Earl of Ilchester kept records. But John MacLennan, a keeper on Guisachan, the Scottish seat of Lord Tweedmouth, recorded that the 1st Viscount Harcourt, one of the first exhibitors of the breed from his Culham kennel, bought his original brace of pups from a

litter bred by MacLennan out of a daughter of a bitch owned by the youngest son of Lord Tweed-mouth. Lord Harcourt's Culham Brass and Culham Copper, born in 1904 and 1908 lie behind most modern golden retrievers.

Another early strain behind many of today's dogs is Mr D. MacDonald's Ingestre's (1904-1915) which he started from a liver flat-coat bitch. The well-known Yellow Nell, owned by Mr W. Hall, said to have been of close Guisachan blood, was out of Ingestre-registered parents, bred from unregistered stock. MacDonald bred a number of 'yellows' sired by black flat-coats. The liver-coloured flat-coat win-ner of the 1904 IGL F.T. stake was sired by Lucifer, a golden flat-coat – an unregistered dog bred by the 2nd Lord Tweedmouth at Guisachan. Mr J. Kerss, head gamekeeper to the Duke of Buc-cleuch, has recorded that the Duke imported some retrievers direct from Labrador but later on (i.e. in the middle of the 19th cen-tury) crossings took place with flat-coats and Tweed Water Span-iels. But he stressed the mixed blood of all retrievers in Scotland, claiming that they all had a 'dash of Labrador' in them.

Because the Tweed Water Spaniel was used to improve the developing 'yellow retrievers' it is interesting to examine this lost breed a little closer. In his *Com-plete Farrier* of 1815, Richard Law-rence wrote: 'Along the rocky shores and dreadful declivities beyond the junction of the Tweed and the sea of Berwick, Water dogs have received an addition of strength from the experimental introductions of a cross withe the Newfoundland dog . . . the liver-coloured is the most rapid of swimmers and the most eager in pursuit.' Fifty years later *Stone-henge* described them as small liver-coloured curly-coated re-trievers, but I doubt if he ever saw me. Stanley O'Neill, the flat-coat authority, saw them on the North-umbrian coast at the turn of the century and described them as tawny-coloured water dogs, re-trieverish not spaniel-like.

Another lost breed here, al-though perpetuated in Canada as the Nova Scotia Duck Tolling Re-triever and taken there by colon-ists from Britain, is the red decoy dog, referred to by Wentworth-Day as the 'ginger 'coy dog'. It was tawny-coloured, retriever-like and extensively used before the invention of firearms to lure wildfowl within arrow range or ducks into channelled nets, partly through its gambolling antics but mainly through the enticing flag-waving of its well-furnished tail. The Kooikerhondje does this in Holland to this day. The red de-coy dog was Dr Caius's 'tumbler', used by humbler hunters to-gether with the 'stealer' or lurcher. For me, colour apart, the flamboyant use of the tail by the golden retriever makes it dif-ferent from the other retriever breeds and I believe this comes from the red decoy dog. Modern breeders dislike red in the breed probably fearing red setter blood coming through, but it could be the valuable blood of the very clever red decoy dogs.

First shown in 1864, the golden retriever was not given a separate register at the Kennel Club until 1913, up till then they came under flat-coats, identified only by colour. A notable early breeder was Mrs W.M Charlesworth (Normanby, later Noranby), with her Normanby Beauty (of unknown pedigree) producing two litters, by Culham Brass and then his son Culham Copper, to produce the foundation on which much of today's stock is based. Normanby Sandy, a son of Yellow Nell, was one of the first goldens to take an award at trials. Early field trial winners were Blofield Rufus of blood-

The Golden Retriever must not lose its working role

lines from Ingestre, Ilchester and Tweedmouth; Gosmore Freeman out of Yellow Nell by Culham Copper and Capt. Hardy's Vixie. Important kennels were those of Mr and Mrs J Eccles (Haulstones), Mr W.S. Hunt (Ottershaw), Lt. Col. the Hon. D. Carnegie (Heydown), Mr H. Jenner (Abbots) and the Hon. Mrs Grigg (Kentford)

In 1920 the breed name was changed from Retriever (Golden or Yellow) to Retriever (Golden) but it was not until 1930 that much official notice was taken of size and weight. In 1936 the breed standard was amended to include the colour cream, any shade of gold or cream being permitted but neither red nor mahogany. Today's dogs are for me far far too pale and I can find nothing but

pleasure in a good red-gold dog; the vast majority of the early stars in the breed were darker-coated rather than lighter-coated. 1921 saw the first show champion Noranby Campfire, later a great sire. Soon afterwards Eredine Rufus took his field trial title, with Balcombe Boy bred by Lord Harcourt becoming the first dual champion. In 1938 registrations of the breed with the Kennel Club exceeded one thousand; fifty years later there are some 12,000 a year to make the golden retriever the third most popular pedigree breed.

Since the second world war there have been over 50 F.T.Chs, with Jean Lumsden's F.T.Ch. Treunair Cala winning the 1952 Retriever Championship stake from 18 Labradors, 4 other goldens and a flatcoat, and the 1982 Championship at Sandringham being won by Robert Atkinson's F.T.Ch. Little Marston of Holway from 34 labradors and 2 other goldens, the largest ever entry. Daphne Philpott's Standerwick Thomasine (sired by F.T.Ch. Holway Spinner) is a notable exception in being a trial and bench winner. Today the separation between field and show is wider than ever. I do hope that all those breeding these admirable retrievers will keep in mind what that word means and honour both their distinguished working heritage and the memory of the great pioneers in the breed who respected a retriever for what it could do . . . not just how handsome it was.

The redder-coated Golden Retriever

The Flat-coat

The Retriever with Setter Blood

'He was as black as a raven – blue-black – not a very large dog, but wide over the back and loins, with limbs like a lion, and a thick, glossy, long, silky coat which parted down the back, a long sagacious head, full of character, and clean as a setter's in the manner of coat. His ears were small, and so close to his head that they were hidden in his feathered neck. His eye was neither more nor less than a human one. I never saw a bad expression in it.' So Idstone described the Flat or Wavy-coated Retriever in the middle of the nineteenth century. But this enchanting description does no more than justice to an under-valued breed of dog that combines physical beauty with intelligence, durability and individuality. It surprises me considerably that a breed with such appealing characteristics isn't highly popular and yet seeing the fate of other gun-dogs 'gone popular' I am almost relieved.

Retrievers as a recognised breed of sporting dogs are only in the region of one hundred and twenty years old, almost certainly starting in the 1850s as a result of a cross between the Newfoundland dog and the Setter. 'Stonehenge' wrote extensively on the breed in 1859 saying . . . 'I shall confine myself to a description of the crosses used solely as retrievers, including the ordinary cross between the Newfoundland and the Setter, and that between the Terrier and the Water-Spaniel. The large black retriever is known by his resemblance to the small Newfoundland and Setter, between which two he is bred, and the forms of which he partakes of in nearly equal proportions. His head is that of a heavy Setter, but with shorter ears, less clothed in hair. The body is altogether larger and heavier, the limbs stronger, and the feet less compact, while the loins are much more loose, and the gait more or less resembling in its peculiarities that of the Newfoundland. The colour is almost always black . . . the coat is slightly curly but not very long.'

At the turn of the century, Flat-coats were the favourite retrievers. Then a few noble families, including the Duke of Buccleuch and Lord Malmesbury, championed the Labrador. In 1903, the Hon. A. Holland Hibbert, later Lord Knutsford, introduced Labradors to a wider public by exhibiting at the Kennel Club show and running them at field trials. Gradually the Flat-coat was supplanted as favourite and has only survived due to the ceaseless interest of a few devotees. Mr S.E. Shirley did perhaps more to produce the modern Flat-coat than any other man – indeed, the breed was often referred to as the 'Shirley Retriever.' Then Mr H. Reginald Cooke championed them in the show ring for some 50 years before concentrating on the breeding of utility dogs. And utility dogs they should be. A hundred and thirty years ago, Pointers and Setters were entrusted with the duty of retrieving game when shot as well as finding it for the guns, then it occurred to sportsmen that it would be more convenient to have what was termed a 'regular retriever' of game.

Retrievers first appeared in field trials in 1870 when the first organised trial for them took place on Mr Assheton Smith's shoot at Vaynol. In 1900 the Retriever Society was founded. Nowadays the popularity of breeds such as the Labrador and the Golden Retriever knows no bounds. In recent years too, Continental gundogs have found favour for their value in the field, if not for their looks. Yet the Flat-coat has always combined superb service in the field with considerable handsomeness, as J. Wentworth Day has testified, 'But Black Bess . . . was my father's dog, a magnificent flat-coat who shone in the sun like a raven's wing, who walked the grass with the gait of a queen. She was all good looks, good breeding and good heart.'

To obtain this magnificent black coat and perhaps to eliminate water-holding in too wavy a coat, it is likely that some Border Collie blood was introduced. To my horror, recently, I have heard talk of making the Flat-coat rather like the Golden Retriever in physical characteristics. No disservice to the Golden Retriever, but the two breeds have separate identities and distinct differences. If the Flat-coat is to resemble any physical style, then the old 'Landseer Retriever' outline would be a preferable model.

The Flat-coat should be constructed on flowing well-proportioned, symmetrically handsome lines, racily yet powerfully built. He must be built on lines that permit easy movement and provide endurance. He must move purposefully but gracefully. He should move enthusiastically but never clumsily. He must carry no lumber of any sort. He should have a nicely moulded head, a broad skull, a good nose, long

Ernest Smith — gamekeeper, Oakedge, Staffs c.1900 with two flat-coats

strong jaws, a square muzzle, small ears close to the sides of the head and dark, kindly but alert eyes. The chest should be broad and fairly deep, the body short-backed, square and well ribbed-up with muscular quarters. The forelegs must be perfectly straight with good bone, the feet round and strong. The stifles and hocks should be well bent, the latter placed low.

The tail should be strong and not too long with ample feathering. The coat must be fairly long but flat with a fairly dense under-

The early Newfoundlands resembled the flat-coat much more than today's breed

coat and feathering on the legs. All this should compose a really handsome, companionable working dog, as responsive to instruction as a working sheepdog but without that quivering stalking restlessness. Flat-coats are strong, intelligent, loyal and powerful, being faithful and courageous watchdogs as well as fine gundogs. But above all they must be energetic, willing, lively and responsive, with deep reserves of stamina – like their Newfoundland ancestors.

J. Wentworth Day has said 'There is nothing feminine about a retriever. He is utterly masculine' . . . going on to say, 'I said that the retriever was all mas-

culine. So he is. He has none of the lap-dog qualities of the spaniel, the readiness of the terrier to adapt himself to house life. The retriever always gives you the impression that the house, even if he is allowed in it, is merely a place wherein to eat and sleep. Even in fireside dreams he twitches in ghostly hunting.' To me, in looks, characteristics and performance, the Flat-coat is the supreme retriever. I would like to see him renamed 'The English Retriever' and restored to his rightful position as principal national gun-dog. He certainly has the appearance and qualities to justify such a distinctive title.

Gentleman with a black Retriever

The Origin of the Sporting Spaniel

No one has ever produced any real evidence of the spaniel originating in Spain. Over the centuries the Spanish origin and the theory that the word 'spaniel' comes from 'espagnol' has been handed down. But if you look at Spanish paintings down the ages, read books on Spanish country sports and consult Spanish literature you will find no evidence of a spaniel in Spain as an indigenous breed. There is no modern native Spanish breed of dog which remotely resembles a spaniel. Over the years, inadequate research, perpetuated myths and a serious lack of cynological scholarliness has led to breeds being dubbed Alsatians, Dalmatians, Great Danes and nearer home, Kerry Blues and Norfolk Spaniels, in spite of and not because of their facts surrounding their origin. I believe there is a similar situation over the word spaniel.

Most authorities, including the various Encyclopaedias, state that the French word 'épagneul' comes from 'espagnol' meaning Spanish or of Spain. But I believe that this is not so and that epagneul comes from an ancient French verb 'espanir' – to crouch or flatten, rather as our setters do when at work. I am also inclined to believe that 'spaniel' is a similar corruption of the Latin word 'explanere' – to flatten out, from which the Italian word 'spianare' – to flatten comes. It is of some significance that the Italian name for the old Piedmontese Spaniel is the Spinone, one of the Continental gundog breeds which hunts, points and retrieves. I believe therefore that it is worth looking to Roman times when researching the origin of the Spaniel, not just to the Roman Empire itself but the trade routes, especially those to the Far East.

The Romans conducted trade with China through the Parthians. The Old Silk Road linking China with India, the Middle East and the Western world was used. Traces of Han silk have been discovered in Roman remains in the Middle East. At this time small, long-haired short-faced dogs, ancestors of the Pekingese, were used as prestige gifts by the Chinese to particular traders, emissaries or travellers. In due course, pure white varieties of these dogs were found in Northern Italy (the modern Italian breeds of Volpino and Bolognese), the islands of the Mediterranean (hence the modern breed of Maltese) and even Tenerife (the Bichon Tenerife) and Cuba (the Havanese). They were subsequently used as prestige gifts between the European courts; Aristotle refers to them as the 'ladies' favourite'. But there were other coloured varieties too, red and white, black and white and whole fawn – the colours of our modern Pekingese, Pug, Japanese Chin, Tibetan Spaniel, Shih Tzus and Toy Spaniels.

In the period 201 BC to 400 AD, the Iberian peninsula was part of the Roman Empire, modern Portugal being roughly the province of Hispania Lusitania. In Roman times, although perhaps originating much earlier, small dogs were used for driving game birds and waterfowl into nets and for finding game to which falcons could be flown. Spaniel-work was therefore very much a feature of Roman hunting and sporting life. In seeking an origin for the word 'spaniel' it is interesting to note an old Italian verb 'spaniare' — to get out of a trap or net.

The Romans are known to have introduced some breeds of dog into Britain, the researches of R.A. Harcourt indicating the presence of 'the Maltese dog', more like the Volpino of Italy (and, incidentally, the Japanese Spitz) than the modern Maltese. The dog depicted on a Greek vase from Vulci and labelled 'Maltese' is remarkably similar to that illustrating the Roman villa at Hemel Hempstead and on a bronze handle at Cirencester. Wherever man travelled, dogs accompanied him. Dogs from China would appear to be the great travellers, one theory suggesting the sea-faring people of the China dynasty of China who flourished in 400 BC introduced the Chihuahua and the Mexican Hairless Dog into South America. There are distinct similarities between the Chihuahua and the Toydogs of the Far East and later in Europe (such as the Papillon) and identical characteristics between the Chinese Crested Dog and the Mexican Hairless Dog. But the prized Chinese dogs were the short-faced

The early Spaniels were the falconers' dogs — small flushing Spaniels

'Palace' or 'Lion Dogs'.

From the earliest records available, the Chinese referred to these small short-faced dogs as 'Lion-dogs' and clipped them with a mane, shaven torso and tufted tail in the image of the lion. For the Romans, the Lion-dog was similarly clipped, the ancestors of our modern Lowchen (Little Lion).

It is of great interest to note that in the Japanese screen painting 'Lion Dogs', attributed to Kano Eitoku (1543–1590) depicts a pair of Japanese 'spaniels' in the classic lion-dog clip with a mane, tufted tail and leg tufts. In Britain, Gervase Markham writing in 1621 described in picturesque detail the 'water-dogge' and how to clip or

Thomas Bewick's large Water Spaniel of 1790

trim, beginning '. . . Now for the cutting or shaving him from the Navill downward, or backward, it is two wayes well to be allowed of that is, for summer hunting or for the water; because these Water Dogges naturally are ever most laden with haires on the hinder parts, nature as it were labouring to defend that part most, which is continually to be employed in the most extremity, and because the hinder parts are very deeper in the water than the fore parts . . .'

But 'water-dogges' were known all over Europe at this time, *The Sketch Book of Jean de Tournes* published in France in 1556, featuring a lion-headed 'Great Rough Water Dogge' retrieving a shot duck from a pond. The modern Barbet perpetuates the water-dog in France, as do the Wetterhoun in Holland and the Irish Water Spaniel in Britain. The little Lion-

Dog or Löwchen is a member of the miniature Barbet or Barbichon (now shortened to Bichon) family which embraces the Maltese, the Bologness and the Bichon à poil frisé, the latter now becoming a firm favourite in Britain.

The first written account of a Portuguese Water Dog is a monk's description, in 1297, of a dying sailor being brought out of the sea by a dog with a black coat of rough long hair, cut to the first rib and with a tuft on the tip of his tail.

Water-dogs came in two types of coat, the long flat lank oily coat and the tight curly coat, as exemplified in the Portuguese Water dog to this day. In France the long coat was maintained in the Barbet, the curly version in the Canne Chien (from Canard Chien or Duck Dog), later to become Caniche, the French name for a poodle. The Germans similarly had a Wasserhund and a Pudel, the Russians had a Pod-Laika. In Britain it is likely that water-dogs were crossed with land-spaniels to create water-spaniels with distinctly curly coats. Today the curly coats of the Poodle, the Bichon à poil frisé and Irish Water Spaniel perpetuate this variety. Water-dogs, not surprisingly, were favoured by the sea-going fraternity, the fishermen, the sailors, the traders.

Hamilton Smith in his *Dogs* of 1840, following earlier writers, mentioned four kinds of Pug, the Roguet, and the Artois Mongrel from France, the little Danish Dog, and the Spanish Alicant - which had a pug-like muzzle but the coat of a water spaniel.

Bearing in mind the small short-faced dogs found around the Mediterranean in Roman times and the fact that Alicante is a Spanish coastal town and province on the Mediterranean, which was Lucentum, a Roman trading post, this Spanish Alicant pug, with the coat of a water spaniel, is of some considerable interest. It is a fact too that breeds of sporting spaniel (and I include the épagneuls or Continental setters) and only found in countries which formed part of the Roman Empire. The early sporting spaniels were of course much smaller than their modern counterparts.

As far as 'spaniels' coming from Spain are concerned, I believe that far too much has been made of Caius and de Foix on this subject without stressing the qualifications they made. Caius wrote: 'Plenty of the same sort were engendered (also) in England . . . the common sort of people call them by one general word, namely Spaniells, *as though* these kind of Dogges came originally and first of all out of Spain,' de Foix wrote: 'Another manner of hound here is, called hounds for the hawk and Spaniels, for their kind came from spain *notwithstanding that there be many in other countries.*' We can discover from Turberville, writing in 1575, that he often quotes Master Francesco Sforzino Vicentino, Gentleman Falconer of Italy on the subject of 'Spanels'. Since then writers have quoted these authors to substantiate the Spanish origin theory.

My own view is that the sporting spaniel originated in China, from the short-faced ancestors of modern day Pekingese, Pugs and Shih Tzus, as well as Japanese Chins, Tibetan Spaniels and Llasa Apsos. In due course, in Roman times, these Chinese short-faced dogs were introduced into South Europe as the ancestors of the modern Maltese, Bolognese, Papillon, Phalène and Toy Spaniels. These Southern European short-faced dogs became the small

sporting spaniels and water-dogs of the 1300–1600 AD period, the ancestors of the Blenheim Spaniels, Canne Chiens and Epagneul Nains, and then 'Cocking' and 'Setting' spaniels. I don't believe that the world 'spaniel' has anything to do with the word 'Spain' but comes from the 'flattening down' or 'setting' of the épagneuls when indicating unseen game. If I am correct however 'setting' the record straight may end up being a matter of, as far as the Chiens Couchant are concerned, letting sleeping spaniels lie!

A re-creation of the old English sporting Spaniel

English Springer Spaniels

Lusty and Nimble Rangers

The Spaniel was probably first manifested, in an identifiable breed-type as a development of the falconer's dog but has at times in its history become blurred with the setting-dog, with interbreeding between the two regularly recurring. It was popular in the last century to consider the setter as an 'improved spaniel' but I believe the use of setting-dogs precedes the use of hawking dogs. In Ancient Rome for example, hawking was well known but I know of no reference to dogs assisting the falconer in those times. There is a reference however to the tuscan, a shaggy-haired dog which would actually point to where the hare lay hidden. Such dogs were used with the net, which was widely used in the hunting field by the Greeks and Romans. The art of hawking was first developed in the East, with the Tartars and Parthians introducing it into Asia Minor then into Europe. In more recent times the hawking dog was associated with Spain but I suspect it was introduced into Spain by the Moors for I can find no reference to such dogs there before the Moorish invasion; the Arabs were in Spain for seven centuries.

In due course, the hawking dog came into use all over Central Europe, the Bavarians having their 'hapuhunt' or 'canis accipitoricus' to flush quail and partridge for the falconer in the hunting field, the French having their 'chien oysel'. In 1387 Count Gaston de Foix wrote that the chien oysel was white or tawny with a fairly rough coat. These dogs were also used to put up duck and diving birds from water and to drive quail and partridge into nets by approaching them 'couchant'. Those used in water were crossed with the ancient water-doggees, usually curly-coated and often liver or liver and white in colour. This texture and colour persists in the descendants of such water dogs today, the Barbet, the poodle, the Irish Water Spaniel, the curly, the Wetterhoun and some breeds of spaniel.

Master Francesco Sforzino Vicentino, Gentlemen Falconer of Italy wrote in the 16th century: 'How necessary a thing is a Spanel to the Falconer . . . Without Spanels the Sporte would be but cold . . . For a good Spanel is a great Jewel, and a good Spanel maketh a good Hawke'. He also advised breeders to 'cutte off a little of the Spanel's Tayle when it is a Whelpe . . . it will bush out gallantly'. Such tail-docking became the fashion, a change from the spaniel-like dogs depicted earlier in the Bayeux tapestry.

A great deal of nonsense was written in the 19th century about the origin and history of the springer and spaniels generally. It is absurd for spaniel breed historians to claim a traceable purity of lineage for their breeds.

Dr Caius divided spaniels into 'two sortes, The first findeth game on the land, The other findeth game on the water . . .' going on to divide the land variety into those working with the net and those working with the hawk, with the latter sub-divided into dogs for the falcon, the pheasant or the partridge. Nicholas Cox in his *Gentleman's Recreation* of 1967 wrote of land spaniels as 'being of a good and nimble size . . . of a courageous mettle . . . lusty and nimble rangers, of active feet, wanton tails and busie nostrils.'

Sydenham Edwards in his *Cynographia Britannica* of 1801 wrote that the land spaniel . . .. 'may be divided into two kinds, the Springing, Hawking Spaniel or Starter and the Cocker, or Cocking Spaniel.' It would be wrong however to think of the land spaniel down two centuries as a consistent type; it was referred to by Gervase Markham in 1621 with these words: 'It is reasonable that people should cross Land Spaniels and Water Spaniels, and the Mungrells between these, and the Mungrells of either with the Shallow-Flewed Hound, the Tumbler, the Lurcher and the small bastard Mastiff . . . all of which are yet inferior to the truebred Land Spaniel — if one could still find one of those.' Not much evidence of line breeding here!

Vero Shaw, writing in 1880, on land spaniels stated that 'The Last variety of the Springer family which we shall treat of is the Norfolk Spaniel . . . this dog is, when found pure, most usually a liver and white, the white spots being heavily flecked with liver . . . a blaze of white up the forehead adds a great deal to this beauty.'

It is not uncommon however to find the existence of Norfolk spaniels denied in books about spaniels. Yet liver-coloured *Norfolk retrievers* with half docked tails were much favoured by Norfolk game keepers in the 19th century. Idstone, writing in 1872, recorded 'Almost any liver-coloured-and-white moderately large dog is called a Norfolk, more Norfolk Spaniels being used than any other . . . Most game-keepers keep a liver-and-white one, and it goes by the name of

The Norfolk Spaniel (c.1900)

the Norfolk dog'. Thirty or so years later, the forthright Dr. Gordon Stables in his *Our Friend the Dog* wrote . . . 'Norfolk Spaniels are very common – indeed, the name is given indiscriminately to nearly all liver and white or liver and white mottled Spaniels . . .' The much-quoted *Stonehenge* in his *The Dog* of 1867, wrote: 'The Norfolk spaniel resembles a thick-made English Setter in shape and general proportions, but is of smaller size, seldom exceeding 17 or 18 inches in height. The colour is black and white, or liver and white, accompanied by ticks of either on the white. This is a very useful breed, and it is now generally spread throughout England, where, however, it is not kept very pure . . .'

The names of modern spaniel breeds could all be very different. We could so easily have had Welsh Cocker, Norfolks, Devon Cockers, Land and English Water Spaniels instead of the modern Kennel Club-recognised breeds. The earliest classification relied on weight and colour. A Land Spaniel over a certain weight was a Field, under that weight, it became a Cocker. Mary Scott, a famous springer breeder of a generation ago, had a Welsh Springer, Corrin of Gerwin, first registered as a Welsh Cocker and after re-registration as a Welsh springer, produced a son, Guy of

Gerwin, which was registered as an English springer. Frank Warner Hill of Beauchief springers was fond of relating twenty years ago of how he competed against a certain dog one weekend in the English Springer ring and then saw it the next weekend as a Field!

For the official Kennel Club-approved of the English Springer to claim that the breed is 'the taproot from which all our Sporting Spaniels (Clumbers excepted) have been evolved . . . breed of ancient and pure origin, and should be kept as such . . .' is rather absurd.

In his *The Complete Farrier* of 1816, Richard Lawrence used the term English Springer, stating that the true one 'differs but little in figure from the setter, except in size; varying . . . from a red yellow or liver colour, or white . . .' By this time a consistent strain of these English Springers was starting, for by 1812 a linebred kennel had been established by the Boughey family on their Aqualate estate on the Shropshire-Staffordshire border near Newport producing, for example, Mop I – rather hefty, a little too curly-coated but of the desired Springer type. Another well-known if much criticised dog was Sir Hugo Fitzherbert's Tissington Flush, exhibited as a Norfolk spaniel around 1857. Flush was setter-headed, leggy and liver and white.

In 1899 the recently formed Sporting Spaniel Society held working trials on William Arkwright's Sutton Scarsdale estate and B.J. Warwick's Little Green estate at Havant, where the winner was a liver and white bitch, Mr Hearnshaw's Burton Duchess. It was not until 1902 however that the name English Springer was authorised when the kennel Club officially recognised the breed. Early field-triallers in the breed were the greatly-respected Isaac Sharpe of Northumberland and the very enthusiastic C.C. Eversfield of Denne Park near Horsham. The latter had purchased most of the Boughey fam-

(left) a successful and contented Springer

(right) English Springer Spaniel — a 'lusty and nimble ranger.'

ily's surviving dogs and in due course produced the redoubtable F.T. Ch.Velox Powder, Ch. Denne Duke, Amberite Powder and Denne Jester. Velox Powder began his winning career at trials in 1904 and continued, never being unplaced, until 1912.

In the 1900s spaniels looking like Springers were registered as such, with Guy of Gerwin being registered as an English Springer from a Welsh Springer father which had been first registered as a Welsh Cocker. A black and tan bitch sired by the first winner (Beechgrove Will) of a Challenge Certificate in English Springers was registered as a Field Spaniel. Several years later C.A. Phillips of Rivington fame developed his own strain of springers by mating an over-sized cocker bitch to a local working springer to produce F.T. Ch. Rivington Sam, whose grandson F.T. Ch. Rex of Avendale features early in many of today's pedigrees. A famous stud dog just after the Great War was William Humphrey's Dual Champion Horsford Hetman.

But the most famous name in the breed must be Selwyn Jones's F.T.Ch. Spy O'Vara, who between 1932 and 1935 won 17 firsts and 11 other honours in single stakes. With Spy, Don O'Vara won the K.C. brace championships from 1934 to 1936. Lorna, Countess Howe had a formidable team for some years, with her Banchory Bright and her son Boy excelling. After the Second World War, Spurt O'Vara qualified as a field trial champion to give Selwyn Jones, with his gifted trainer and

handler Joe Greatorex, his fourteenth title and other prominent triallers were John Kent, Thornell Browne, Mrs Beale and A. Wylie. A renowned stud dog of the 1950s was F.T.Ch. Rivington Glensaugh Glean, very nearly free of O'Vara blood, with F. T. Ch. Markdown Muffin, the greatest of his progeny. Other influential stud dogs have been Lord Biddulph's Conygree Simon, his offspring F.T.Ch. Markdown Mag, F.T.Ch. Saighton's Swing a very clever dog, F.T.Ch. Pinehawk Sark, Hales Smut, F.T.Ch. Gwibernant Ashley Robb, F.T.Ch. Sliguy of Ardoon and F.T. Ch. Rivington Santa Claus. But I wonder if we are not storing up future problems by the over-use of a few sires. Half our field trial springers nowadays come from only three or four sires or grandsires each year. Perhaps the time has come for the kind of outcross our sporting ancestors carried out in order to give us the great breeds we have today.

Here is an outstanding gundog which has become the foremost spaniel breed on sheer field merit. From a rich heritage, probably combining the blood of the hawking dog of the Arabs with water-dog blood – most likely coming from the Far East, with an infusion of hound blood in the last few centuries, the English Springer combines great energy with endless enthusiasm, a gentle nature with a determined manner. The writer in Bewick's *A General History of Quadrupeds* of 1790 on the springer summed up rather picturesquely both the

value and the style of this excellent sporting dog: 'Is lively, active
and pleasant; an unwearied pur-
suer of its game; and very expert
in raising woodcocks and snipes
from their haunts in woods and
marshes, through which it ranges
with amazing perseverance.'

*English Springer bitch and litter
of 50 years ago — no sign of the
'Cocker-type' then*

The Cocker Spaniel

Docility with Individuality

A prize-winning Cocker Spaniel of 30 years ago

Spaniels, as Espee de Selincourt wrote in the 17th century are the falcons, hunting with the nose low, following by the track. The Spaniel was the falcon-dog, flushing the game for the falcon, which once cast off, would gain height and hover for winged game to be flushed, when it would stoop and strike. Winged game is difficult to net and so the partnership of dog and bird gave scope to the human hunter in the type of country favoured by woodcock. It is not surprising therefore to find the best 'Cocking Spaniels' in places like Wales and Devonshire a century or two ago.

The Sportsman's Cabinet of 1803 recorded that 'the smaller is called the cocker or cocking-spaniel, as being more adapted to covert and woodcock shooting, to which they are more particularly appropriated and by nature seem designed . . . The smaller spaniel has also the advantage of getting though the low bushy covert with much less difficulty than the larger spaniel, and in that particular department may probably not tire too soon' . . . Our spaniel breeds evolved as a result of the varying demands made on them in different countries and are therefore specialists; it is not always fair therefore to compare breed with breed without mention of the country being hunted. But whatever the country, hunting in close thick undergrowth with overlong leathers, well furnished with wavy hair, can hardly help the spaniel to perform its task.

A thousand years ago there were red and white spaniels performing their task of flushing or springing game in Wales. I have seen some excellent working cockers with this colour combination in recent years and of course the separation of the spaniel into the modern breeds is comparatively recent. It is also foolish to claim purity of breeding in the various spaniel breeds. Outcrosses to English setters, Border collies, Springers and even toy spaniels have taken place; the use of field and Sussex spaniel blood

Working cockers of 100 years ago — a shooting party at Good Easter, Essex.

was also resorted to in the pursuit of a better Cocker. And I support such measures wholeheartedly, with over 300 inherited defects already identified in pedigree dogs and the gene pool closed in every breed in line with modern pure-breeding, the seeking of better healthier dogs always makes sense. Distiachiasis (extra eyelashes on the inside of the eyelid) causing sore eyes, chronic ear infections resulting from long hairy ears, a higher than normal incidence of epilepsy, progressive retinal atrophy (PRA), congenital cataract, cranial defects, elbow dysplasia, cryptorchidism and abnormal aggression have all occurred in Cocker Spaniels, either here or in North America, but not so far to any alarming degree. It is now up to the breed clubs, working with the veterinary surgeons

and geneticists, supported by the Kennel Club to eradicate such defects through revised breeding programmes. Good sound dogs usually come from a traceable family history of show-ring or field-trial success; it takes several generations of planned line-breeding to fix a type. We should now be looking more and more for those lines free of inheritable defects rather than those well-clad with glittering names in the breed.

The most famous first name in the breed is undoubtedly that of James Farrow's Obo kennel. His dogs formed the tap root of the modern cocker. Up to that time, 1880, a cocker spaniel was merely a land spaniel (as opposed to a water spaniel) that weighed less than a field. Master breeders of one hundred years ago then bred away from the rather squat Obo type with the thick neck and the low head carriage of the Sussex Spaniel style to what the renowned A.W. Collins (of Colinwood) later called . . . 'Square little dogs without exaggerations, built on robust lines, of short cobby appearance, but lots of substance'.

Recognised by the Kennel Club as a separate variety in 1892, Cocker spaniels in well under fifty years of that displaced Wire Fox Terriers as the country's most popular pedigree breed. In 1935, 7,656 were registered, and fifty years later over twelve thousand, with a peak of 27,000 in 1947. The entry of cockers at Crufts in February 1950 exceeded one thousand. In recent years however the numbers registered annually have fallen away, from 9,891 in 1980 to 7,697 in 1982 and then 7,121 in 1986.

Talented breeders like James Farrow and Richard Lloyd did valuable work at the end of the last century, to be followed by C.A. Phillips (Rivington), C. Caless (Bruton), R. de Courcy Peel (Bowdler) then T. Harrington (Trumpington), E.C. Spencer (Doony) F.C. Dickinson (Rocklyn) and F.A. Hickson (Sherington). The early influential sires were Farrow's Obo, Caless's Toots and Phillips's Rivington Signal and Toronto, the latter from a Canadian sire to breed out a tendency to snipyness. Between 1912 and 1917, Peacemaker of Ware, Rocklyn Magic, Fairholme Rally, Corn Crake and Pinbrook Scamp laid down the working lines from which most modern working skill is inherited. Between the two wars, a few breeders started to stabilise the reds or goldens, using the Pinbrook strain and blood from Toronto and Rufus Bowdler. During this period on the working side Charles Phillips's Rivington cockers won no less than 38 single stakes. The record number of 46 stakes (single and brace) was won by the Fews kennel of Dr W.J. Dawson; 12 of his dogs becoming F.T. Champions. The Silverlands kennels of Mrs. Berdoe Wilkinson won 29 stakes in seven years. Between the wars the most influential working stud dogs were Foel Joe, Rivington Dazzle, Pat of Crishall, Barney of Ware, Raeholme Rally and Dyron's Sunstar. In recent years field trial champions Templebar Blackie, Monnow Mayfly, Ardnamaurchan Mac, Carswell Zero and Speckle of Ardoon and the Jordieland dogs have had a considerable impact on the development of contemporary cockers.

Their compact well-proportioned build, backed by the most attractive range of coat-colour available in the breed and highlighted by the effusive nature and companionable qualities of the breed, has led to the Cocker spaniel becoming well-known the world over. Their warmth and loyalty have long endeared the breed to generations of owners and is likely to go on doing so for many years to come.

In his introduction to Carlton's work *Spaniels, Their Breeding for Sport and Field Trials* published in 1914, William Arkwright, the famous pointer man, wrote of the four natural qualities essential in any spaniel. He put docility, the wish to learn, the desire to please his master first, ahead of courage, nose and style. It is this quality which has led to the enormous popularity of the cocker throughout this century both in the field and as a companion dog, although their field use is not as extensive as it once was. (I suggest that the differences in temperament between Cockers and English spingers comes from the greater degree of hound blood in the former, as against the infusion of water-dog blood in the springer.)

Nowadays they are still one of the ten most popular breeds of pedigree dog in Britain, although registrations decreased by 40 per cent in the United States. Around 7,500 are registered annually with the Kennel Club, with well over a hundred being shown at Crufts's each February. In America, it was the most popular breed in the 1940s and was rarely out of the top ten there in the first half of this century. In the gundog group in Britain it has been overtaken by the Labrador and Golden Retriever and is now rivalled by the English Springer in the spaniel section. The American Cocker Spaniel, a different pedigree breed, has also become established in this country but not as a working dog and should not really be considered to be a sporting breed.

The club which safeguards the best interests of the breed was formed in 1902 at Conway Castle

The Cocker Spaniel (a 1958 head study)

and has progressed from a membership of thirty five to over one and a half thousand today. The first rule to be established by its club is a quite admirable one: 'to promote the breeding of Cocker Spaniels, to publish a description of the true type, to urge the adoption of such type on breeders and judges and to establish field trials'. Physically, as far as type is concerned I believe the club has been successful, but I do have concern over temperament in golden cockers and over the length of the ears in the breed generally. The breed standard lays down that the leather should reach the tip of the nose but no further; I regularly see cockers with ears at least an inch longer than this and further exaggeration is inevitable unless curbed. I do hope the cocker will not go the way of the show bassett hound as far as length of leathers is concerned. There was a case in a show ring recently in which a basset hound trod on its own ears and performed a graceless somersault. Shame on the breeders involved.

The breed standard was laid down by those with knowledge of sporting dogs and has largely survived to this day. By 1909, the club noted an improvement in the breed both in uniformity and correctness of type and the breed became the most popular of all the sporting spaniels. An arrangement was made with The Spaniel Club for two field trial stakes for Cockers to be included in their programme, with prizes up to £15 on offer. The judges were re-quested to disqualify any dog which they considered did not conform in appearance to the standard. If this happened in regard to English Springers at trials these days I should think about half would be disqualified!

After the Great War, the Club prospered under the joint leadership of two famous cocker breeders, C.A. Phillips (of Rivington) and H.S. Lloyd (of Ware). By 1922 the entry at the club's show was 332, a quite remarkable figure in those days and the largest entry of any one breed up to that time. In ten years registrations had quadrupled and the breed was a firm favourite both in the show ring and as a pet.

After the Second World War, half a dozen high class field trial cockers like Buoy of Elan, Jordieland Bunty, Carswell Solomon, Stockbury Elizabeth and Deewood Wendy kept the breed to the fore but in the 1960s there was a considerable decline. Today the position is improved overall, whereas I believe in English Springers, despite a number of top-class specimens, the across-the-board quality is not there. I suspect that some spaniels are rushed into field work before the basics are right and if bred from top field trial champion stock can be too fast and difficult to handle for the average shooting man. I believe however that even if traditional breeds and their style of hunting are being steadily but significantly infiltrated by Continental all-rounders, we will always need our spaniels for thick cover.

The Hunting Dogs of Clumber Park

The association of the Clumber Spaniel with Clumber Park in England and the lack of evidence of their precise Continental origin has accompanied their being regarded rather wastefully, as a rather ponderous gundog fit mainly for the older sportsmen and a style of shooting no longer practised. The name spaniel too gives many contemporary shooting men an immediate picture of a fast English Springer winning yet another spaniel field trial with dash and style. But, whilst all our spaniels are likely to have originated on the Continent, there is a world of difference between the spaniel as a gundog in the United Kingdom and the epagneul as a hunting dog in say France, as the devotees of the Brittany readily point out. I was once taken to task by a renowned Dutch sportsman for describing the Brittany as the only spaniel which points; he had a point, pun apart, which I acknowledged but I was attempting in a phrase to establish the essential difference between the words spaniel and epagneul, with 'hunt, point and retrieve' setter being a useful short definition of the latter.

I have long regarded the Clumber as a hunting dog rather than a spaniel in the true sense, designed for use in dense undergrowth and more suitable as a resolute beater than a quick finder of game. In General Hutchinson's masterly *Dog Breaking* of eighty years ago he recalls two notable instances of a *team* of Clumbers being utilised to hunt turnip and potato fields for fur and feather and in Yorkshire for partridges without the aid of pointers or setters. The Clumbers hunted mute, retrieved to hand and dropped instantly to shot. The Clumbers 'worked quietly and ranged close, alarming the birds less' but required 'very judicious management'. In the days when firearms had a very restricted range, there was little point in using fast wide-ranging dogs which sent game well clear of the guns. Hutchinson records that the Duke of Newcastle, who owned Clumber Park, used a team of spaniels reinforced by a retriever so that the spaniels could concentrate on hunting. At the turn of the century in those parts of Kent and Sussex with extensive woodland a type of 'hunting-shooting' was practised using small beagles to hunt rabbits for the gun. The beagles were used because they were slow and hunted so low, especially in gorse. This is very much the continental style of 'chasse à tir' in which hounds are used to drive the game to the guns. In the Kent and Sussex experience however it was noticed that the 'music' of the beagles alarmed game considerably; they really needed a team of Clumbers!

We forget in these days of fast communication, easy means of travel, a densely-populated Western Europe and the development of pedigree breeding that in the

past hunters in isolated areas produced the type of cross-bred dogs
which suited their country,
sought excellence of performance rather than conformation
and depended on the assistance
of dog to fill their pots more than
we have ever needed to. We can
afford the luxury of judging dogs
purely 'on the flags'; for them it
was solely in the field *and* in the
local field conditions, this being
how the different breeds were
evolved.

We overlook too how hunting
dogs were often inter-bred especially in France. When I look at
such a lemon and white hunting
dog as the Clumber originating
on the Continent I think of
hounds like the Griffon Vendeen,
gundogs like the Korthals Griffon
and the Spinone and their ancestors, some of which were once
referred to as 'Alpine' Spaniels.
Lemon and white is very much a
hound colouration. The similarities between the head of say a
Clumber, a Griffon Vendeen Petit
Basset and an Alpine breed like
the St. Bernard is marked. The
heavy-headed so-called Alpine
Spaniels were used from the Dor-
dogne, Monts du Limousin,
Haute Loire, Dauphine, Basses
Alpes, Alpes Maritimes, Piedmont
and Lombardy into the Bernese
Alps of Switzerland. As the German pointer breeds demonstrate
today, such hunting-dogs could
come in short-haired, wire-haired
or longer silky-coated varieties.
The Spinone has been linked with
the Piedmontese spaniel. The
Duke de Noailles who is alleged
to have sent his dogs to Clumber

Park in the 18th century had his
seat in the Limousin region.

We seem to ignore so often
when researching dogs the constant migration of peoples and
their dogs across the whole of
Europe especially in the period
A.D. 300–700 when for example
the Lombards moved from southern Scandinavia through the
Luneburg Heath area of what is
now West Germany to settle in
Northern Italy. How many researchers have linked the Spinone with the old heavy-headed
dewlapped Danish gundogs and
hounds with this breed and say
the Bracco Italiano? Similarly how
often do you read in words on the
Clumber of the distinct similarities with the Epagneul Francais, nowadays more like a Red
and White Setter but more akin to
a St Bernard in days gone by. For
me the old heavier-headed type
of Epagneul Francais is the link
with the Clumber; in the seventeenth century in France it was a
heavy-headed, lavishly-lipped
rather ponderous retrieving hunting dog.

The present Duke of Newcastle
has written, on hearsay from his
father only, that the 9th Earl of
Lincoln obtained dogs from the
Continent between 1760 and
1768, the year he became the 2nd
Duke of Newcastle. He has also
written that 'the dog we know as
the Clumber Spaniel is not very
like what Lincoln imported. He
brought in breeding stock for
crossing to produce a stronger,
however, slower moving Spaniel
than then existed, but one suitable for working in the under-

growth of Sherwood Forest'. If this is an accurate record then it can be seen that the modern dog is unlike the original imports and that cross-breeding ensued. Certainly the celebrated painting by Wheatley, *The Return from Shooting* of 1788 shows four Clumbers which are more like the Brittany Spaniels depicted in England by George Horler in the second half of the 19th century and the Clumber Spaniels 'Brass' and 'Judy' which illustrated Stonehenge's *The Dog* in 1867. Interbreeding between the different

The Clumber has always been a handsome, sensible, highly individual breed

varieties of sporting spaniel was of course commonplace about this time. It is important to keep in mind too how the use of hunting dogs and the method of hunting is always relative to the development of firearms from the 16th century onwards. The wheel lock, the spring lock, barrel-rifling and the repeat-shot facility all affected the way in which shooting was conducted and therefore the role of the sporting dog. We must remember too the sheer scale of hunting in the past centuries, in 1748 for example Duke Ernst August of Saxe-Weimar kept, only for hunting, 1,100 hounds and 373 horses. In the 18th century English noble-

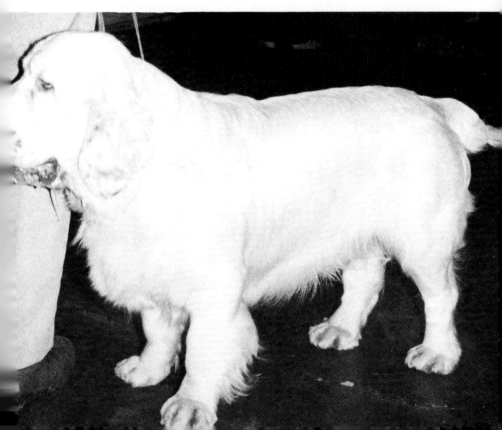

men went on Grand Tours to the Continent and I wonder whether it was on such a trip that the Earl of Lincoln discovered the success of the Duke of Noailles in developing a hunting dog in similar woodland to that of Sherwood Forest and arranged a shipment. It would be unwise however to suggest that today's Clumber resembles the dogs imported in the 18th century.

At the turn of the century if the Clumber fanciers quoted by Compton in his *The Twentieth Century Dog* are anything to go by there was some disquiet about the way the breed was being perpetuated. 'There are no Clumbers large enough to-day, and very few have the true Clumber expression

Clumber Spaniels in their classic role as beaters

. . .' wrote one; 'I do not consider the ordinary Clumber of today a credit to the breed . . .' wrote another with a third pointing out 'I am not satisfied with present type . . .' My own concern today about the breed would not be rooted in size, expression, correctness of type or even historical accuracy in its origin but over its well-being, for I see excessive haw and far too much loose forehead skin in just about every show specimen. This must cause discomfort to the dog, is most desirable in a hunting breed and does not reflect well on contemporary show breeders. There is for me an enormous difference between the breed standard which reads: 'heavy brows' and eyes 'slightly sunk, some haw showing but without excess', and the rather distressing condition of Clumber's eyes which I see at shows. Do modern breed fanciers really have the physical soundness of their admirable breed at heart?

It is good however to see some of today's fanciers trying hard to promote the working qualities in the breed. A few years ago James Darley trained a Clumber from show stock as a gundog *in London,* teaching him to discipline his hunting instincts along road verges at dead of night. That kind of dedicated interest can only do good. I'm not sure that the Welsh Springer, and I believe a Basset hound, outcross has had any marked effect on the working

Clumber Spaniels in the mid 1800s — lacking the massive build of the modern pedigree breed

qualities of the breed since World War 2. I can see Mr W.J. Ironside's Tollylog Angus Mor of Belcrum, at one time the only living qualified Clumber Spaniel champion and his Ch. Scarsdale John Barleycorn of Belcrum contributing a great deal to the breed. I hear too of excellent Clumbers in Sweden.

The Working Clumber Spaniel Society has recently been established with plans to get back to the smaller, physically sound, exaggeration-free dog and I applaud such a step. I rather warm to highly individual, rather independent, long-established breeds like this and welcome a dog which offers that extra challenge to a trainer. In country where thoroughness matters more than pace, here is your gundog breed. When I next see a well-trained Clumber at work in the field then I'll see with admiration the fruits of a *really* talented trainer's labours.

Clumber Spaniel of 1905, less heavily timbered and higher on the leg than today's breed

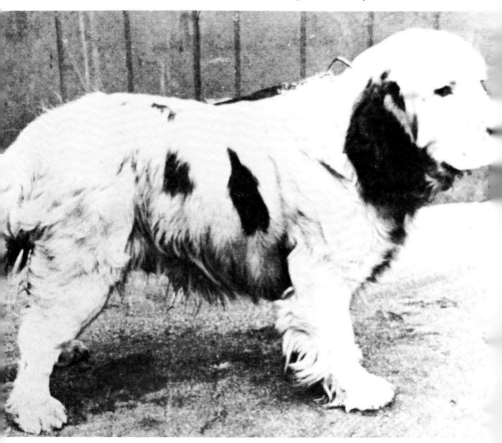

The Field Spaniel

It is not always easy to recommend a breed of gundog to an individual what with differences of temperament, terrain and handler-capability but when the country being shot-over calls for the resolute *flushing* of game then give me one of the old-fashioned spaniel breeds – ideally, a strongly-constructed field spaniel of Rhiwlas breeding. A combination of low-growing bramble and bracken or thick gorse is more than a match for a fast whippety field trials' dog whose instinct may be to try to go over dense prickly undergrowth rather than get his head right down and bore his own trail. A sturdy field spaniel with a powerful low drive is the breed for such a task.

In making a plea to the shooting fraternity to utilise this admirable breed more, my mind goes back to a story told by that great spaniel fancier, Mr C.A. Phillips. He was recalling an occasion in Ireland in the 1920s when the Kildare Hounds were drawing the new gorse at Castletown and finding it most difficult to work with no foxes prepared to bolt for them. Colonel Claude Cane, from his adjoining property, teased the Master and said his spaniels would shift them. Invited by the Master to attend next time, Colonel Cane did so with six spaniels, four being black fields, all well-known show winners, one of them Champion 'Celbridge Chloe'.

With hounds and field gathered together some distance away, the spaniels were sent in. A good deal of ribald comment came from the hunting people, but, in a few minutes only, out came not just pheasants, rabbits and the odd hare, but no less than six foxes and a grateful hunting field set off in pursuit.

The instinct has always been there, the physique has now been stabilised and perfected, the character is simply admirable; it would now be a just tribute to this staunch, praiseworthy but unheralded breed for them to be recognised by many more gundog fanciers for what they are - a fine unspoiled native breed only too willing to be used in the shooting field or to provide selfless companionship to their fortunate owners.

Evolved in the 1860s from a cocker-Sussex cross with some old black springer blood added, the breed has suffered greatly at the hands of well intentioned but misguided sportsmen and exhibitors. Irish setter blood was introduced to achieve a greater length of leg and many English springer crosses in an attempt to produce a faster gundog. Perhaps most unwisely, basset hound blood was introduced around 1880, to obtain a range of attractive colours but principally to shorten the leg. With crooked fronts, absurdly and long and low, they became the subject of ridicule and interest in them waned. It would be unjust to lay the blame for this on show fanciers entirely. There was a theory amongst sportsmen of the time that a low-set spaniel would be more effective in low thick cover, would not range too far or too quickly for the guns and have improved scent from the hound blood. This theory manifested itself in other spaniel breeds too, in the Old Norfolk for example.

In the first volume of the Kennel Club studbook, ranging from the year 1859 to 1875, all spaniels, for convenience sake – except the Clumber and water spaniels, were lumped together as field spaniels, which included springers, cockers and Sussex. Only gradually did they become classified into the varieties we know today. The dividing line between cocker spaniels and field spaniels was for some time of one weight only, with a hard and fast rule of cocker spaniels having to be under 25lb in weight – anything over being classified was a field spaniel and at one time, if it was liver-coloured, as Sussex. At that time, the cocker spaniel as making only slight headway and was far less popular than the field.

Writing in 1867 however, the celebrated Stonehenge used the expression 'the field spaniel' to embrace all sporting spaniels other than water, rather as Dr Caius 300 years before had used the expression 'The Land Spaniel'. 'Stonehenge' divided these field spaniels into ' . . . two leading divisions: one known as "the Springer", and including the Sussex, Clumber and Norfolk Spaniels, besides several others confined to their respective localities; and the other called "the Cocker" . . .' but giving the colour of the latter as ranging from plain liver or black and tan, white and black, white and liver, white and red or white and lemon. Spaniels had an ancient function but it would be most unwise to talk of purebred spaniels more than 100 years ago. Gervase Markham, back in 1621, recorded 'It is reasonable that people should cross Land Spaniels and Water Spaniels and the Mungrells between these, and the Mungrells of either with the Shallow-flewed Hound, the Tumbler, the lurcher, and the small bastard Mastiff . . . all of which are yet inferior to the true-bred Land Spaniel - if one could still find one of those'.

The field spaniel is to my mind the truest model for all our modern English breeds of sporting spaniel. He is the sturdy active present-day version of the old land spaniel and to avoid confusion between field (the name of the breed) and field spaniels (i.e. spaniels used in the field) it might have been preferable to have called the breed 'The English land spaniel'. The present title is rather a nondescript name for a breed that is anything but nondescript. Today's lively, well-proportioned, fine looking breed certainly deserves a suitably distinctive name. Field spaniels have made enormous strides in physical conformation as a sporting spaniel this century and I know that the modern fanciers will never again permit the antics of the 1890–1900 period, the peak of the 'Bassetised' era, in which exhibitors could be seen at shows actually aiming to impress the breed judge with the sheer length of back of their exhibit, to claim as on one occasion, that Rother Queen was half an inch longer in the back than Undeniable, as a point of merit in a working breed!

The main breeders of the last century were Mr F. Burdett in the 1850s, Phineas Bullock who was just about unbeatable from 1861–1874, then Mr T. Jacobs of Newton Abbott, who also ran a famous Clumber spaniel kennel, from 1890–1900 and Mr Moses Woolland into the early years of this century. From 1900–1910

Champion Wribbenhall Whitewash *owned by Mr G. Mortimer Smith of Bewdley, a fine example of a blue roan Field Spaniel, born 1928*

there were well-filled classes of both blacks and coloureds at shows, then, after the 1914–18 War, the better proportioned construction was produced by more sensible breeders by introducing crosses to English springers led by Mr R. R. Kelland with his Black Prince and Mr G. Mortimer-Smith's renowned Wribbenhall strain; in due course the Field Spaniel Society, formed in 1923 was able to organise field trials where Major Beaumont's Strouds kennel became highly successful. But the immense popularity of the cocker spaniel and the sustained interest in the English springer spaniel kept even the improved breed of field spaniel in the background until the Second World War and its disastrous after-effects on so many pedigree breeds. The Kennel

Club studbook for 1949 listed only one dog but thanks to the dedication of a determined bunch of devotees, the breed rallied with increased registrations for a few years, only, sadly, to sink again in the early 1960s when no fields were entered for Crufts. The breed has now rallied again with a steady increase in Kennel Club registrations from 57 in 1979 to 85 in 1985.

It is enormously gratifying to learn that a renaissance of the Field spaniel as a working dog is being promoted especially it seems in the Welshpool areas with Peter Spilsby a keeper on the Powys Castle estate, Bernard Beech of Brooklyn Kennels and Clive Rowlands the treasurer of the Field Spaniel Society all employing the breed on local shoots. Indeed Bernard Beech's bitch Hyfrydle Emma, a handsome liver specimen has recently produced her first litter and I have not seen better spaniel puppies for some ten years. The sire was another liver dog, Clive Rowland's Rhiwlas Garth Shade Oak and the result is really something special. With beautiful heads, excellent temperament, strong hunting instincts, really sturdy young frames with superb bone, I could see such stock producing a genuine resurgence of working Fields, not flashy field trial dogs but rough shoot trojans with strength, determination and old-fashioned spaniel characteristics.

Peter Spilsby is using a liver roan Bacanti Bridget (from an Adamant of Westacres - Dayhouse Kate of Bacanti mating, with the late Champion Adam of Elmbury, who won 12 C.Cs all under different judges, as grandsire) and her son (from a mating with Clive Rowland's liver roan Rhiwlas Likely Lad, out of Jack Tannant's stock) on the estate shoots. He admires their stolid temperament, robust build and the fewer demands they make on a handler than say today's springers. He acknowledges however that they are slow to mature and need to be two years old before they are ready for full training. His dogs are often confused with English springers at conformation shows by ignorant judges and penalised accordingly. He particularly values the way a Field spaniel lasts a long day in the shooting field, doesn't dissipate energy needlessly through highly-charged nervous activity or waste effort by pursuing casual distractions; in other words they concentrate on the real work. Jack Tannant, now in his seventies, confined by a stroke but still spirited, knowledgeable and wise, has passed on his Rhiwlas name to Clive and Pam Rowlands, after contributing enormously to the breed since World War II. Jack's black dog Gormac Teal has had a marked influence on the breed since the early 1960s, being responsible for the famous 'A' and 'J' lines in the breed. Jack bred for temperament and substance, producing sound working dogs with excellent heads and good bone. He insisted on working strength in his dogs and found them superb companions as well as great workers. He freely concedes they are

slower to learn and less frenetic in the field than springers but found them more dependable, better in water, more methodical, more thorough in their search and a better bet for the average shooting man. He expresses concern, with his wife Blodwyn, over the lack of body strength in many contemporary Fields . . . 'they're too shallow, too small boned, too cocker-like
. . . the bitches of ten years ago were bigger than today's dogs.' He said that Gormac Teal would 'go through anything' but rates Kip of Kiondroughad (born 1950) as a superb worker.

Kip won his first ticket under Joe Braddon in 1957 and was awarded nine championship certificates, three at Crufts. I was interested to hear Jack advise giving a bitch at least 15 months be-

A Field Spaniel of the 1900 period when the breed was 'Bassetised' . . .

tween litters and keeping pups under the dam's influence until they are 11–12 weeks old. His renowned Gormac Teal was in the first litter (1962) registered as pure fields, four generations after the outcross to an English Springer dog with Escott Cox's field bitch. The Rowland's bitch Gele Girl of Rhiwlas, who has the best head I've seen on a contemporary field is a granddaughter of Teal, with Peter Spilsby's dog, a grandson through Rhiwlas Likely Lad. The sire of Bernard Beech's really outstanding litter, Rhiwlas Garth Shade Oak when he was but nine months old was predicted by Jack Tannant to be a 'great sire' and a 'good winner'. I believe he is well on the way to achieving both prophesies. His other litter, out of Gele Girl of Rhiwlas looked highly promising even at eight week's old when I saw them at the Rowland's cottage. Jack's wife incidentally is the Patron of the Field Spaniel Society, a very apt and

well-deserved choice.

The other officials in the Society, which now has over 100 members, are Peggy Grayson (Westwind then Westacres) the President and Mrs A.A. Jones M.B.E. (Mittina) the Secretary, both of whom have made a major contribution to the breed in the last thirty years or so. Peggy's dog Adamant is winning well in Sweden; Mrs Sowton's Merry Megan of Gamefell has gone to the Cantas, who have one of the leading kennels in Holland where there is a lively interest in the breed. Predictably the Americans have also shown interest in our best dogs but they seem unable to comprehend the correct type and true movement essential in a proper Field spaniel. Current winning kennels in the show ring are Lydemoor (the Nicholls from Bristol), Coralmist (the Mowbrays of King's Lynn), Shermal (the Fowkes from Northampton, Donholme (Mrs J.K. Grant of Billingham), Nadavin (the Holgates of Essex), Nantddu (the Prossers of Merthyr Tydfil), Silksheen (Mrs Grattan of Chepstow), Bajenta (the Butlers of Swindon) and Gamefill (Mrs R. Sowton of Bromsgrove). The last full champion bitch was pre-war but there have been several full champion dogs, Peggy Grayson having 2 and the Muirheads of Norwich (Shipden Kennels) who do so much to keep the working capabilities of their Fields (and Sussex spaniels) alive, another.

The modern field spaniel satisfies both the eye of the exhibitor and the purpose of the rough-shooter, an active, robust, lively, contented and yet largely unacknowledged sporting dog. Now nicely built for activity and endurance, the field spaniel is a natural retriever with an excellent nose and the great perseverance of all the best spaniels.

Although I very much admire the sheer handsomeness of this breed, I value them most for their innate character. There is nothing flashy about the breed, they are steadfast and stable in temperament, with all the good points of the spaniel family yet none of the wildness of some strains of the more popular breeds. As companions, they have few rivals, combining devotion to their owners with a healthy streak of impishness and a very affectionate nature. Good car dogs, clean house dogs, not at all fussy feeders, very much wanting to be in their owners' good books and enthusiastic members of the family, I find them quite charming and incapable of malice. I cannot understand why a breed with such a pleasant character isn't more favoured. Even if they were to become more popular, I cannot see their dedicated followers allowing this fine old breed to be spoiled.

CHAPTER SIX

Terriers

*'Body and limb go cold,
Both foot and hand go bare;
God send teroures so bold,
   so bold,
Heart will harbour no care.'*

This little piece of verse written by Dr Still in 1543 shows very clearly that the terrier was valued well over four hundred years ago and that his boldness was his striking feature even then. The terrier-family of dogs has made its name throughout history as a group of brave, determined, alert, energetic, willing, bright-eyed little workers. It is both surprising and disappointing therefore to read the various terrier-authorities in the last one hundred years linking the modern terrier-breeds with the agassaean dog, a British 'breed' referred to by Oppian.

He described this animal as small, like the little table-dog (the lap-dog of today), exceedingly ugly, shaggy-haired, dull of eye, with sharp claws and venomous tusks. If I were a terrier-authority I would strive mightily to dissociate my dogs from such a creature, it sounds more like a nasty little yard-dog to me. I can see no reason to link this dog so firmly with the terrier, despite Oppian stating that they were used to follow beasts into their holes and emphasising their smallness by saying that the whole body of one could be contained in one hand. Sounds like a good meal for brock and charlie to me! I have heard of pekes, chihuahuas, poms and papillons 'following beasts into their holes', as indeed did our show-quality Persian cat!

But these varieties were not in the British Isles two hundred years before Christ and the agassaean dog could have been the forerunner of the terrier in Britain, although Oppian knew next to nothing of Scotland and Ireland, long famed for their terriers and long known to have great need of terriers.

Of greater interest to terrier-researchers is the ordnance of Dagobert, King of the Franks, some eight hundred years later than Oppian, which refers to the bibarhunt, or beaver-dog, as hunting underground. We ourselves once had an otter-terrier, as the engraving of W. R. Smith in 1846 indicates. The Earl of Cadogan possessed the breed, Sir Walter Scott knew of it and gypsies prized them; Jesse however confused many by referring to this dog as an otter-hound. The beaver and the otter are fearsome adversaries for a small dog. British beavers probably disappeared around the end of the 12th century, victims of ruthless commer-

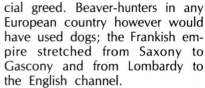

cial greed. Beaver-hunters in any European country however would have used dogs; the Frankish empire stretched from Saxony to Gascony and from Lombardy to the English channel.

The fourteenth century brought accounts by Gaston Phebus, Count of Foix, of hunting fox and badger underground though little of the dogs which carried out this hunting; a translation of his work by Edward, second Duke of York, referred to 'small curres that fallen to be terryers.' There was no description of such dogs however and a suggestion that there was no distinct breed or particular value in them. This was of course a book mainly on hunting in France not Britain. Also in France and a little earlier, in 1359, Gace de la Vigne wrote that the hunter, in hunting the fox:

> *'Le va querir dedans terre*
> *Avec ses bons chiens terriers*
> *Que on met dedans les*
> *terriers.'*

Whilst the author could have been referring to the task rather than the dogs, it is the first use of the word 'terrier' with dogs that I can find. One should remember in all terrier research however that terriers were mainly owned and used by the peasant class not the nobility; this explains the ab-

(left) a common rough-haired Terrier in Shropshire, with a gamekeeper, 1870

(right) the shorter-backed longer-legged Dachshund of 80 years ago

sence of literature down the centuries on terrier-work, whilst hunting and shooting has spawned bookshelves full of information.

At the end of the fourteenth century in France there were many sportsmen specialising in the chase below ground of the fox and badger, the Dukes of Burgundy for example utilising bassets and 'petits chiens Anglais', with the latter likely to be terriers. Terrier-work has long been part of the chase with dwarf hounds being used in Northern Europe in the terrier-role, as the dachshund illustrates. At the end of the fifteenth century there is reference in France to 'petits chiens taniers', small dogs which pursued the fox into his taniere, an earth or hole in old French.

Caius listed the terrier with the hounds and his contemporary the Bishop of Ross referred to them as 'another kind of scenting dog' as indeed they are, eyesight not being much use underground and hearing, however sharp, inhibited by the digging of the terrier and the quarry not moving at all. Also in the sixteenth century, Du Fouilloux, a sportsman from Poitou wrote of little bassets hunting underground, his work being exploited by George Turbervile in his *Noble Art of Venerie* but with basset translated as terrier. Du Fouilloux recognised two types of basset, the crooked front (torses) and the straight front (droites) with the former generally short-coated and better earth-dogs and the straight-fronted ones usually rough-coated and better able to run game above ground.

Much later de la Blanchere listed bullterriers as bassets à

jambes droites and Scottish terriers as bassets à jambes torses in his *Table of French Breeds* and their British Counterparts. The French-English dictionary of 1632 defined a basset as a terrier or Earthing Dog. It is very important to appreciate that modern pedigree basset hounds are very different from their ancestor breeds, although the Fauve de Bretagne has been remarkably unchanged for a long long time.

Sir Thomas Cockaine in his *A Short Treatise of Hunting* of 1591 described the 'entering of young Terriars' on fox cubs in a specially dug trench and also how to blow for the 'Terriars' in the hunting field. By 1803, Taplin in his *Sportsman's Dictionary* was describing variations: 'Terriers of even the best blood are bred of all colours: red, black (with tan faces, flanks, feet and legs), brindled sandy; some few brown pied, white pied and pure white; as well as one sort of each colour, rough and wire-haired; the other soft and smooth'. . .

I always think of terriers in four sub-groups: the basset hound/dachshund type as exemplified in the Dandie Dinmont, Skye, Clydesdale or Paisley and some so-called Jack Russell terriers; the beagle or small scent-hound type as in the foxterrier and the pinscher; the 'griffon' or coarse-haired type as in the border, lakeland, Scottish, Irish, Sealyham, schnauzer (once called the rough-coated pinscher), cairn, Kerry blue, the smoushond of Holland and the Airedale; and then the hydrids — the English white, Man-chester and Bedlington terriers.

It is of interest that the same factors which apply to the inheritance of scent-hounds apply to wire and smooth-haired foxterriers. A narrow head is dominant over the broader houndlike head. The sharp nose is dominant over the blunt nose; wire hair is dominant over short hair and the short legs of the dachshund, basset hound and Scottish terrier are (incompletely) dominant to the normal longer legs of the foxterrier. The colour of the dachshund whether wire, long-haired or smooth, is determined by the same determiners which affect scenthounds. In 1916 Wellman wrote of experimental crosses between foxterriers and basset hounds in which the vast majority of the progeny were black and tan and short-legged. From these facts it can be seen that in time it would not be difficult to produce a narrower-headed, sharper-muzzled, shorter-legged, wire-coated earth-dog from a hound origin.

Our terriers are likely however to have more than just a hound background. As Darwin himself once wrote: 'A breed, like a dialect of language, can hardly be said to have a distinct origin. A man preserves and breeds from an individual with some slight deviation of structure, or takes more care than usual in mating his best animals and thus improves them . . . When further improved by the same slow and gradual process, they will be spread more widely and will be recognised as something distinct and valuable, and will then probably first receive a provincial name'. In this way we developed our Rothbury, Manchester, Aberdeen, Reedwater, Glen of Imaal, Patterdale. Norfolk, Poltalloch, Clydesdale and Yorkshire terriers. The root stock of many being the old rough-coated black and tan common terrier of Britain, used by most hunts before hound-marked dogs became fashionable.

I have not made use of the many authors who covered this subject in the nineteenth century, partly because they copied from each other and partly because they themselves only quoted authors of previous centuries who were wittingly and unwittingly

Arthur Wardle's Border Terriers of 1890

plagiarising Du Fouilloux's masterly work. A modern author like Brian Plummer, who has exhaustively researched working terrier origins, again and again comes across the influence of terrier blood from Ireland. I have not mentioned what is perhaps the common terrier of Britain today, the so-called Jack Russell. I say so-called because strictly speaking a Jack Russell should be 14 inches high, stiff-coated and have an undocked tail! I don't see too many like this . . . or indeed too many pure-bred genuine earth-dogs. A real terrier must never have too short a back or its work underground cannot be carried out, yet very short backs seem favoured in showring terriers.

But whether descended from hounds or yard-dogs, developed in a Lake District valley or an Irish

glen, prick-eared or drop-eared, short-legged or long-backed, it is the terrier *spirit* which distinguishes the group. As a veteran sportsman recorded in 1802: 'Size is not so indispensable as strength, but invincible fortitude must be equal to both.' The quite invincible fortitude of the British terriers has made them respected all over the world, a uniquely British contribution to the dogs of the world.

Terrier-men have all the character of their dogs. Lewis Williams, a celebrated fox-catcher of Powys, 1937

The Good Sportsman

'First of all make certain that you have the sort of terrier whose build will enable him to do his job efficiently and with ease to himself', that telling advice was tendered fifty years ago by the field sports' enthusiast and working terrier devotee, Major G. B. Ollivant. But what build does enable the earth-dog to do his job not only well but more easily? Mr O. T. Price that much-loved old terrier man who maintained his own type of terrier from 1896 to the 1950s, opted for a dog '. . . twelve inches in height, about three and a half in breadth and weighing about twelve pounds. I like a narrow eel-like terrier' . . . he used to counsel. Certainly his favourite dogs 'Tartar' and 'Worry' and his little bitch 'Twinkle', famed over many counties, were on these lines. Geoffrey Sparrow in his classic The Terrier's Vocation goes for a dog . . . 'weighing from twelve to sixteen pounds, with a strong jaw – not snipy like the show breeds – a good back, neck and shoulders, and fairly long legs. The length doesn't matter. They can be folded up while bad shoulders cannot.' Ron McCoy, south-west representative of the Fell and Moorland Working Terrier Club, prefers . . . 'a dog with a nice straight leg, twelve to fourteen inches high, with a narrow body and not too deep in the chest.' His dog Trimmer is a fine example of a working terrier. Paul Luckhurst of the West Kent Hunt stresses that a working terrier must be . . . 'not too deep in the chest or too heavy-boned'. Bert Gripton of the Albrighton has also emphasised to me the undesirability of heavy bone.

But I'll go back to Major Ollivant for a most interesting description of the physical build of his terriers . . . 'the conformation I have always found the best for a Working or Hunt Terrier is that which approaches the nearest in build to the short-backed short-legged hunter . . . like the short-legged hunter he must have long, well-laid back, sloping shoulders, a short back and big long galloping quarters. This conformation will make him stand over a lot of ground, in spite of the fact that his back is short and not long.' Modern hunters are often less cobby than they used to be but, for me, that description 'says it all'. Dan Russell in his admirable Working Terriers, states . . . 'Fourteen pounds should be the weight to seek for . . . length of leg does not matter a great deal. A long-legged dog can get down a surprisingly small hole if he is narrow chested . . . The dog to refuse instantly is the one with loaded shoulders or turned-out elbows or a wide, cobby chest.' Mr William Baker, one of the breeders who developed the Sealyham, in the same vein, stated . . . 'In my opinion, no Terrier for underground work should be coarse in his shoulders, but my experience teaches me that nature decrees that a certain width of chest is always there in the gamest of them. The Sealyham of today is verging on a fancier's craze — straightness, length of head, great bone and cloddiness. If these are carried to excess, goodbye to him as a working Terrier'. Prophetic words!

But the expression 'gamest of them' applied to Sealyhams resurrects an old worry of mine. Having read of the method used by Captain John Tucker-Edwardes to 'prove gameness' in his terriers when fashioning the Sealyham as a distinct breed, it has always appeared to me the perfect recipe for producing brainless canine psychopaths and I cannot understand his standing as a terrier-man if the stories about his selection tests are true. Terriers which when not at work are expected to kill captive pole-cats will hardly appeal to ratting men and their valuable ferrets! It matches however the story of the poltroon who returned a fine Border Terrier pup to the highly-respected breeder as 'useless', because it declined to slaughter a neighbour's tom-cat which he had put into a barrel with his newly-acquired pup. I have never heard a proper terrier-man admire a dog that was 'too hard'. usually the reverse is true. O. T. Price once stated: 'Don't let your terrier get too hard. Remember that a terrier's job is to *bay* the fox or badger not fight it.' Dan Russell has written . . . 'No, the hard dog is as big a nuisance as the coward. He spends half his working life in hospital'.

Major Ollivant, writing in the early thirties, again, for me,

summed it up more than adequately: . . . 'In addition to the right conformation it is absolutely essential for the terrier to possess good pluck, nose, voice, endurance and intelligence, for those are all indispensable in his work. The terrier's pluck must not be the bravery of the Bull Terrier that goes in regardless of consequences, but the brave, fearless kind of pluck that knows its own danger, and yet has the grit to stay there.' But I like too the words of Roger Free in his informative book *Beagle and Terrier* . . . 'Choose the dog which is not afraid to look you in the eye and stands as if he owns the piece of ground he stands upon and half the battle is won. In the fullness of time the rest should be easy.' Restrained fearlessness based on self-confident determination, garnished with respect for his adversary and flavoured with a mutual owner-terrier regard is what gameness should amount to in a sound terrier. The 'holy terror' is usually nothing more than a blessed nuisance!

But how does the newcomer find the correct conformation allied to the desired temperament? What does our Major Ollivant have to say about that? 'To breed certain working points into working terriers that will improve their conformation and prevent them being handicapped at work by faulty build, we must go to blood where these points have already been stamped for generations, so that they will be reproduced,' he wrote. And Geoffrey Sparrow, in similar vein, records in his *The*

Terrier's Vocation: . . . 'but then she had a working pedigree back to the nineties on both sides. The real blood must be there or the pups are sure to throw back to soft lines.' No surprise to those who breed animals of any kind, yet again and again you meet those who choose puppies on their appearance rather than from their ancestry. And then there are those who swear by this breed of terrier or that – as if every single human from say Devon or Dur-

Today's smooth Fox Terrier — very different from hunt terriers

ham had similar qualities. The most consistent breed of working terriers I ever came across was the Glen of Imaal Terrier, whilst working in Ireland for a couple of years. No dog of that breed could gain show champion status until he first had his 'Teastac Misneac' – certificate of 'dead gamenesss'. The consistency came from the blood-lines.

Yet our breeds of terrier were developed in times when otters were hunted and badgers dug. Do we now need a Mink Terrier or even a Coypu Terrier? Will the Airedale, developed to kill a spate of pole-cats near Bradford in

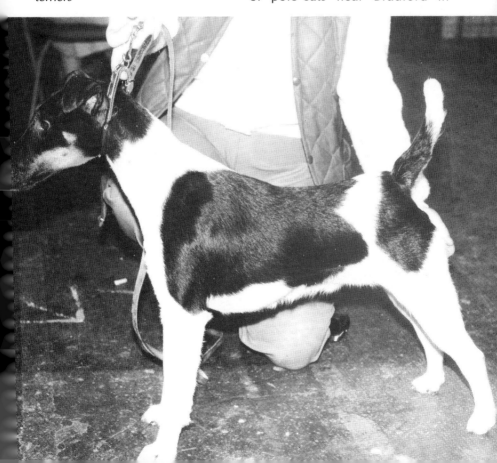

Yorkshire make a sporting comeback? If the Working Bedlington Terrier Club can recreate Squire Trevelyan's dog Old Flint of 1782 – long before the whippet cross took effect, the ancient 'Foulmart Hound' type of sporting dog may be seen again. Shades of Mr Gladdish Hulke's celebrated pack of stoat-hunting Sealyhams! At least the Bedlington has a tail you can get hold of, unlike the modern Norfolk and Norwich Terriers. But tail or not enough tail, let the Major have the last word: 'A terrier that has to work underground must have his heart in the right place; then if his body permits him to do so, he will get there like the good sportsman he is.'

'Other working terriers' depicted by Arthur Wardle in 1896

The Myth of the Jack Russell Terrier

'I firmly believe that if someone were to choose as apple-headed, crooked-fronted, broad-chested, flat-sided, short-necked, bulgy-eyed a terrier as he could find in all the progeny, say, of our best Terriers, and call it a Parson Jack terrier, which it certainly would be, for they all are, that he would find enough admirers of it to form a new Parson Jack Russell Terrier Club, and make a small fortune in stud fees and pups. It has been done before. It is curious how a once great name is used to bolster up a modern fad . . .' So wrote Dr Rosslyn Bruce, the famous Fox Terrier breeder in writing to *Dog World* sixty years ago; it could have been only a year ago. Parson Jack Russell should be remembered and revered as the father of the Wirehaired Fox Terrier and not, mistakenly, as a breeder who developed the short-legged hound-marked smooth-coated so-called working terriers bearing his name as a distinct breed around the Lurcher and Terrier shows of England and now, sadly, recognised by the Kennel Club.

Parson Jack Russell favoured a terrier with length of leg (as it had to keep up with the hounds), a narrow chest, a well-boned skull and a thick hard dense close-lying coat. He modelled his terriers on Rubie's and Tom French's Dartmoor Terrier and his first terrier Trump was the size and height of a full grown vixen with legs as straight as arrows and a coat that was thick, close and a little wiry. He selectively bred from good working dogs to produce more good working dogs - not to establish a physically-identifiable type as a distinct breed. Many fox-hound kennels have perpetuated the Parson Jack Russell style of hunt terrier, but it is essentially a Working Wire-haired Fox Terrier, not a separate breed. In short, a Jack Russell is a Wire-haired Fox Terrier and a Wire-haired Fox Terrier is a Jack Russell.

It may well be that the modern show ring Wire-haired Fox Terrier, with its bushy trousers, exaggerated muzzle and undesirable ultra-straight front is far removed from Parson Jack's idea of a fox terrier. But even more so is a broad-chested, crooked-legged, smooth-coated, Dachshund-terrier with a lack of good bone in the skull. Yet at the Jack Russell Terrier Club of Great Britain's National Show held at Tushingham, near Whitchurch, Shropshire on August the 17th, 1980, I saw at least twenty such dwarf terriers which seemed perfectly eligible for classes at the show. Now this was a quite admirable show, run by a well-organised club which has regional clubs from the Isle of Wight to South Wales and from the Thames Valley to the North West. But what they were promoting was not a Jack Russell Terrier but a Working Fox Terrier. Tan Tivi Tess, Mr Brian Male's 18 month old bitch which was judged supreme champion at the show would in fact have gladdened the Parson's heart, having a strongly boned head with powerful jaws, a stiff-haired broken coat and good straight legs. The Supreme Champion of the 1980 Harrogate Terrier Show, Mr D. Hume's Grip, was a very similar dog. Both are of the same type as the famous Spider, used by Arthur Heinemann with the Culmstock Otter hounds at the turn of the century.

But about that time, there were Cheshire Terriers, Shropshire Terriers, Patterdales, Elterwater Terriers, Suffolk Terriers and Reed-water Terriers. John Benson had some really hard terriers running with the West Cumberland otter hounds, as did the renowned Tommy Dobson in the Cumberland lakes, Tom Andrews the Cleveland huntsman, the Earl of Macclesfield in Warwickshire and Squire Danville Poole at Maybury Hall in Shropshire. All are lost to us as distinct strains but many are perpetuated in the K.C. registered terrier breeds – Lakeland, Welsh, Border and Norwich Terriers. It would be far

Local farmers out fox hunting near Llyn Ogwen, Gwynedd — 1930s

more appropriate to call short-legged hound-marked hunt terriers, Cowley Terriers, for Mr J. H. B. Cowley of Callipers, King's Langley developed a magnificent strain of such dogs, maintaining his own Stud Book and attempting to breed to physical type, something Parson Jack never did. But of the longer legged variety of rough-coated white hunt terriers used in the last century, even more celebrated than the Rev J.

Russell's pack in North Devon was that of another clergyman, the Rev A. Peyton of Doddington in Cambridgeshire. They were the envy of every terrier-man who saw them, were of an even type, breeding true.

Round about 1890, an 'Old English Terrier Club' was formed seeking to draw attention to the hardy hard-bitten varieties of ultra-game terriers from the various country districts. The worthy people behind this club were well-intentioned and genuine enough in their zeal but so often the best dogs brought for-

The Fox Terrier of 1900: stiff-coated without 'leggings' and exaggerated muzzle-length

ward in this way won their class in their own right as an Airedale or a Welsh Terrier, for the various breed-types had stabilised in this way. The Patterdale and Fell Terriers are nowadays embraced by the Lakeland Terrier, the Elterwater and Reedwater Terriers by the Border Terrier, Tommy Dobson's strain lives on in the Lakeland – the chocolate coloured dog still often being referred to by his name; the superb hunt terriers bred by the two sporting parsons Peyton and Russell live on in the Wire-haired Fox Terrier. Parson Jack Russell was inordinately proud of his Fox Terrier and if that was good enough for him then it should certainly be good enough for the rest of us.

Working terriers of 'Russell' type

Terriers of Scotland

For centuries Scotland has had small, rough-haired Terriers, reference being made as far back as 1436 by John Leslie, in his *History of Scotland,* to a 'dog of low height, which, creeping into subterraneous burrows, routs out the foxes, badgers, martens, and wild cats from their lurking-places and dens.' H. D. Richardson writing in 1853 refers to three varieties of Scottish Terriers, one 'sandy-red and rather high on the legs', and called the Highland Terrier; a second, the same size but 'with the hair somewhat flowing and much longer, which gives a short appearance to the legs. This is the prevailing breed of the Western Islands of Scotland;' and a third 'the dog celebrated by Sir Walter Scott as the Pepper and Mustard or Dandie Dinmont breed.' In her surviving breeds of terriers, Scotland has much to be proud of, from the irrepressible impertinence of the Cairn Terrier to the quite unforgettable Skye Terrier and from the sheer vivaciousness of the West Highland White to the stubborn 'diehard' character of the Scottish Terrier itself.

Colonel Hamilton Smith writing in Volume Ten of the *Naturalists' Library,* published in 1840 considers the Scottish Terrier to be the oldest representative of what he terms the cur dog race in Great Britain, stating . . . 'Our diminutive modern terrier, particularly the Scottish or rough-haired breed, is therefore the race we look upon as the most ancient dog of Britain . . . and in no part of Europe has the rough-haired breed retained so completely as in Britain all the traits which constitute a typical species. No dog carries the head so high . . .' Known for some years as the Aberdeen Terrier, the Scottish Terrier was originally much more like a black Cairn Terrier, without the exaggerated muzzle of the modern specimens. The heavier head was introduced in an attempt to counter the 'snipey' muzzles prevalent at the end of the last century. Mr W. L. McCandlish, famous for his champion bitches was fond of saying that the breed was 'engineered'. But with their modern 'cubist' outline, quite undesirable leglessness and over-

profuse coats, the breed is nowadays less in favour with the general public.

But this game, highly independent little breed is packed full of plucky attributes and deserves revived interest. The very fetching silver-brindle coat is not seen so much these days; the wheaten-brindle shade also seems to have lost favour. Perhaps a return to the traditional breed, both in length of leg and muzzle and in colour of coat would attract potential owners again to this fine old breed. 'A heart of gold and a soul of glee-Sportsman, gentleman, squire and gallant – Teacher may be of you and me,' as Hilton Brown sang of Hamish, the immortal Little Black Devil who remains to this day held representative of all Scottish Terriers.

The Cairn Terrier of 1948

Thompson Gray in his *Dogs of Scotland* (1891) refers to a visit made by a Captain Mackie to Poltalloch for the purpose of seeing a white variety of Scottish Terrier. The West Highland White was first called the Poltalloch Terrier and at one time bred as White Scottish Terriers with longer narrower heads and low cloddy bodies. They were also known as Roseneath Terriers, after a strain owned by Mr Clark of Roseneath in Argyllshire.

There was another strain called the Pitterween Terrier — identical in type. But for many years in Scotland, white and pale cream pups of the 'Cairn' type were destroyed at birth as unlikely to prove game enough as 'earth-dogs' or vermin-killers underground. But Colonel Malcolm of Poltalloch, whose family had used these small white dogs as hunting terriers for generations, brought his particular strain to public notice and the breed has never looked back.

The modern Westie is immensely popular, well over 4,000 being registered with the Kennel Club annually, and rightly so, for it has all the good qualities of the very best type of small family dog. There is still a tendency however for the tail to curl too far over the back and some strains are still prone to skin disease, but unlike many other highly popular breeds, the West Highland White has survived 'improvement' by show fanciers and remains a lively, friendly, quick-witted and remarkably adaptable little breed.

But just as Poltalloch produced its own strain of terrier and the Blackmount part of Perthshire, the Moor of Rannoch and surrounding districts developed the show type of Scottish Terrier, so

West Highland White Terriers before the First World War. Colonel Malcolm's Sonny *and* Sarah

too did Clydesdale, Paisley and Skye. The three latter varieties are now embraced in the modern Skye Terrier, now twice its original weight and longer-coated even than any of its hairy predecessors. No longer a sporting terrier but still full of fire and terrier spirit, the Skye seems to have been left for show fanciers to exaggerate the breed's physical characteristics almost to the point of absurdity. With only 38 entered for Cruft's in 1980 and only around 150 being registered annually with the Kennel Club it seems that even the show-breeders are turning away. It now needs a devoted Skye fancier in Scotland to recreate the original working breed and save part of his nation's heritage . . .

Arthur Wardle's portrayal of a Scottish Terrier in 1890 — longer in the leg and shorter coated

W. C. L. Martin in his *History of the Dog* (1845) records: 'The Isle of Skye Terrier is covered with long, coarse hair; its limbs are very short, but muscular; its back is long, and its ears erect; the eyes are large and bright; the muzzle short and pointed. The colour is sandy brown, reddish or white. The latter breed is much used for otter hunting on the wild shores of the Western Isles of Scotland, and though the dogs are of small size, their courage is equal to any encounter . . .'

Also small and brave and once known as the short-haired Skye Terrier, is the ever popular Cairn Terrier, the smallest working terrier but as game as any and quite fearless. Arguably the oldest authenticated breed of terrier in the British Isles — a Waternish strain being known in 1600, they were maintained as steel-grey short-coated Skyes until early in this century. Then in 1908, Mrs Al-

astair Campbell from Tigh-an-Rudha, Ardrishaig, Argyll began to promote them as short-haired Skye Terriers, which provoked a strong reaction from breeders of Skye Terriers, as classified. In 1909, Lady Aberdeen suggested that they be called West Highland Terriers as they were undoubtedly related to the West Highland White. But from 1911 the breed achieved championship status in its own right and with its final name. The first champion very appropriately being owned by Mrs Alastair Campbell.

Cairn Terriers seem to attract the very best breeders of dogs and I very much admire some of the present day Cairn strains. It is a breed which has changed little in 100 years and that in itself speaks reams for its resilience; and 100 years ago, Dr Gordon Stables paid this fitting tribute to the breed in *The Live Stock Journal*:

*'For pluck and pith and jaws
   and teeth,
And hair like heather cowes,
Wi' body lang and low and
   strong,
At hame in cairns or knowes.
He'll range for days and ne'er
   be tired,
O'er mountain, moor and fell;
Fair play, I'll back the brave wee
   chap
To fecht the de'il himsel'.'*

The Scottish Terrier at the turn of the century

Erin's Dare-devils

The Irish Terriers

. . . 'In form, it is, as it were, a perfect English terrier; in colour it is a blueish slate-colour, marked with darker blotches and patches, and often with tan about the legs and muzzle. It is one of the most determined of its race, and is surpassed by none in the skill and activity with which it pursues and catches its game, and the resolution with which it battles and destroys it.' In writing these words on the Harlequin Terrier, in his *Dogs, their Origin and Varieties* of 1847, H.D. Richardson goes on to state that Mr. Nolan of Dublin and Mr Wilcox of Palmerston had good specimens. Edward Ash in his *The Practical Dog Book* mentions a show being held in Limerick in 1887 with a class allotted to 'silver haired' Irish Terriers. Herbert Compton in his *The Twentieth Century Dog,* published in 1904, in describing terriers in Ireland, writes '. . . there was a terrier in County Wicklow (preserved distinct, and highly prized for a century) that was long in body, short in leg, and of a blue-black colour; there was a slaty-blue or silver-haired terrier in County Limerick; there was a black terrier in County Kerry' . . . Dalziel, doyen of dog writers at the end of the last century, suggests that Richardson's Harlequin' terrier could be reproduced by crossing a small Dane bitch of the desired colour and a black and tan terrier! But why stop there? Why not go back to the Harlequin

Pinscher introduced into Ireland by soldiers of the House of Hesse when serving in Ireland? Why not link them with the blue merle collies and the 'Blue Heelers' of the Irish drovers?

There is no doubt that the modern breeds of pedigree terriers from Ireland have common ancestors and became distinct breeds through county or locality specialisation in coat colour and length of leg. It could so easily have been that today's Glen of Imaal terrier became known as the Wicklow terrier and the Kerry Blue as the Limerick Blue. I believe that Irish Blue terrier is more apt a name than Kerry Blue. In 1919 a club was formed in Dublin to promote the interests of the Irish Blue terrier; it was not until 1921 that the name Kerry Blue was given to the breed. I have doubts about Richardson's 'harlequin' terrier being a true harlequin in the sense of the gene that produces in the Great Dane, Dunkerhound, Dachshund and some others, the so-called harlequin pattern – irregular, large or small, roundish black spots on a white or grey background in dogs possessing the factor for a black coat. It is interesting to note that Scottish terriers can be black or steel/iron grey, sandy and wheaten. The Irish Terrier, before the standard was revised at the end of the last century could be bright red, yellow, wheaten or grey. Grey was subsequently omitted. Twenty five years ago blue puppies still occurred in red and wheaten litters.

But whatever the origin of the

colour and the appropriateness of the breed-title, the Kerry Blue has a type, versatility and temperament worth perpetuating. The breed has been utilised as a ratter, cattle dog, sheep dog, watchdog, earth-dog, tracker and companion; the Irish have always expected a great deal of their terriers. Essentially an upstanding dog, the ideal Kerry should never be low-slung but be a well-knit well-balanced dog, around 36lbs and 18 inches high. The Kerry colour is highly individual, clearing from an apparent black at birth to the mature grey blue (or blue grey) but passing through one or more transitions, a blue darker than deep slate often with tinges of brown. Black on the muzzle, head, ears, tail and feet is permissable at any age but solid black is never permissable in the show ring. The coat texture is soft, dense and wavy, never harsh or bristle-like.

The Kerry Blue has never been spoiled by over-breeding through over-popularity. 221 were registered with the Kennel Club in 1978, 315 in 1980, 299 in 1982 and 315 in 1986 – more than twice as many as the Irish Terrier. There are usually just under 50 entered for Crufts each year. But in Ireland especially before the Second World War the Blue Terrier was pre-eminently a working terrier. He was judged at Irish shows from this viewpoint and field trials were held on rat, river work and rabbit, as well as drawing the badger, with no Blue Terrier becoming a full champion unless he won his certificate as an efficient working terrier.

The three characteristics of the Blue are his build, his coat and of course his unique colour. He should be sturdily built and never feature the narrow front, narrow skull and long foreface which spoils several of the English terrier breeds. The Blue is a one coated dog. He has no undercoat. His coat should be very full all over the body and lie in almost ragged broken waves with a distinct tendency to curl possibly from water-dog blood from way back, rather as the Irish Water Spaniel features to this day. Like the light blue terrier of Northern England, the Bedlington, the blue is all-rounder rather than a classic earth-dog and both have been used 'in the ring' as fighting dogs. A breed from such a heritage must never become 'coffin-headed' or over-coiffured as so many longer coated terriers have in the pursuit of show ring prizes. This blue terrier is part of Ireland's sporting history and must be perpetuated essentially as a working dog, a functional animal. It is surely an insult to a breed bred to a gameness so they can tackle wild cats and with the stamina to accompany the drovers across Limerick and Kerry for it to become a baggy-trousered straight-fronted be-fringed exhibit valued only for its colour and its coat. This is a highly versatile, extremely spirited breed of great character, part of the rich heritage of Ireland itself.

Less terrier-like is the Wheaten Terrier and since there is only one wheaten terrier by name, it does seem superfluous to add 'soft-coated' to the breed title. Both the Wheaten terrier and the Glen of Imaal could so easily have been lost to us as pure-bred dogs and it is good to see such character breeds being conserved.

The national breed, the Irish terrier itself, has a reputation the world over for pluck and spirit, in many ways epitomising the dare-devil nature of Irishmen themselves. There is a lovely very Irish term which expresses with whimsical understatement that the Irish terrier is averse to anyone 'treading on his coat'. At the end of the last century, a fearsome red-coated crop-eared very sharp ter-rier defended many a paddy's patch against intruding pigs, wandering goats and marauding dogs, as well as keeping the inevitable rat population well under control. But colour did not seem to matter one hundred years ago.

Killiney Boy, the founder sire of Irish terriers had a black and tan dam; the two early champions Bachelor and Benedict were from a litter of one grey, three red and five black and tan puppies and one of three red and five black and tan puppies respectively. At Belfast in 1816 a dog named Slasher was unbeatable, being described as a 'pure old *white* Irish terrier, a splendid field and water dog.' Show dogs in those days were still revered for their character: Limb, a bitch, being famous for having jumped from all the

Glen of Imaal *Terrier*

highest bridges in and around Dublin; Daisy, another bitch, was respected as quite the gamest in all Ireland. But then nothing bred out of Ireland is likely to avoid a good 'mill' or shindy, as the *Livestock Journal* of 1876 commented in verse:

'An Irish Terrier I was called
And sent on bench to show,
But oh! how little they believed
I should cause such a row.'

This spirited temperament is valued too in the Glen of Imaal terrier, a breed from an area in the Wicklow mountains where all living creatures have to be determined, resolute, tough and durable. Described by Jowett in *The*

Irish Terrier as . . . 'not recognised, being mostly blue and tan, with an occasional wheaten and black and tan, short of leg, long in body, and not straight in front but dead game, being bred and kept for nothing but vermin destroying,' the Glen of Imaal is progressing as a modern show dog with only 7 registrations in 1980 but 56 in 1986. I rather like the way this breed is prized for its silent work and that less attractive terrier-trait, 'yappiness', is frowned upon by the devotees of this breed.

The fourth Irish breed of terrier is also increasing its numbers in the modern show ring, with 148 registrations (11 more than the Irish Terrier) of soft-coated Wheaten terriers in 1986 after only 50 in 1980. Despite starring fifty years ago in the field trials held by the Working Terrier Association of Ireland, the 'blond terrier of Ireland' looks more like an old drovers' breed than an earth-dog. But then the Irish have always expected their longer-legged terriers to be multi-purpose. With a red, a white and a blue terrier, spanning wire-haired, soft-coated and wavy-coated varieties, the Irish have never been guilty of having inflexible views on the appearance or cosmetic attraction of their terriers, but their views on temperament have always been fixed. Spirit, gameness, pluck, even recklessness, has been demanded from each and every

The soft-coated Wheaten Terrier

breed. We may not need our modern terriers to work underground these days but to be true terriers they must have not only the conformation but also the guts to do so. This essential and absolutely characteristic terrier spirit in the Irish breeds is neatly conveyed by the lines:

'The lion and the unicorn fighting for the crown,
Up jumps a wee dog and knocks them both down'

Long may the terrier-spirit live and a long life to those highly individual breeds of terrier out of Ireland.

The Irish Terrier . . . a continental specimen

The Hunting Dog from the Vale of Aire

'The Airedale is not of ancient origin. He was probably first heard of about the year 1850, and he is undoubtedly the product of the Otterhound and the old black-and-tan wire-haired terrier. Yorkshire, more especially that part of it round and about the town of Otley, is responsible for the birth of the Airedale'. These firmly-written views of the prolific Robert Leighton, from his *The Complete Book of the Dog* of 1922 would appear to rule out any further argument but Leighton, although much quoted down the years is not the most reliable of dog-breed historians. Leighton was however merely echoing the widely-held view about the origin of this breed. I have a number of doubts, partly because the Airedale is, like the Otterhound, around two feet at the withers whilst the old black and tan terrier was only half that size and rough-coated rather than specifically wire-coated. If sportsmen in the nineteenth century were seeking a two foot high hunting dog why use a twelve inch terrier? And why use a twelve inch terrier with an otterhound when for over one hundred years there had been a northern breed of rough wire-haired hound, sometimes called the Lancashire Otter-hound?

In *Essays on Hunting* of 1781, edited by William Blane, this hound was described as 'of northern breed and in great esteem being bold dogs and by many huntsmen preferred for the otter and marten'. The Airedale was developed in response to the need for a dog to tackle the sweet-mart or pine-marten, the foul-mart or polecat and the otter. Sir John Buchanan-Jardine in his *Hounds of the World* of 1937 writes 'I am inclined to think, then, from the foregoing opinions, that there was really no true breed of otterhound to be found before about 1880.' He was guided partly by Johnson's *Sportsman's Cyclopedia* of 1830 which stated . . . 'Any hounds may be trained to hunt the otter; but the dogs generally used for this purpose are rough-coated, bred most likely between the hound and the water-spaniel' . . . Blaine wrote ten years later that . . . 'We have seen many otter packs, but we do not remember to have seen one that gave unequivocal marks of descending in any one immediate line or strain.' If there was no true breed of otterhound before 1880, but there was around 1850 when the Airedale was developed, a rough wire-haired hound in the north of England used against otter and marten, is it not more likely that the blood of the latter would be used by the water-side vermin-catchers of Yorkshire? It was wire-haired and the Airedale evolved as a wire-haired breed. The use of terrier blood would of course have provided a stiff-coated factor too. But the terrier work in otter-hunting has always differed from that of the hound,

demanding a much smaller dog. A water-terrier as such could have been provided by the old black and tan broken-coated terrier without any need of hound at all. But if a water-hound was being sought then what better source than the northern breed of rough wire-haired hound, proven against water-based vermin?

Down the centuries however, the canine specialist in water was the water-dog, often confused and indeed later inter-bred with the water-spaniel. But you only have to read Bewick and look at the Barbet in France to realise that the distinct breed-type of water-dog existed all over Europe, exemplified by the Cao D'Agua in Portugal, the Wetterhoun in Holland, the Irish Water 'Spaniel' in Ireland and the Curly-coated Retriever in Britain. Bewick illustrated the Large *Rough* Water-dog in his *History of Quadrupeds* of 1790 as a shaggy-haired medium sized dog, quite like the otterhound of today. Stubbs painted the 'Rough Dog' in 1790 and in doing so produced a dog which the first Airedales must have resembled, black and tan and shaggy-coated. The Large Rough Water-dog was accepted as being the best dog in water and is likely to have been the first resort of any breeders wishing to develop a waterside hunting dog in the first half of the 19th century. But of course once this dog was named a terrier, breeders down the years have set out to breed it to look like one.

I believe it was an enormous pity that the Airedale became regarded and then classified as a terrier in times when that collective noun was used to describe such diverse breeds at the Maltese, the Tibetan, the Boston and the Silky. A terrier can only be an earth-dog designed and equipped to go to ground; for a dog standing two foot high to be called an earth-dog is patently absurd. The Airedale should be regarded as a waterside hunting dog. It is the nearest English equivalent to the griffon breeds of the Continent, rough-haired , full of devil and great hunters. Nowadays the Airedale is rather like a king-sized

The Airedale of fifty years ago, widely used as a guard-dog

Lakeland terrier, although I still wince when I hear the Airedale described as the 'king of the terriers'. The Airedale has been used to hunt in pack in India after jackal and in the western states of North America to hunt the brown and grizzly bear. This is a hunting breed with a good nose, perseverance and stamina.

In due course and inevitably once the breed was accepted as a terrier, the hound ears, big feet and longer back were bred out and todays smart, upstanding epitome of a terrier was developed. Mr E. Bairstow of Bradford, one of the most prominent breed-enthusiasts of the 1880s and '90s always promoted the breed as an all-rounder, able to

act as a gundog if need be, an excellent water-retriever, but excelling as a companion-guard. In the Great War, the breed was used as sentry-dogs, messengers and ambulance-dogs, emerging as the best all-round wardog breed. Colonel Richardson, who was Commandant of the British War Dog School in the Great War, wrote in his *Watchdogs* of 1924: 'I have owned and trained at one time or other, nearly every kind of dog suitable for guarding work . . . but as the result of all my work of years it is my considered judgement, that for all-round watching and guarding work, the most reli-

able dog in size and character is the Airedale Terrier'. Coming from a man with his unrivalled experience that is some tribute. In 1920, the Airedale was the most popular breed of dog in the United States, but their popularity both there and at home has suffered at the hands of imported German dogs, initially the German Shepherd Dog, then the Dobermann Pinscher and more recently the Rottweiler. It saddens me to look at the registration tables for 1985 and see that against over 21,000 German Shepherd Dogs, over 9,900 Dobermanns and 6,800 Rottweilers, we can muster only 1,300 Airedales and 752 Bullmastiffs, our two famous native guarding breeds, both the choice of gamekeepers all over the British Isles. This may be an example of market forces at work but I hope and pray we will still have something in the region of 2,000 of our own two watch dog breeds in the year 2000 A.D.

I was delighted to read however of the first annual hunting and working workshop of the Airedale Club of America in April 1986. Using the Killdeer Plains Wildlife Area in Ohio, a three day working trial was held for Canadian and American dogs. Day 1 was for upland bird hunting, Day 2 was for trailing and tracking fur and Day 3 for retrieving. I do hope waterwork was included but commend the enthusiasts concerned in this

The Airedale has given valuable service to man — but is no longer utilised — the German dogs reign supreme

admirable venture. I have read too of Airedales being used by American hunters as specialists, ahead of the Walkerhound, at running very fresh trails and treeing bears. I believe that the Russians, after extensive research, used Airedale blood in the development of their new breed, the Black Terrier, intended for use with their police and armed forces.

Looking at the modern breed, apart from some concern about over-large eyes and sometimes a rather soppy expression, heads which are too long and some unfortunate Hackney carriage-horse front actions, stemming from incorrectly placed shoulders, I find them in good shape. I do ask however for some 'devil' to be retained in the breed, a sound temperament shouldn't be confused with softness – a breed famed as a watchdog should be instinctively protective not immediately welcoming. I have admired this breed since being an unpaid 'Vet's assistant' and going along to see Miss Harbut's dogs in the late 1940s and I have always found that my admiration has been very much deserved by this excellent English breed of dog.

Bring Back the Real 'Yorkie'!

Small black and tan working dogs have been known in Yorkshire for over two centuries, the little 'Halifax' terrier and the Yorkshire heeler being commonplace before the advent of breeding for 'the pedigree'. But whilst the former is perpetuated in the Yorkshire terrier of today – the tiny ornamental breed of that name, the black and tan diminutive cattle-heeler has been lost, whereas in adjacent Lancashire the Ormskirk or Lancashire heeler, also black and tan, has recently been saved. Yet the terriermen of Yorkshire are much respected in the working terrier world, with the annual Harrogate show the mecca of all committed earth-dog men. I have seen some really top-class 'Russells' in Yorkshire over the last ten years and some really game stiff-coated black and tan working terriers there too, midway between the Border and the Lakeland terriers in appearance and fine little dogs. It is really beyond the skill, perseverance and county-pride of the breeders of such stock to resurrect the old working terrier of Yorkshire?

The modern show Yorkshire 'toy' terrier is very much a manufactured breed which materialised around 1860 and in time its devotees hi-jacked the breed name for the ornamental exhibitioners' type of seven-pound dog. In due course the Yorkshire Terrier Club was founded in 1898. I do not believe it is at all historically correct for a long-coated dog with a coat of such silky texture, so tiny physically and so often with its top-knot beribboned to be dubbed 'The Yorkshire Terrier'. Originally this terrier was a bigger more robust dog with specimens from 10 to 14 lbs., and early shows had classes for over and under 8 lbs. For most of this century 6 lbs., has been the weight of most of the bigger specimens in the show ring and today we see a wee scrap of a dog with a suppressed terrier spirit in a highly ornamental container.

Now I have nothing against small companion dogs which bring comfort to so many older or lonely people. I have nothing but admiration for the Yorkie; a dog of that size needs all the support it can get! I do object however to the name 'Yorkshire Terrier' being misapplied in this way. This is not the earth-dog of that great sporting country.

The pedigree Yorkshire Terrier of today is extremely popular, with over 9,000 registered in 1988 but then 23,500 registered in 1989. With the American Kennel Club, registrations of the breed increased by 26 per cent between 1979 and 1983. But however much in demand, this is a breed from Scotland not England's biggest county.

When the Industrial Revolution took place, a large number of Scots especially from the industrial west, made their way to Yorkshire and Lancashire, bringing with them their Clydesdale and Paisley Terriers, forerunners of today's Skye Terrier. Some of this stock inter-bred with the small terriers which were favoured in the Halifax and Bradford districts. The Clydesdale was a soft-coated Skye Terrier, a bright steel blue colour with a clear golden tan on the head, legs and feet. In due course at the Islington Show of 1862, Scotch terriers under six pounds were exhibited and a year later in London, white, fawn and blue Scotch, under seven and over seven pounds were shown. Among the blues was Mr Platt's Mossy, No. 3628 in the Yorkshire Terrier stud book. In 1869, the famous Huddersfield Ben made his first appearance, being placed second as a Scotch Terrier. He subsequently sired many of the 'Toy Terriers (Rough and Broken-haired)' entries and is a founder of the modern breed of Yorkie. The links between the Clydesdale, Paisley, Skye, Dinmont and the Yorkshire terriers are many, with a common root-stock likely. Long-backed, short-legged terrier-like dogs with a top-knot are likely to have a common origin; the Scottish origin of the Yorkshire terrier as a pedigree breed is undeniable.

The descriptive noun 'terrier' can only be accurately applied to earth-dogs with a working origin. The Maltese terrier's name was wisely shortened to Maltese; the Tibetan Terrier is not correctly named. It would be very sensible for the breeds of Yorkshire and Tibetan terrier to be renamed. The pedigree Yorkshire terrier is nearly always called a 'Yorkie' anyway. It is worth noting that in the value of points in judging Yorkies in the show ring only 15 points out of 100 are given for 'formation and terrier appearance', whereas 50 out of 100 are given for the colour and quality of coat. This is very much an ornamental breed.

How timely it would be if the skilful artisan breeders of Yorkshire's working terriers could produce a true terrier of the county, preferably blue and tan, 12–14 inches at the withers, 12–14 lbs.,

Yorkshire Terrier in today's show ring

stiff-coated and unexaggerated. For this was essentially the common terrier of England, the old broken-coated black and tan. What would make it distinctive and different from the Lakeland type of working terrier, would be the *blue* and tan coat. The old Halifax terrier featured this combination and truly handsome it must have been.

I fear that by the end of the century we will have lost several of our famous terrier breeds, like the Sealyham and the Dandie Dinmont. To recreate the blue and tan of Yorkshire would be a notable contribution to the heritage of that great county . . . and to that of the nation's terriers.

The Fighting Dog of Staffordshire

The county of Staffordshire figures prominently in the history of barbarous sports in Britain. Dr Plot's *Natural History of Staffordshire* written in 1686 makes mention of a machine then in use in the county for gauging the size of fighting cocks . . . 'the most curious was an instrument shown me by the Right Worshipful Sir Richard Astley of Patshull, baronet, of his own invention to match game-cocks, discovering their size, both as to length and girth . . .' At Rushall near Walsall, 'duck in the hole' was the favoured game, in which the wretched duck was placed in a hole in the ground, with only the head and neck visible and used as target for a throwing match using short hard sticks.

Sedgeley, Tipton, Wednesbury, West Bromwich, Bilston, Walsall, Willenhall and Lichfield were very popular bull-baiting venues. The Lichfield Mercury of October 1828 recorded . . . 'The cruel and disgraceful scenes at Greenhill Wakes on Monday and Tuesday nights were the subject of investigation at the Town Hall of this city yesterday . . .' after a particularly brutal bull-baiting incident involving Wednesbury men. Darlaston once possessed a much admired town bull and a famous black bull was baited at Tettenhall, usually leaving the scene 'dotted for miles with dead dogs.' Bull-running was the speciality of Tutbury, where the bull had its horns cut off, was smeared all over with soap and his nostrils filled with beaten pepper.

Dog-fighting was a popular attraction all over England, with Lancashire, Yorkshire and Staffordshire producing famous champions. But it was Staffordshire which produced its own distinctive breed, which survives to this day, the Staffordshire Bull Terrier. Louis Becke, the Australian novelist, utilised the experiences of a Darlaston apprentice in his novel *Old Convict Days* . . . 'I was apprenticed early to one Toby Duffell, living on the Leys near the Ranter's Chapel in Darlaston . . . My master was an inveterate fancier and breeder of bulldogs and gamecocks. Bull-baiting on Monday and Cock-fighting on Tuesday was the order of the week . . . So keen was Duffell about dog-fighting that before a match I have seen him run his tongue all over his opponent's animal to make sure that no bitter aloes, or other drug, had been applied to prevent his dog seizing and holding.'

In 1834 at Wednesbury a dog-fight took place for a five pound purse. After a match lasting an hour and a half, one dog dropped down dead and the other died half an hour later. A little later when this winning dog was about to be buried in the back garden, an admirer exclaimed, 'Wait a while! I'll run and fetch a bible and read the burial service over him! It's sure no Christian ever deserved a-more than he did!' Such was the reverence for a winner in this barbarous sport. Fighting dogs often had their ears cropped off and Staffordshire colliers sometimes drew the incisor teeth of their dogs to enable the dog to bite deeper.

Dog-fighting has long been outlawed but there are still clandestine matches. At the turn of the century a case of permitting premises at Darlaston to be used for a dog-fight was tried at Wednesbury Police Court. Twenty men were present in a club-room while two dogs were 'played' at each other by two men who held them by their hind legs. One of the dogs used had its muzzle almost torn away. Whenever such

A red-tan Staffordshire Bull Terrier from Ireland

contests are held Staffordshire Bull Terriers are used, whether it is South Africa, the United States or Great Britain. In America, 'Pit Bull Terriers' also known as Staffordshire Terriers have been selectively bred and are now recognised by their Kennel Club as a pedigree breed. Last year, two pedigree Staffordshire Bull Terriers, well known in the show ring were stolen from a parked car in an area where secret dog-fights are still allegedly arranged.

The breed of Staffordshire Bull Terrier was always markedly different from the national breed, the Bull Terrier. Developed by the county's ironworkers by crossing working bulldogs of those times with various types of local terrier, the new breed evolved as a 28lb

dog, about 15 inches at the shoulder; red, fawn, white, black or blue or brindle of any shade but never black and tan or liver. The 'Dudley' or flesh-coloured nose is discouraged nowadays. It is quite wrong to think of this breed being developed from the modern type of bulldog, a grotesque caricature of the original breed. The bulldogs of a hundred years ago had to be lightning fast, remarkably agile and physically sound and were quite unlike the sad exaggeration offered as a bulldog in today's show rings.

Many everyday expressions widely used today originated in the dog-fighting world. 'Top dog' and 'coming up to scratch' being perhaps the best known examples. But 'throwing in the towel' comes from the gesture used to spare a losing dog for another day. The rules used in dog-fighting were few and yet even those are a little spine-chilling . . . 'In any case of a Dog being declared dead by the Referee, the living one shall remain at him for ten minutes . . .' and 'Both Dogs to be tasted before and after fighting if required': modern dope-tests are not exactly new! Famous fighting dogs of those times were well-known to the sporting public and were much acclaimed. One dog was Trusty, a fine fawn example, bought by Lord Camelford for eighty-four guineas and reputed to have fought and won fifty contests, killing three celebrated dogs in the process. A dog pit was usually about nine feet across, round or square, with a line marked or 'scratched' across the centre. After weighing, which itself led to considerable subterfuge, both dogs were washed in fresh milk ready for the 'tasting'. Much chicanery went on over applying strange mixtures to a dog's coat to discourage its opponent form holding on too long.

Each part of Staffordshire tended to favour a colour of coat, a breeding line or a particular style of build, the Walsall type for example being lithe and 'reachy'. But the blood of this reformed breed is used to this day, to instil gameness into a working terrier line and even to give more devil

Staffordshire Bull Terrier by Maud Earl

to some lurchers. It is said of the old fighting dogs that they had to be muzzled to mate a bitch, their keenness to fight was so powerful. With three of four thousand registered annually with the Kennel Club, this is one old breed in no danger of extinction and although they no longer lust for a kill, there is no doubt that this is

Cover the head and the anatomy of this mid 19th century Bulldog is pure Staffordshire Bull Terrier

about the gamest of all breeds of dog. And if Staffordshire can take no pride in its regrettable record in the practice of cruel sports, it has every reason to be proud of its own breed of dog, a bundle of sinew and muscle admired all over the world for its staunchness, equable temperament and loyalty to its master. Unlike many other old terrier breeds, the Cheshire, the broken-coated black-and-tan and the English White, now lost to us, the Stafford is very much here to stay.

75 Years of the Sealyham

If the Sealyham Terrier were a breed of farm animal rather than a pedigree terrier, it would by now feature on the most urgent list of the Rare Breeds Survival Trust and be placed as a 'Category 1: critical' breed. With less than 50 exhibited annually at Crufts and with annual registrations illustrating the worrying decline in numbers i.e. 140 (1981), 123 (1982), 107 (1983), 114 (1984), 100 (1988) and 182 (1989) steps need to be taken now to ensure the survival of this game little breed.

Only known as a pedigree breed for 75 years, the popularity of this breed rose to its zenith in the 1920s and 1930s with the best specimens changing hands for £1,000 on a number of occasions. Princess Margaret was fond of the breed and one of her dogs won his class for three successive years at the Sealyham Terrier Breeders' Association's Annual Championship Show held in Windsor Great Park. Princess Margaret's dog was usually handled on these occasions by Sir Jocelyn Lucas, who also bred him. Sir Jocelyn was a great devotee of the working Sealyham as his advertisement in *The Times* in 1921 indicates:

'Captain Jocelyn Lucas is prepared to back a team of not less than 10 couple nor more than 15 of his pedigree Sealyham terriers, underground to badger, in water to otter, etc., and on land to stoats, rats, etc., against a similar number of any breed, pedigree or not, from any one kennel . . .'

But it was another Captain and working terrier fancier, Captain John Tucker Edwardes on his Sealy Ham estate in Pembrokeshire who is alleged to have first developed the breed in the middle of the 19th century. It was a third Captain, Jack Howell, Master of the Pembrokeshire Foxhounds who was largely instrumental in their being recognised by the Kennel Club as a distinct breed in 1910.

Edwardes wanted to improve the local strain of working terrier and produce a compactly-built, strong-jawed dog, low on the leg and principally white. It has long been argued that white working terriers are less likely to be mauled by the hounds in mistake for a fox or otter, especially after a prolonged underground battle when the dog smells strongly of its prey. But I cannot follow this argument; white terriers soon become brown when working underground, hounds are specifically bred for their expertise in detecting the scent of their quarry and it is an insult to their capabilities to suggest that they cannot tell a muddy dog from a fox. This argument too doesn't seem to impress those using Border, Lakeland, Irish, Norwich, Cairn, Dandie Dinmont or Glen of Imaal terriers I believe that many hunts preferred their terriers to match the markings of their hounds, nothing more.

It is also recorded that Edwardes used Pembrokeshire

Welsh Corgi blood as his foundation stock, together with the blood of local rough-haired terriers. Whilst the Pembroke corgi was once much more terrier-like than the modern pedigree breed of that name, I find the use of corgi blood difficult to follow. Here was a fanatical terrier-man who shot any young dog unwilling to face a pole-cat, resorting to cattle-dog blood at a time when he must have known of the best terriers for fifty miles around Sealy Ham. If he was after a white terrier, why start with a brown heeler? Edwardes, too, was a proud old Welsh sportsman, living as far west into Wales as he could and seeking a superlative Welsh terrier. Quite why he should have resorted to Dandie Dinmont blood from several hundred miles away, and again not a white dog, at a time when West Wales abounded with game work-

Today's Sealyham — too short-legged and too long in the back

ing terriers, mystifies me - if the story of Dandie Dinmont blood being used in the early evolution of the Sealyham is actually true.

I can appreciate his resorting to Cheshire terrier blood but whilst agreeing that these were white and widely used as fighting dogs, I can find no evidence of their being closely allied to the bull terrier but smaller. I believe that the Cheshire terrier was much more like a pure white smooth-haired fox terrier. Much more likely to me than the use of untried England and Scottish terriers and cattle-dog blood would be for Edwardes to have located the best terrier blood in West Wales, probably the old broken-haired gamekeepers' dogs and then selectively bred for gameness as he desired. In this way, the silky topknots as also seen in Dandie Dinmonts, bull terrier heads and leggy shaggy-coated off-spring would have been produced even without the presence of blood from distant breeds. Certainly at

the Pembrokeshire Hunt Hound puppy and Sealyham terrier shows at the turn of the century, it was not unusual to find terriers 16 inches at the withers, short-muzzled and featuring long woolly coats.

In the early days of the breed as a show-dog, various outcrosses were tried, some admitted, some not. In this way the West Highland White cross was used to reduce size and a cross with Clumber Spaniels tried to increase head size. But I have never understood the craving for 'boot-box' heads in Sealyhams, no other working terrier breed features this exaggeration. Nor too can I see much sense in producing a terrier so lavishly-coated or short-legged. Such a coat is most undesirable in an earth-dog and for a breed whose standard decrees 'a general appearance of a freely moving and active dog' to be just about legless defies comprehension. It would be good to see a

more balanced dog produced, higher on the leg, shorter coated and shorter-muzzled. This would at least keep faith with John Edwardes who is proudly hailed as the breed's founder.

It might well be that the general public would prefer a 16lb., 14 inch, stiff-coated, not long woolly-coated terrier as a companion dog rather than a breed, however attractive, displaying a hovercraft-like appearance with a coat needing so much attention. The widespread popularity of the Jack Russell terrier, with a trouble-free coat yet similar characteristics, would tend to indicate this. I also favour hound-marked Sealyhams rather than pure white, although I understand that all-white is usually favoured in the show-ring.

In Canada a dog about 10 1/2 inches at the withers and 21 lbs. in

The early Sealyham, longer-legged and shorter-coated

weight is desired, with a head length to withers height ratio of 3/4:1. I would be very much against such a low-slung relatively heavy and long-headed dog, it is not the traditional breed. From Sweden it is disturbing to learn of two puppies in a litter suffering from Retinal Dysplasia, admittedly from a half-sister half-brother mating. On the Continent, they seemed to be obsessed with black eye-rims rather than true type and anatomical soundness. The American standard lays down that the length of the back from withers to set-on of tail should roughly equal the height at the withers, which to me indicates a short-coupled build not always desirable in a terrier which if true to type must have a flexible back. I don't want a Sealyham to look like a drop-eared Westie! Freeman Lloyd, an authority on

A Sealyham 30 years after Kennel Club recognition

the breed, claimed to have traced the Sealyham back to the 15th century when the Tucker family is said to have imported a small white *long backed* Flemish terrier into Wales. The Tuckers were the ancestors of Captain Edwardes.

I am very glad that the present standard omits some of the follies of the past such as : 'Black is objectionable, even on the head and ears. A large black spot on the body should be almost a disqualification as showing Fox Terrier blood' and on the desired type: 'The ideal being a combination of the Dandie Dinmont with a Bull Terrier of twenty pounds, otherwise any resemblance to a Fox Terrier in either make, shape, character or expression should be heavily penalised.' Not particularly fond of fox terriers were they, those early Sealyham fanciers!

Captain Edwardes died in 1891 and so never saw the breed he stabilised develop into a show

dog. I don't believe he would have approved the heavy furnishings the modern specimens display but would have found a commonality of spirit with those who have done so much for the breed over the years, Mr Fred Lewis, Mrs Winnie Barber, Lady Baylay and her daughter, Miss Frida Chenuz, and more recently Phoebe Cuming, Nancy Bilney and Pat Crick. This is an admirable breed of dog, a great companion, full of good canine qualities. I do hope that the modern craving for fad foreign breeds is tempered with a regard for our own native breeds which so much deserve our attention. I pray that the poem of the Reverend William Williams found in Freeman Lloyd's *Dog Breeds of the World* published over fifty years ago is prophetic:

'Just as old as the hills is the Sealyham,
Mars was his sire and Diana his dam,
Near Treffgarne Ricks he was nurtured and bred,
And there on the milk of the wolf he was fed . . .
When Sir Gwen Tucker, of Poictier's fame,
(He served the Black Prince) back to Sealyham came;
He laid his sword down – so the old books we read –
To found and to foster the Sealyham breed,
For ever and ever, his fine dog shall live,
And tho' he can't hear us! 'tis three cheers we give!'

The Terrier from the Rothbury Forest

'I was perturbed by quite a few of the exhibits. The standard does call for a lithe muscular dog but many were in a really flabby condition with hindquarters feeling like a piece of dough - no strength there . . . several also had narrow chests or pinched fronts, where has the horseshoe front gone? Several too were light in bone and didn't look as if they could do a hard day's hunting; we must remember that a Bedlington is a working dog not a dressed-up lap-dog . . .' This rather hard-hitting judge's critique in *Our Dogs* a few years ago on Bedlington terriers attracted my interest immediately for it followed close on the heels of a reader's letter to the *Shooting Times* which read: '. . . although the dilettante breeders of today have retained the breed *names* of the dogs which established such a high reputation for working ability, the actual animals they breed are of a very different order. I am at present engaged in the process of reconstituting a strain of working Bedlingtons . . . for the efficient fulfilling of its multi-purpose role the real working Bedlingtons needs a long, sprung back and not a short roached one; a close, hard, non-trimming coat of a deep, solid colour and not a soft, open, woolly, off-white one . . . well-angulated stifles and strong hocks not too close to the ground and a skull of adequate width to contain brains . . . the present-day "lamb fanciers" are barking up the wrong family tree.' I then took a trip to the National Terrier Club Championship Show at Stafford in April to look at the Bedlington Terrier classes myself. After two hours of studying the exhibits there I too was perturbed by quite a few of the exhibits and also felt that the wrong type of Bedlington Terrier was being displayed.

This is a breed I have always admired and I was saddened to see some of the exhibits, for underneath their show ring smartness of coat condition and appar-

The Bedlington Terrier of fifty years ago

ent perfection of presentation, there were some truly dreadful faults. A unique combination of lurcher and terrier, with dog-fighting heritage thrown in, the Bedlington must be built as a working dog, well-balanced, strong and hard-muscled but flexible in the back, keen-eyed and purposeful when on the move. Far too many of the Bedlingtons at Stafford had no drive from the hocks, a near-Hackney front action and soft muscles; one was so unsound that the word 'cripple' came to mind. The coats too were far too open and lacked the 'lintyness' so necessary in this breed. If these specimens epitomise the modern breed then I am not sur-

prised to read of an enthusiast attempting to reconstitute the breed.

As a breed the ancestry of the Bedlington Terrier is, relative to most breeds, well-documented and free from myths – no claims for this breed originating in dogs swimming ashore from wrecked ships! Some writers however, still perpetuate the Dutch origin story which arose from one researcher believing that old references to Bedlingtons as 'Holland's dogs' meant the country and not the breeder, Mr Taprell Holland. From the celebrated hunt terriers, Peacham and Pincher of Edward Donkin of Rothbury to the nailer's terriers in the Northumbrian village of Bedlington itself, from Joseph Ainsley's dog and Christoper Dixon's bitch and their offspring, the prototype Piper and Coate's Phoebe came the foundation of the modern breed. The cross with the small Otterhound was never pursued, the bull terrier blood was soon dispensed with but the need for rabbit-dog meant the regular use of miner's whippet blood over many years. But for me, the highly individual coat, the distinctive top-knot and the range of self-colours have never been convincingly traced.

It is a fact, as Mrs Stonex documented when tracing quite admirably the origin of the Golden Retriever, that there was a dog with a top-knot, a linty-twisty coat and a light liver coat on the Berwick coast and up into the Cheviot Hills, at the time the early types of Rothbury Forest Dog were ermerging as a distinct type; it was referred to as the Tweed Water Spaniel, but Tweed Water Dog would have been more accurate. Dogs like this, sharing a common ancestry with the poodle, were renowned for their versatility and cleverness; much favoured by gypsies they could locate truffles, catch fish and were the earliest retrievers all over Europe. Perpetuated today in the Wetterhoun, the Portuguese Water Dog and our own Irish Water Spaniel, such dogs are considered to be equally at home in water as on land.

In the last century, a show held by the old British Kennel Association featured a water-rescue competition which not surprisingly was won by a Newfoundland but a Bedlington won the third prize and was equal second in the speed trial. In a much-quoted letter in the The Field in 1869, an authoritative and well-informed correspondent, in a long description of the breed's development stated that 'the Bedlington Terrier is fast, and whether on land or water is equally at home.' The Bedlington Terrier is the only terrier to have its tail shaved – significantly, like the 'whiptail', the Irish Water Spaniel. The white chest marking of the water-dog, seen in the Portuguese Water Dog and to a lesser extent in the Newfoundland, also manifests itself in the Bedlington.

Gypsy families like the Jeffersons, the Andersons and the Faas lived in the Rothbury Forest at the start of the last century and were famous for their long-dogs, water-dogs and terriers. I believe that the most unusual and very un-terrier like appearance of the Bedlington Terrier comes from water-dog blood.

But whether a blend of hunt terrier, nailer's dog, miner's whippet and gypsy water-dog or just a leggier Dandie Dinmont, the Bedlington Terrier is a highly individual member of the terrier family, part of the sporting heritage of Northumberland and a unique blend of working abilities which deserves to be preserved. This breed, of all breeds, must not be allowed to deteriorate into a 'dressed-up lap-dog' fit only for 'lamb fanciers'.

It is therefore encouraging to learn that the National Bedlington Terrier Club for the first time in 30 years is to sponsor in its open show schedule two classes for working Bedlingtons and two cups for Bedlingtons holding

Arthur Wardle's Bedlington Terriers of 1890

working certificates. Once known as the Northern Counties Fox Terrier, this breed in which pedigrees have been traced farther back than in any other terrier breed, in fact in any breed of dog except greyhound and fox-hounds, must be perpetuated in a working mould. From Squire Trevelyan's Old Flint, a dog whelped in 1782, we have inherited over the intervening 200 years a unique breed of sporting dog. It is not enough however to produce the show-type Bedlington which works, as George Newcombe, the Chairman of the Working Bedlington Terrier Club, has pointed out; a proper terrier must have the instinct to work backed by the physical conformation to enable it to do so. There can only be one type of Bedlington Terrier, the dual purpose sporting dog from the Rothbury Forest and I pray that the show fanciers of the breed will honour its working pedigree.

Can We Have Our Terrier Back?

'The Case for a National Terrier'

The writer would like to see really serious attempts made to revive the English White Terrier, because it is a type, or rather variety, of dog which makes an excellent companion, combining many of the best features of the Bull Terrier without the aggressive qualities not uncommonly present in the breed last referred to.' These words were written by Darley Matheson sixty years ago in his *Terriers*, published by The Bodley Head, but can be echoed today. For if you look down the list of the Kennel Club-recognised terrier breeds, there is no English Terrier, named as such. In the British Isles we have the Irish, the Scottish and the Welsh Terrier; from abroad there are Australian, German Hunt, Czech and even Tibetan Terrier, yet in the land which has produced more breeds of terrier than any other, there is no national terrier breed.

It could be argued that the Manchester Terrier, at one time called the English Black and Tan Terrier, has a claim to the national title, the miniature Black and Tan Terrier still being called the English Toy Terrier, although not featuring in the Kennel Club's list of terrier breeds. There was once a Black and Tan broken-haired working terrier too, now lost to us as a distinct breed, but perpetuated in our pedigree breed, the

Lakeland terrier, and as a working variety in some hunt terriers such as those working with the Eskdale and Ennerdale. The Welsh equivalent was stabilised and then recognised as the modern pedigree terrier breed of that name. But of the English breeds of terrier which emerged in the last century, the one with the best claim to be identified as the national breed was the English White, as favoured in Cheshire and in the Midlands as the Black and Tan was in Lancashire and part ancestor of both the modern Fox and Bull Terriers.

The son of the creator of the all-white Bull terrier, James Hinks of Birmingham, described his father's blend in these words: 'The forebears of my father's dogs presented a comical appearance with their short thick heads, blunt muzzles, showing a certain amount of Bulldog layback, bow legs, thick set bodies and overhanging lips . . . Around the end of the fifties a great change came about: my father, who had previously owned some of the gamest of the old stock with which he had been experimenting and crossing with the white English Terrier and Dalmatian, bred a strain of all white dogs, which he called Bullterriers by which name they became duly recognised. These dogs were refined . . they were longer and cleaner in head, stronger in foreface, free from lippiness and throatiness and necks were longer . . . in short they became the old fighting dog civilized . . .'

Forty years later in the 1890s the

portraits of Bull terriers and English White Terriers by Arthur Wardle showed all too clearly the considerable influence of the rather refined English White on the formerly coarse and often grotesque fighting breed. Writing in the 1860s, the celebrated Stonehenge described this rather refined English terrier as '. . . a smooth haired dog . . . body very symmetrical . . . shoulders generally good . . . Fore legs straight and strong in muscle, but light in bone, and feet round and hare-like. Hind legs straight but powerful. Tail fine . . . Such is the pure English terrier, a totally different animal from the short, thick muzzled, spaniel-eyed, long-backed, cat-footed, curly-tailed abomination so prevalent in the present day.' Cynics might say that 100 years later we have preserved far too many of such 'abominations' in the pedigree breeds of dog yet allowed the once much-admired English White to lapse.

Writing on The White English Terrier before the First World War, Robert Leighton, in his *Dogs and all about them*, recorded: 'This dog, one would think,

The smooth-haired, white, leggier Terrier is an ancient type — detail from interior from the Grimani Breviary (1515)

ought, by the dignified title which he bears, to be considered a representative national terrier, forming a fourth in the distinctively British quartette . . . Possibly in the early days when Pearson and Roocroft bred him to perfection it was hoped and intended that he should become a breed typical of England . . . It is a pity that so smart and beautiful a dog should be suffered to fall into such absolute neglect. One wonder what reason of it can be . . .' The principal reason was undoubtedly the edict from the Kennel Club in April 1898 outlawing the cropping of

dogs' ears, neither the Manchester Terrier nor the White Terrier could retain their previous popularity and in time the Manchester Terrier was almost lost to us and sadly the English White became extinct.

But there were other reasons too for this sad decline and then loss, Dr Lees Bell, who bred many fine specimens of the breed, recording in 1893: 'All breeders have, I daresay, experienced the

The English White Terrier from a sketch by Arthur Wardle in the 1890s

same difficulty of breeding pure white puppies with level heads and fine skulls, together with proper English terrier lines of body. The puppies are either foul-marked, or have domed skulls and whippet bodies, or they have level heads, with the thick skull and wide chest and general stoutness of body of the bull terrier.' Unfortunately, too, congenital deafness was also present in the breed, as in some other all-white breeds. Regrettably, too, Whippet blood was used by show fanciers with the intention of producing a "daintier" dog and this without doubt led to some loss of terrier character in the breed. Some fanciers even crossed the 'Cheshire Whites' with Italian Greyhounds to produce a finer smoother coat. Soon the English White was a fragile breed, difficult to breed true to type and its followers turned to other breeds.

Two years ago, Dr Alan Walker put forward the view that a new breed of dog was needed to suit modern living, a purpose-bred

The English White Terrier with cropped ears

family dog. Among his listed characteristics for such a dog were these: 'short coat, about 17 inches high, with a 12 inch tail (something to wag!), with no exaggerations to cause veterinary problems, free from inherited abnormalities, not hyperactive, outgoing without being effusive, affectionate and faithful'. The English White was about 16 inches in height, with a short sleek coat, a whip-like foot-long tail, a symmetrical build and had a gentle yet lively nature. Such a breed — recreated possibly from a blend of the White Bull Terrier, the Smooth Fox Terrier and the whippet, need certainly not have inherited abnormalities and would probably be more robust mentally and physically than many surviving pedigree breeds. A white terrier might look grubbier than a coloured one after a walk in the rain but that doesn't seem to deter the several thousand owners of other pure white breeds like Samoyeds, Maremmas and the Japanese Spitz, all with much longer coats.

Terriers have always had a great reputation as companions. In *Breaking and Training Dogs* of 1903, this quality was very aptly and quaintly summed up by Pathfinder in these words '. . . they will come to understand your character as well as your nearest and dearest friend, and adapt themselves to your circumstances with even greater patience. Many a man will tell you that his pipe has solaced many a lonely hour and pulled him through many a bad time. I have known a terrier act as an anodyne where a boisterously cheerful companion would have been a bore. To bachelors, to sufferers from the 'blues', if they do not smoke, then I recommend a terrier . . .' Perhaps we could combine both a need for a new 'companion' breed with the need for an English Terrier — the gap in the list of British terrier breeds is clearly there.

CHAPTER SEVEN

Wider Aspects of Heritage

The Dying Art of Decoying

The invention of firearms and the subsequent improvements in the range and accuracy of guns in the shooting field brought about a large measure of redundancy in the ancient art of decoying, now rarely known about by sportsmen let alone practised. We still of course put out bird-dummies to entice feathered game like wood-pigeon and duck, but it is extremely rare to come across decoy-dogs at work, despite their time-honoured employment in this field in many different countries. In Canada, in Holland and certainly in one place in England however, this ancient canine skill is being perpetuated.

From medieval times the antics of the 'tumbler' have been well documented, although I notice that writers on lurchers often use the pseudonym 'tumbler' whereas this should, more accurately for them, be 'stealer'. The tumbler aroused the curiosity of furred and feathered game by its histrionic performance, lowering their guard, reducing their caution and then enticing them, sometimes into nets or within range of the guns, and sometimes seizing them itself.

In Bewick's *A General History of Quadrupeds* of 1790, the tumbler was described as being ...'so called from its cunning manner of taking rabbits and other game. It did not run directly at them, but, in a careless and inattentive manner, tumbled itself about till it came within reach of its prey, which it always seized by a sudden spring.'

Dr Caius, in his long letter to the naturalist Conrad Gessner of 1570 used these words to describe similar antics...'When he comes to a rabbit-warren, he does not worry the rabbits by running after

*The red decoy-dog completes
its task*

them, nor frighten them by barks, nor show any other marks of emnity, but casually and like a friend he passes by them in artful silence, carefully noting the rabbits' holes...'

Phrases like 'careless and inattentive manner' and acting 'casually and like a friend' describe most perceptively the crafty technique of the decoy dog whether 'tumbling' or leading ducks astray. The dog used as a decoy in duck hunting often worked in partnership with tame ducks to entice their wild relatives along ever-narrowing netted or caged channels until they were made captive. Jesse in his exhaustive *Researches into the History of the British Dog* of 1866 described how in the fens of Essex dogs resembling the 'colly' were used with tame ducks to entice wildfowl into tunnel-nets.

The skill of the decoy dog lies in giving the inquisitive ducks only fleeting and seemingly tantalising glimpses of its progress through the reeds and undergrowth, taking great care never to frighten them or even give them cause for suspicion. Before the use of firearms and indeed in the days when their range was very limited, these dogs must have been enormously valuable to duck-hunters.

The distinctive feature of dogs used in this way was the well-flagged tail. Their colour was usually fox-red, leading to some being referred to as fox-dogs, partly also because foxes will entice game by playful antics in a very similar vein. Clever little fox-like dogs have been used in many different countries in any number of ways in the pursuit of game: in Finland, their red-coated bark-pointer spitz transfixes feathered game by its mesmeric barking whilst awaiting the arrival of the hunters; in Japan, the russet-coated shiba inu was once used to flush birds for the falcon and the Tahl-tan Indians in British Columbia hunted bear, lynx and porcupine with their little black beardogs, which were often mistaken for foxes.

At the end of the last century 'ginger 'coy dogs' were frequently to be seen alongside the lurchers in gypsy camps, especially in East Anglia. Because no pedigree breed in this mould has been handed down to us, very little reference is made nowadays to these gifted and at one time invaluable dogs, rather as the ancient waterdogs are rarely acknowledged in the histories of our gundog breeds. Both decoy-dogs and water-dogs were usually handled by the humbler hunters like gypsies and so very little has been written about them.

In Europe it seems that the Dutch in particular had perfected the art of duck decoying, with the word itself coming from their word 'endekoy', a duck cage. The first duck decoy in Britain was built by a Dutchman, Hydrach Hilens, just over three hundred years ago in St James's park for Charles the Second. Such a decoy usually consists of a small shallow pond secluded by trees with a number of 'pipes' leading off it, each about 60 metres long. These pipes or caged tunnels are six metres wide and four metres high at their entrance but narrowing right down to the decoyman's net.

Along the curve of the pipe the decoyman (or kooiker in Holland) is concealed behind reed-screens. One of the few remaining in Britain is a joint venture between the National Trust and the Berkshire, Buckinghamshire and Oxfordshire Naturalists' Trust at Boarstall. This decoy is marked on the 1697 map of the Manor of Boarstall in the Buckinghamshire County Record Office. Tame 'call ducks' are no longer used here but Daniel White who once worked this decoy for over 60 years used six large Rouen call ducks. The yearly average of duck taken at the end of the last century was 800. The present warden-decoyman at Boarstall, Jim Worgan, is using a decoy dog. I believe there are only four kooikers still operating in Holland but they have retained their specialist breed of decoy dog, the kooik-erhondje, a small red and white spaniel-like dog with a tail very much like that of the Cavalier King Charles spaniel. I understand that the Wildfowl Trust has the only full-time decoyman in Britain, Tony Cook, at the Borough Fen decoy. There is a decoy at Slimbridge but I gather that their decoy 'dog' is a stuffed fox on a broomstick! We appear to have lost our native red-coated decoy dog which surely could still have been useful if only to those wishing to ring, photograph, paint or just study wild duck.

In Canada, probably taken

there by European colonists, there is the Nova Scotia Duck-Tolling Retriever, a golden-red medium-sized dog with the distinct look of our golden retriever about it. This Canadian dog is about 20 inches at the shoulder with a compact muscular build, alert, agile and determined, a strong swimmer, easy to train and a natural retriever. To be a successful duck-toller, such a dog needs a playful nature, a strong desire to retrieve and a heavily-feathered tail which is in constant motion.

The Canadian kennel club recognised the tolling retriever as a distinct breed in 1945 but since then only about 1500 have been registered. There are around 60 of the breed in the United States. Avery Nickerson has been breeding, training and hunting with tolling retrievers for most of this century from his Harbour Lights kennel in Yarmouth county, Nova Scotia. He builds blinds or screens on the shore of his local lake in areas where ducks come ashore from deep open water. He then creates a winding path from the screen to the shore of the lake. When ducks swim close by he begins to throw sticks for one of his dogs to retrieve. The ducks are attracted by the waving tail of the disappearing dog and come closer to investigate.

The skill of the hunter lies in throwing the stick for the dog the right distance at the right moment so that the ducks are not frightened away by the menace of an advancing dog, but made curious by the enticing waving of its bushy tail. The dog makes a normal retrieve of the stick but does so in a playful manner with plenty of tail-wagging. This decoy dog does not entice the birds by deliberately frolicking about, as foxes have been seen to, but is used essentially as a retriever of sticks. This playful retrieve however does lure the duck within range of the hunter's gun. I strongly suspect that this Nova Scotia

The ducks are made captive at the end of the decoy

duck-tolling retriever is our 'ginger decoy dog' exported and I think it likely too that the latter was part-ancestor of the modern breed of gundog, the golden retriever.

So the next time you throw a stick for your golden retriever to bring back to you, you may be re-enacting the role for which the dog's ancestors were greatly valued rather than merely idling away time and providing exercise. The golden retriever always seems to have its well-furnished tail in perpetual motion and this may come from its long-lost role with the decoyman. Perhaps some enterprising wildfowler will now try his hand at reviving what may well be a dormant instinct in the breed.

The concealed decoyman
checks on the ducks' progress

On What Men Do To Dogs

*'What have I done, to be thus
  mocked,
By my own lord and master
  docked?
Oh, the unspeakable disgrace!
To other dogs how dare I show
  my face?
Ye Kings, nay rather tyrants of
  my race,
If such a trick were played on
  you . . .!
Thus the young mastiff Towzer
  rent the skies
When with small heed for his
  shrill anguish'd cries
They seized his ears and shore
  them through . . .'*

The young mastiff Towzer of the La Fontaine poem was, despite his 'disgrace', relatively fortunate to have lived in the 17th century, for if he had lived six hundred years earlier he would have had his knees cut, if his owner dwelt within ten miles of a royal forest, under King Canute's Old Forest Law. A century later, under Henry I all dogs kept near the forests were disabled by the amputation of a claw and under Henry II's subsequent law were disabled through 'expedition', the severing of three claws at one stroke, using a broad chisel, from the right fore foot. The methods of disabling potential hunting-dogs varied in degrees of dreadfulness from 'hoxing' to 'hamling' and 'hock-sinewing' to 'lawing', with the practice of the time. But

the mutilation of dogs, whether the cropping of the ears, the docking of the tail, the severing of the hamstring or the removal of several claws of a foot has been a practice throughout recorded history. In the so-called 'sporting' field, it was not however that dogs were singled out. In the hunting field, carted-deer were released, after one foot had been removed, to train tyro-hounds in the chase and kill; young 'unentered' terriers were taught their trade on bagged foxes whose lower jaw had been sawn off and on boxed badgers whose teeth had been filed flat.

Such appalling practices are thankfully long behind us as are the complete removal of the ears of both the ornamental Pug and the dogs used in dog-fighting contests. But whilst the pursuit of 'sport' and the preservation of royal game occasioned much of the amateur surgery on dogs, superstition and ignorance in earlier times played its part too. For a thousand years it was believed that the little rod of gristle on the underside of a dog's tongue was a 'worm' causing rabies. I believe it was Gratius nearly two thousand years ago who first recommended that this 'worm' be cut out with a knife but from the time of Aristotle it was held that this 'worm' if not removed would grow and grow and then strangle the life out of the dog. But about this time Columella too believed that rabies was caused by parasites embedded in the flesh and recommended biting off the tails of *forty-day* old pups then pulling out the sinews so bared. And there is some resemblance in sinews separated out from the amputated tail of a dog to a bunch of glistening white worms. The modern practice of docking puppies' tails in certain breeds may well have originated in this belief. Perhaps more firmly based was the belief that the castration of male farm dogs lessened the chance of their wandering off and neglecting their pastoral duties. The castration of bitches or 'spaying' has been going on for a surprisingly long time but the removal of dew-claws, the dog's vestigial 'thumbs' has never been either consistently advocated or indeed always been considered necessary. The practice of 'rounding' hounds' ears both to avoid their being torn on bushes and achieve a uniform pack has been out of fashion for a long time but many Continental hounds and pointers have their tails 'rounded' i.e. the end vertebra or two cut off.

In more recent times Mr Michael Young, a Veterinary Surgeon, in his paper on *The Mutilation of Pet Animals* listed procedures carried out for non-therapeutic reasons and pointed out that some of these operations were carried out in order to change the appearance of an animal so that it would conform with the standard expected in the show ring. Mr Young wrote 'The veterinary surgeon must always resist demands and requests which conflict with

his professional integrity and conscience . . .' The Director of the Animal Health Trust, Mr W.B. Singleton M.R.C.V.S. in his *Ethics of Certain Surgical Procedures in the Dog* (Veterinary Record of 21 March 1970), recalled a vet in Yorkshire who, in an area densely populated by dog breeders, used a cataract knife 'to sever partially the dorsal caudal ligaments. Most of the cases were terriers but St Bernards . . . were frequent visitors to the premises . . . such a procedure was unethical because it was intended to deceive the judges or prospective purchaser and it was also unethical on the grounds that unnecessary pain was inflicted on the animal. The same vet used to

Basset Hound — sunken eyes, disabled body, absurd ears

Ear-less pug . . . once the fashion in England

sever partially the ear cartilage of fox terriers in order to make the tips drop down in a manner befitting the breed standard.' Clearly the B.V.A. has to obtain a consistently ethical approach in their work on dogs if their professional standing is to be safeguarded.

There is undoubtedly a great deal of work to be done too over the worrying increase in congenital deformities in the domestic dog. Already over 300 inherited defects occur in dogs, nearly all the fault of man and new ones crop up almost annually.

Diseases like retinal dysplasia now affects English springer spaniels; in the U.S.A. inherited cerebellar abiotrophy affects Gordon setters and neuro-axonal dystrophy affects rottweilers; in Canada renal failure in Samoyeds has recently been reported; our own sealyhams now have cases of pro-

gressive retinal atrophy; hereditary cataract affects American cocker spaniels; the 'rage syndrome' has been identified in cocker spaniels; pancreatic insufficiency is now in many breeds including German shepherd dogs; spina bifida occurs in bulldogs; solar dermatitis is found in collies; dentition problems occur in many broad-mouthed breeds, like the boxer, such as the production of additional incisors, whilst cases of undescended testicles seem to be increasing and probably have genetic causes too.

The B.V.A. and K.C. co-operate over such as the P.R.A. and H.D. schemes. But are voluntary schemes, mainly relying on the goodwill of breeders, enough? Not if the annual increase in inherited canine diseases is anything to go by?

Some years ago, at the instigation of Dr Malcolm Willis, a geneticist from the Agricultural department of the University of Newcastle and a German Shep-

Our unhealthy, unathletic Bulldog

herd Dog fancier, the Kennel Club formed an Inherited Abnormalities Sub-committee. This body was charged with carrying out an investigation into the many abnormalities in dogs which might be heritable and finding ways of reducing their incidence.

For a number of reasons this sub-committee was not successful. Most of the various schemes devised for the control of inherited diseases in dogs have failed to achieve anything worthwhile. There is no evidence to indicate that the methods sought by breeders to counteract the more drastic results of 'bad' genes have had widespread corrective effect in the last few years.

Over the 12,000 years that man

and dog have developed their unique partnership, man has exploited to the full the many mutations which appear quite naturally in dog-breeding. In this way we have produced nearly 400 distinct breeds varying from the 4lb Chihuahua to the 184lb English Mastiff, from the 'smashed' muzzle of the Bulldog to the elongated aristocratic muzzle of the Borzoi and from dogs that are barkless to those ridged and crested. We would be well advised to stop the pursuit of exaggeration and 'oddities' in dogs and instead of seeking eccentricity and uniqueness go for soundness both in temperament and physique. This may sound like going back to the beginning but there is plenty of evidence to support the school of thought which holds that man has exploited dog quite enough.

The Dobermann with cropped ears and docked tail

The Northern Dogs

Utility First

There is nothing ornamental about the northern dogs, the climate, the terrain and the perpetual priority of survival over pleasure have ensured that the usefulness of dog is the major criterion when allocating time and resources to them. Whether herding reindeer, pulling sleds, hunting elk, keeping wolves at bay or even locating puffins' nests, utility has always been their worth, although their companion value too has long been acknowledged. The latter, combined with their handsome appearance, has resulted in breeds like the Samoyed, the Siberian husky, the Elkhound and the Finnish Spitz being favoured much further south.

The Finnish Spitz is proving a very popular import into the United Kingdom with well over fifty registrations with the Kennel Club in each of the last five years. Finland's third most popular breed, increasing in popularity in Canada and close to recognition in the United States, the Finnish Spitz is a most unusual hunting dog in a style not pursued in Western Europe, that of the 'bark-pointer'. The dog is used in heavily wooded areas where it uses sight, scent and unusually good hearing to locate feathered game, upland game such as grouse or the capercaillie. The location of the quarry is pointed by a special stance, four-square with tail up twitching with excitement, head back and giving voice - a singsong crooning bark which is clear and consistent.

This 'point by bark' has two distinct purposes, one to draw the attention of the human hunter who could be some distance away and secondly to 'freeze' the bird. The Finlanders say that the tone of the bark, the agitated almost hypnotic waving of the tail and even the small white spot found on the dog's chest, holds some kind of fascination for the bird which watches intently from the temporary safety of its perch. The work of the bark-pointer is even mentioned in the *Kalevela,* the national epic poem of Finland. But if the dog is indicating game and not chasing and killing it then it is surely a gundog rather than a hound. This line of reasoning could also be applied to Norway's Elkhound.

Just as the Finnish Spitz is the national dog of Finland so too is the Elkhound of Norway. Archaeological finds at the Viste Cave at Jaeren, West Norway include two skeletons of dogs dating from 4000 to 5000 B.C. which are remarkably similar to the Norwegian Elkhound. In Viking times, towards the end of the first millennium A.D., such dogs were used to hunt bear, elk, reindeer and wolf. But it was not until 1877 that the breed was awarded official status in their home country, where only those dogs which qualify in Hunting Trials may be awarded the full title of champion. The Elkhound hunts mainly by scent and silently to locate its prey which it then holds or drives towards the hunters. But as it does not actually 'catch and kill' its quarry, strictly speaking it should not be classified as a hound.

The black elkhound comes from the Finnmark region and with a shorter coat looks lighter and taller than the 'grey elk-dog'. In Sweden the Jamthund has the same function but is 4 inches taller. The Laplander has his Lapphund, a handsome heavy-coated usually black reindeer-herder whilst the Finns use the Laplandic

Eskimo Dog

herder, less heavily-coated and not always pure-bred. Further east, the Russians have their own laika or barking gun-dog breeds with regional differences between the West Siberian, European and Karelian varieties.

The Karelian breed which attracts increasing interest however is the imposing Karelian Bear Dog, a strapping mainly black breed used for hunting the bear, lynx and elk. A stubborn, fiercely-independent and very determined breed, which is hardly surprising if they have to hunt such quarry, they have a very acute sense of smell and superb long-sight, picking up movement at extreme distances.

Canada's equivalent breed, the Tahltan Bear Dog may well now be extinct. The last Tahltan to be registered with the Canadian Kennel Club was born in 1948. The breed originated with the Tahltan Indians of British Columbia, in an area south of the Yukon and flanked by Alaska, and although Finnish Spitz-like in appearance and size was used to hunt black and grizzly bears and the lynx. They hunted in small packs with a fox-like yap but a coyote yodel. Scientists examining a skeleton of one of these dogs declared that structurally it was closer to a fox than a dog. Once heading for extinction too was the Eskimo Dog of Canada, shown at the Manchester Show of 1868 as Esquimaux Terriers. At one time the best known breed of sled-dog in the world and quite distinct from comparable breeds like the Alaskan Malamute, the Eskimo Dog or Husky was used for centuries as a primitive but very sensible form of native transport and as a hunting dog for caribou, musk, ox and polar bear. Their role was undermined by the advent of over-snow powered transport, air and rail travel and the establishment of large settlements rather than smaller separated villages. Last registered in the United States in 1942 and in Canada in 1966, it was fast disappearing in its natural habitat, the arctic regions, until a Canadian biologist established the Eskimo Dog Research Foundation in 1974 with 40 dogs. His

Karelian Bear Dog — tough and fearless

work has since led to a breeding base being set up in the North-west Territories, with several established dog-breeders playing their part in ensuring the survival of this historic breed, surely the toughest breed of dog in the world. The Eskimo Dog Club of Great Britain is playing a role too in conserving these outstanding dogs.

Apart from their remarkable feats on polar exploration trips, dog teams have made astonishing journeys. One sled-team driver left Nome, Alaska in 1905 and covered the 8,000 miles to Wash-ington D.C. in under two years. In 1973 Colin Irwin retraced the route taken by Greenland's pioneer-explorer Knud Rasmussen 50 years earlier, leaving Repulse Bay in early February and getting to Tuktoyaktuk by dog-sled by mid-June, nearly 2,000 miles further west.

Irwin described the astonishing rapport which his Eskimo companion had with the massive lead dog, a huge grey bitch, and then her quite astonishing reaction to being hit, going out into the storm and standing still, defiantly facing into the wind, until she died of exposure. Two famous American kennels utilised the different sled-dog breeds together;

The large German Spitz . . . The Barge-dog of the Rhine

the Toklat kennel near Aspen employing light-weight Siberians to head the team, medium-sized Eskimos to tug from the middle with the powerful Malamutes bringing up the rear. The Chinook kennels in New Hampshire similarly uses 80 pound Alaskan Malamutes for heavy freighting in rough terrain, big Eskimo dogs for the eastern Arctic areas of North America and lighter Siberian huskies for speed work.

The absolute degree of pride displayed by Colin Irwin's lead dog manifests itself in different ways amongst the Northern dogs, from the fierce nature of the Karelian Bear Dog to the affectionate friendly nature of the Alaskan Malamute, but each has a rather special dignity as the extremely handsome Siberian Husky and the thicker-coated Samoyed display. The latter is also a Siberian breed, much used as a sled-dog by sable traders. The Samoyed was developed by the tribe of that name in Tundra country whereas the husky was developed by the Chukchi people of the Kolyma River Basin in northern Siberia. I have heard of Samoyeds being used as sheepdogs and one as a most efficient gundog but I wonder if the sheer impact of their canine beauty isn't to their disadvantage at times. I suspect that the breed could be judged on subjective assessments of cosmetic appeal rather than physical soundness. A breed with the less romantic name of Russian Sledge Dog is now being promoted in Germany, shorter-coated, black and white husky-like dogs.

Another good-looking Northern dog is the Norwegian Buhund, used as a cattle-dog or sometimes a sheep-herder and for rounding up ponies. The smaller tail-less Swedish Vallhund, so like our corgi, and the bigger long-tailed Laponian Vallhund of Finland are other herding breeds from the frozen north. The comparable Iceland Dog was also used for driving horses and sheep but I have not seen one outside Iceland for over 30 years. The Greenland Dog too is rarely seen outside its home country and I doubt if it is still being kept pure and its individual type retained.

Amongst these many regionally-developed breeds, there are many similarities, the prick-ears, the thick coat, the fox tail which can be used as a wrap at night, the distinctive bark and above all a desire to work. Without this usefulness to man, their evolution would not have happened at all. This usefulness should not however be allowed to lapse and I am delighted to see sled-racing being perpetuated in many widely separated countries despite the ease of modern living. For the the ultimate usefulness of the Northern dogs is exemplified to this day in our collie breeds which I believe to be an off-shoot of the Northern dog breeds. I find many of the Spitz characteristics in our own working sheepdogs, in their pride, their determination, their alert assertiveness, but above all in their willingness to work.

Dogs in Japan

Although it is common to find in expensively-produced and illustriously-attributed *Encyclopaedias of the Dog* all manner of ludicrous statements about the origins of pointers, spaniels, sheepdogs and mastiffs and equally absurd claims about the history of such breeds as the St Bernard, the Newfoundland and the Great Dane, these are relatively minor when it comes to the coverage of the Japanese native breeds of domesticated dog. For I know of no book produced in Europe which describes these breeds either with accuracy or comprehensively. And this is forgivable when one is aware of the paucity of information from previous generations of Western writers on dogs. But this should be a challenge to the diligent researcher if not to the casual plagiarist.

I have long been intrigued by the native breeds of Japan, sparked initially by the information that genetically Japanese breeds with one exception originated from a common ancestral type (in which both A and B haemoglobin alleles were present) whilst the European breeds originated from a different ancestral group (in which the A allele was absent). My interest was heightened more recently when I read that Joe Braddon, the well-known dog-show judge, rated a Japanese

The Japanese Spitz — from nearby Russia

Akita which he made best-in-show in Norway seventeen years ago, the best dog he ever saw. In a career now approaching forty years, he must have sized up hundreds of thousands of pedigree dogs, at home and abroad. The Akita was recognised by the kennel club in 1954 and the American Kennel Club in 1956. Recently the breed has gained considerable popularity in the West, although the medium and smaller Japanese breeds are still virtually unknown outside Japan.

The indigenous Japanese dog is believed to have been introduced by the people who migrated to the Japanese islands in the Jomon period (around 10,000 – 300 B.C.) with the first domesticated dog bones recognised as authentic in

Japan being excavated from early Jomon sites dating around 5000 B.C. Several waves of migration have contributed to the diversity of types of native dog and resulted in cross-breeding among them. When using the term indigenous Japanese dog I exclude relatively new breeds like the Chin (Japanese Spaniel) developed during the Edo period (1600 – 1868), the Tosa Inu (Japanese fighting dog) developed during the Meiji period (1868–1912), the Nippon teriya (Japanese Toy Terrier) developed during the Taisho period (1912–26) and the Karafuto inu (Japanese Spitz or Sakhalin dog) which is related to a different strain of northern sled dog. (Sakhalin being the Russian island off Japan, near Hokkaido).

Among indigenous Japanese dogs function and locality have played the biggest role in producing the various types. Their common characteristics are those of a primitive canine type, with small prick ears and curled or upright bushy tails. Their eyes are triangular, small, set on a slant. The coat colour varies but is mostly reddish brown or wolf-grey. They are hardy physically and temperamentally, alert, dignified, resolute and quick to learn but not as sociable as most Western domestic dogs. The Japanese dog prefers by nature to devote itself to one owner.

From the 19th century onwards, the Japanese varieties were mixed increasingly with foreign breeds and some were in serious danger of extinction as pure-breeds. Through the efforts of devoted fanciers however, the Society for the Preservation of the Japanese Dog (Nippon Inu Hozonkai) was organised in 1928 to preserve the native breeds. Standards for these breeds were subsequently produced. About that time, several surviving indigenous breeds won official recognition from the government under the Tennen Kinembutsu Hogo Ho, or Law for the Protection of Notable Natural Objects. Until the 1950s Japanese native dogs were hardly known in the West although there were some sporadic importations.

It is less confusing when describing the Japanese breeds to do so by grouping them into sizes, i.e. large (ogata), medium (chugata) and small (Kogata). In the large type category comes the Akita inu (once called Odate inu), two feet at the withers and weighing around 90 lbs. An imposing breed with immense composure and a detectable presence, the Akita has a natural dignity and proud aloofness which matches its calmness of temperament and rather grandiose manner. At the time in the Akita region when dog-fighting was popular during the Edo period and in the constant desire to seek greater strength and aggression, the blood of the big game hunting dogs (Akita matagi inu) from the nearby mountain ranges was introduced. This led to the production of particularly large animals which was perpetuated later on with the introduction of blood from the newly developed Tosa fighting dog. Such outcrossings were leading to a serious erosion of the traditional characteristics and by 1931 public concern led to the breed being awarded the status of a government protected animal. A breed standard was established to restore the original character of the dog but the modern Akita is different from the local hunting dog from which it originated and should therefore be considered to be a fairly recent breed albeit with extremely ancient origins.

The medium size native dogs are still commonly named after islands or localities, e.g. the Hokkaido inu (ainuken), Koshi no inu, Kai inu, Kishu inu, Shikoku inu etc. The last named being the one truly indigenous breed genetically similar to Western dogs and dissimilar to the other native

The Shiba Inu from Japan

breeds of dog. Some of these breeds are also classified by original function, e.g. Shishi inu (boar-hunting dog), Shika inu (deer-hunting dog), Matagi inu (Tohoku hunter's dog) etc. Since the Japanese word 'inu' (dog) is written with a Chinese character that can be pronounced 'ken' in some compound words, you find the pronunciation ken being used instead of 'inu' for dog in the names of some varieties. In 1934 the Kai inu, Kishu inu and Koshi no inu and in 1937 the Shikoku inu and Hokkaido inu were designated protected animals under the above-mentioned law.

Despite recognisable differences, the medium-sized breeds have often been jointly considered as one, sharing a common standard. They retain the primitive characteristics of a well-balanced muscular entirely sym-

metrical body, sharp senses and good hunting instincts. Around 20 inches at the withers and weighing around 44 lbs., they are courageous in the hunt, having been used against bear, boar and deer, yet admirable in the home, being faithful and even-tempered.

The small type is also called Shiba inu and was found mainly in the mountainous regions, especially the Chubu and Chugoku districts. After the various localities, rather like our own native breeds of terrier, they were variously named Mino Shiba, Shinshu Shiba, Sekishu inu etc. They were used to hunt small game like hare, racoon dog (tanuki), fox, weasel or birds. In ancient times they were used in falconry to flush birds. These small dogs were officially recognised as government protected animals in 1936.

I understand that the Japanese Kennel Club recognises the following Japanese breeds: (in alphabetical order).

Akita, Chin, Hokkaido, Japanese Spitz, Japanese Terrier, Kai, Kishu, Shiba, Shikoku and Tosa. Of these some are easily identifiable and very different from each other, the Akita being rather like a German Shepherd Dog with a spitz tail, the Chin like an oriental toy spaniel, the Japanese Spitz like a miniature Samoyed, the Japanese Terrier like a toy smooth-haired fox terrier and the Tosa, similar to our Bullmastiff. The other five very much resemble each other, apart from size and colour. The Hokkaido is 50 centimetres high and in a whole range of colours: brindle (black or red), black, red, brown, white etc. The Kai is a little bigger and only brindle colour. The Kishu is 50 centimetres high but is mainly white, although reds and brindles are also found. The Shiba is just under 40 centimetres, brindle, black, black and tan or red and white. The Shikoku is 50 centimetres tall but only brindle or red.

From the earlier reference is classification by size, it can be seen that the Hokkaido, Kai, Kishu and Shikoku are medium-sized dogs from those named localities. The Shiba is the group name for small dogs, embracing the shibas from many localities, i.e. Mino-Shiba, Shinshu-Shiba, San'in-Shiba etc. The Shiba is an enchanting fox-like little dog with a hard thick coat, sparkling eyes, alert posture, attentive manner and inquisitive nature being markedly affectionate with a lively, friendly personality. They were the rabbit dogs of Japan but are good ratters too, being determined, quick and extremely agile.

As far as the medium-sized dogs are concerned however, I would not claim to be able to differentiate between, say, the red-brindle colour varieties found in the Hokkaido, the Kai, the Kishu and the Shikoku! But then even some distinguished judges have confused Lakeland and Welsh terriers and perhaps here is the obvious British comparison, i.e. Akita = Airedale, Kai = Welsh terrier, Hokkaido = Lakeland Terrier, with the Shibas equating to our Jack Russells, which seem to vary according to who breeds them.

The native dogs of Japan may not look much like terriers but do have many of their characteristics, being alert and assertive, keen-eyed and observant, sharp-eared and persistent. Many will see likenesses too with the Schipperke and the Finnish Spitz, especially as fox-red is a popular colour in Japanese dogs. But whether as similar to each other as some of our terrier breeds are or as dissimilar in size as the powerful impressive-looking Akita is to the diminutive perky little Mino-Shiba, the indigenous breeds of Japan make a fascinating contribution of the lore of the domestic dog.

The Akita

Do You Remember the British Dog?

If you cast your eye down the Kennel Club list of the pedigree breeds of dog registered annually with them in Britain you could be forgiven for thinking that we are doing a great deal to perpetuate breeds of German dogs and not a lot to conserve some of our once famous native breeds. In 1986 there were 19,000 German Shepherd Dogs, 8,500 Doberman Pinschers, 8,300 Rottweilers, 5,000 Boxers and 3,300 of the German pointer breeds registered here. Eighty years ago these breeds were virtually unknown in the United Kingdom. If you compare these numbers with half a dozen breeds of British dogs: Bullmastiffs 800; Bedlington terriers 232; Curly-coated retrievers 83; Dandie Dinmont terriers 204; Sussex Spaniels 102; Skye terriers 110; then you quickly see an enormous difference in our support for our own products.

But is this worrying situation at all justified? Are our modern Airedales and Bullmastiffs incapable nowadays of police work or security duties? Is the Bullterrier suddenly no longer suitable as a house guard? Is the contemporary British dog-owner's choice of breed a reflection on his copy-cat mentality, insatiable appetite for novelty, ignorance of breed characteristics, inherent fickleness — or are German dogs actually better than ours? One hundred years ago the Airedale or the Bullmastiff would have been the first choice of the gamekeeper, the dockyard policeman or the Armed Forces' dog sections.

General Hutchinson, in his classic *Dog Breaking* of 1909, wrote of the bullmastiff or night-dog . . . 'the appearance of the formidable-looking animal and the knowledge of his powers, more effectually prevented egg-stealing than would the best exertions of a dozen watchers.' Could Herr Dobermann's dog so quickly have outnumbered our own comparable breeds on pure merit? Undoubtedly the German 'breedmaster' policy contributes a great deal to the breeding of better dogs. Breeding programmes in German pedigree breeds in Germany have not only long been better planned and tighter controlled, but have also been pursued in the quest for higher quality dogs rather than financial reward or mere show ring success. Their show ring judges too are better trained and judge much more precisely than ours. Yet we have produced more breeds of dog than any other nation, breeds now revered all over the world. Have we lost our skill with livestock, with so many Dutch dairy cattle, increasing numbers of French beef cattle and so much Danish bacon on offer in Britain nowadays? I suspect that it has more to do with British fickleness than greater foreign facility. Four hundred years ago, Dr. Caius in

The German Boxer has replaced our own Bull Terrier

his book on British dogs considered that . . . 'we Englishe men are maruaious greedy gaping gluttons after novelties. And covetous covrorauntes of things that be seldom, Rare, strange and hard to get.'

The grand European tours of the British nobility brought Dutch paintings, French furniture and Italian sculpture to Britain. Continental service by British Army officers brought Spanish pointers, 'Alsatians' and Munsterlanders to Britain over the years. We also seem curiously attracted to the more bizarre specimens in the canine world: abnormally hairy Hungarian dogs, nearly completely hairless Chinese dogs or absurdly loose-skinned dogs from Hong Kong. Even when these were not on offer we did our best to make the Old English Sheepdog more hairy, the Bloodhound more wrinkled, the Mastiff more ponderous and the Bulldog even more exaggerated than our ancestors ever intended.

The copy-cat mentality too plays its part. How refreshing it would be to see a dog in a Range Rover which wasn't a Labrador. Why rush out and buy a corgi simply because the Royal family favour them? Do many of us truly assess the suitability of a breed mainly because of its role in marketing a brand of paint or toilet paper? I'm eternally grateful that T.V. programmes like 'Dallas' and 'Dynasty' don't feature Kentucky Mousehounds or our quarantine kennels would no doubt be packed with them by now. Perhaps predictably the rural working-class have shown more sense with their steadfast allegiance to working terriers and lurchers over many centuries. It is significant that the well-heeled brigade is now copying them, judging by the wide diversity in the social order at lurcher and terrier shows. But it is sad to see all the social elements of Southwestern Wales neglecting their Sealyham, the county of Sussex not protecting its spaniel heritage and the people of Ormskirk not preserving our sole remaining English heeler. But such neglect is hardly new; the last century saw indecent haste in the promotion of St. Bernards from Switzerland, Borzois from Russia, Pekingese from China, Dachshunds from Germany, Griffons from Belgium, ornamental dogs from Tibet and clever companionable poodles from France whilst our water spaniel, black and tan roughhaired terrier, Smithfield sheepdog and English White Terrier disappeared from view. I would never be against the importation of good dogs but I mourn the loss of our native breeds.

Through the National Trust and English Heritage we are safeguarding our famous buildings and historic sites; through the Rare Breeds Survival Trust we are very commendably conserving our Tamworth and Gloucester Old Spot pigs, Bagot goats, Longhorn cattle, Shropshire sheep and native breeds of poultry, but who

The German Shepherd dog has ousted all British counterparts

is going to protect our native breeds of dog as human whim determines their demise? They too are part of our heritage.

The Rottweiler — now too popular in Britain

Glossary of terms

angulation — the degree of slope or angle of the shoulder-blade in the forequarters and in the sharp angles of the inter-related bones in the hindquarters – thigh, hock and metatarsus.

barrel-hocks (spread hocks) — hocks turning out resulting in feet with inward-pointing toes (similar to bandy legs).

barrel-ribbed — well rounded rib cage.

belton — a colour designation in which white and coloured hair intermingles (blue belton, liver belton, orange belton etc).

bird dog — a sporting dog specialising in the hunting of birds.

blanket — the coat-colour on the back from the withers to the rump.

blaze — a white strip of hair in the centre of the face usually between the eyes.

bloom — the sheen of a coat in prime condition.

bodied up — well developed in maturity.

button ear — the ear flap folding forward usually towards the eye.

cat-feet — the rounded short-toed foot effect.

chiselled — clean cut particularly in the head.

chopping — as for paddling but exaggerated forward rather than out to the side.

close-coupled — comparatively short from withers to hip bones.

cobby — short-bodied, compact in torso.

coupled — hindquarters connected to torso.

cow-hocks — hocks turned toward each other (similar to knock-knees).

dewlaps — loose, pendulous skin under the throat.

dish-faced — concavity in the nasal bone making the nose higher at the tip than the stop.

drive — a solid thrust from the hindquarters, denoting sound locomotion.

drop ears — the ends of the ear folded or drooping forward.

dudley nose — flesh-coloured or brown-nosed

elbows out — the positioning of the elbow away from the body.

even bite — meeting of both sets of front teeth at edges with no overlap.

feathering — distinctly longer hair on rear line of legs, back of ears and underside of tail.

flecking — coat markings from groups of different coloured hairs.

flews — upper lips pendulous, particularly at their inner corners.

gay tail — the tail carried up on high (usually used when carried so incorrectly for the breed).

grizzle — bluish-grey or steel-grey in colour of coat.

hackney-gait (or-action) — high stepping motion of the front legs.

hare-feet — a foot whose third digits are longer, an elongated foot.

haw — membrane in the inside corner of the eye, usually reddy pink.

layback
(used loosely) — the angle of the shoulder as compared with the vertical.
(or strictly) — an undershot jaw with a receding nose.

lay of shoulder — angled position of the shoulder.

leather — the flap of the ear.

level bite (pincer bite) — when the front teeth of both the jaws meet exactly.

linty — firm twisty condition of coat, with

plenty of spring in it.

lumber — superfluous flesh.

mask — dark shading on the foreface.

merle — blue-grey flecked with black, in colour of coat.

occipital crest — peak of upper rear point of skull.

out at elbow — see elbows out.

overshot jaw — the upper jaw's front teeth overlapping (pig-jawed in excess).

overspring ribs — exaggerated curvature of rib-cage.

paddling — a heavy clumsy threshing action of the forelegs in which the feet swing wide of the body when on the move.

pile — dense undercoat of soft hair.

pily — a coat of mixed soft woolly and long wiry hair.

pincer-bite — see level bite.

plaiting (or weaving or crossing) — the movement of one front leg across the path of the other front leg in the dog's gait.

prick-ear — carried erect and usually pointed at the tip.

ribbed up — long last rib.

roach-backed (carp-backed) — with a convexly curved back towards the loin

roan — a fine equal mixture of coloured and white hairs (blue roan etc).

rose ear — a small drop ear which folds over and back.

saddle-backed — with a soft or sagging back (from weak muscles or over-long back).

scissors bite — in which the outer side of the lower incisors touches the inner side of the upper incisors.

set on — join (of say tail root to torso).

short-coupled — see close-coupled.

shoulder lay-back — see layback.

snipiness — condition in which the muzzle is too pointed, weak-looking.

splay-feet — flat, open-toed, over-spread feet.

stop — indentation where the nasal bone meets the skull between the eyes.

straight shoulders — straight up and down shoulder blades, lacking correct angulation.

sway-back — concave curvature of the back line between the withers and the hip bones.

tail carried gaily — see gay tail.

throatiness — an excess of loose skin under the throat.

ticked — small isolated areas of black or coloured hairs on white.

topknot — a tuft of longer hair on the top and front of the head.

topline — the dog's outline from just behind the withers to the rump.

undershot jaw — the malformation of the jaw which projects the lower jaw and incisors beyond the upper (a sign of this in small puppies is that they appear to be grinning).

well angulated — good sharp angle in the thigh-hock-metatarsus area.

well-coupled — well made in the area from the withers to the hip-bones.

well-knit — neat and compactly constructed and connected.

well-laid — soundly placed and correctly angled.

well laid back (shoulders) — oblique shoulders ideally slanting at 45° to the ground.

well let-down — close to the ground, having short hocks.

well ribbed up — ribs neither too long nor too wide apart; compact.

well-sprung — with well-rounded ribs.

well tucked-up — excessively small waist; absence of visible abdomen from the side-view (as in Greyhounds).

yawing (crabbing) — movement with the body travelling in a line at an angle with the line of movement of the legs.

ACKNOWLEDGEMENTS

Illustrations are acknowledged as follows:

Ploon de Raad: Pages, 2, 6, 11, 13, 14, 17, 34, 44, 51, 62, 68, 72, 76, 97, 99, 107, 121, 125, 126, 136, 185, 187, 189, 265, 279, 292, 294 and 295.

Club Portugues de Canicultura: Pages 5, 63 (top), 142, 143 and 201.

Charwynne Dog Features: Pages 7, 9, 15, 16, 18, 19, 21, 22, 23, 30, 33, 35, 39, 41, 43, 46, 47, 50, 55, 64, 66, 69, 74, 75, 78, 79, 81, 83, 84, 87, 88, 89, 91, 93, 95, 100, 103, 104, 105, 106, 109, 112, 113, 114, 117, 119, 123, 131, 133, 138, 141, 144, 146, 147, 149, 150, 153, 154, 155, 157, 158, 162, 163, 167, 169, 171, 172, 175, 177, 179, 180, 182, 183, 186, 191, 192, 193, 197, 199, 204, 205, 206, 211, 212, 215, 218, 219, 221, 223, 224, 235, 236, 237, 238, 241, 243, 247, 249, 253, 254, 257, 258, 260, 261, 262, 266, 267, 269, 270, 273, 275, 276, 277, 280, 281, 283, 285, 287, 288, 289, 297, 298 (top and bottom) 299, 301, 302, 303, 305, 307, 309, 311, 313 and 314.

Editor of *Greyhound Magazine*: Page 130.

D. Copperthwaite: Page 137.

Buckinghamshire County Museum: Page 216.

Kate Watson: Page 225.

Ronnie Crowe: Page 229.

Florence Tilley: Page 63.

Courtesy of Christie's: Page 134.

The author is especially grateful for the generosity of the following for permission to use photographs from their collection:-

Pam Sambrook, Curator, Staffordshire County Museum at Shugborough: Pages 61, 110, 111, 129, 202, 214, 227, 228, 231, 246 and 259.

Lesley Colsell, Assistant Curator, Museum of East Anglia Life: Page 48 (from Suffolk Record Office) Page 49.

R.N.R. Peers, Curator and Secretary, Dorset Natural History and Archaeological Society: Page 52.

Dr. Sadie Ward, Institute of Agricultural History and Museum of Rural Life: Pages 59 and 209.

Bridget Yates, Curator, Norfolk Rural Life Museum: Page 161.

Dr. J. Geraint Jenkins, Curator, National Museum of Wales: Pages 250 and 256.